MW00340467

Black Masculinity and the Frontier Myth in American Literature

Contents

Acknowledgments

Thanks to Iris Smith for her thoughtful suggestions about the manuscript from the earliest stages onward. Also, thanks to Omofolabo Ajayi, William L. Andrews, Doreen Fowler, Melody Graulich, Daniel Gunn, Karen Hellekson, Michael Kowalewski, and Cheryl Lester.

Black Masculinity and the Frontier Myth in American Literature

Introduction

> *The Myth of the Frontier is our oldest and most charac-*
> *teristic myth. . . . According to this myth-historiography, the*
> *conquest of the wilderness and the subjugation or displace-*
> *ment of the Native Americans who originally inhabited it*
> *have been the means to our achievement of a national iden-*
> *tity, a democratic polity, an ever-expanding economy, and a*
> *phenomenally dynamic and "progressive" civilization.*
>
> —Slotkin, *Gunfighter Nation*

> *At the constitutional conventions of almost every western*
> *state, the single most pressing question was the admission or*
> *status of the black population. . . . Both proslavery and anti-*
> *slavery delegates vied with each other in [insisting] . . . that*
> *equality was entirely unacceptable to white residents of the*
> *states.*
>
> *Horace Greeley, the reformer who urged Americans to "go*
> *West, young man," also insisted that the territories "shall be*
> *reserved for the benefit of the white Caucasian race."*
>
> —Katz, *The Black West*

Houston Baker, Jr., comments that "when the black American reads Frederick Jackson Turner's *The Frontier in American History*, he feels no regret over the end of the Western *frontier*" (*Long Black Song* 2). The availability of "free land" to the west encouraged immigration to those areas, Turner argues in his important 1893 essay, "The Significance of the Frontier in American History," and the subsequent meeting of "civilization" and "savagery" on the frontier transformed the pioneer of European descent into "a new product that is American" (Turner 34). David Leverenz points out that Turner represents the frontier "as a natural factory for manufacturing American manhood," as the place where the white male pioneer achieves a masculine identity by transforming unproductive wilderness into profitable farmland (32). According to Baker, such "tales of pioneers enduring the hardships of the West for the promise of immense wealth are not the tales of black America" (*Long Black Song* 2). Because the black man has been "denied his part in the frontier and his share of the nation's wealth," *frontier* is "an alien word" to African Americans, "for, in essence, all frontiers established by the white psyche have been closed to the black man" (2–4). If the black man has been denied the frontier, he has also been denied one of the nation's dominant narratives of the development of masculine subjectivity, a narrative based indeed on the opportunity to share the nation's wealth, the opportunity to exploit the availability of land in the West. If the myths, legends, and narratives of pioneers conquering the West are the exclusive province of the white psyche, and if the frontier myth in its most traditional form provides a narrative of man-making, and a narrative explicitly of making "white manhood," what, we might ask, happens when an African American male writer engages with this "mythic narrative"?

Those few African American males who have written about their western experiences indicate diverse responses to the frontier. Nat Love, in *The Life and Adventures of Nat Love, Better Known in the Cattle Country as "Deadwood Dick"* (1907), tells of a boyhood in slavery and an impoverished post-emancipation adolescence that he leaves behind to journey westward, where he "became known throughout the country as a good all around cow boy and a splendid hand in a stampede" (Love 43).

The frontier was a place where "a man's work was to be done, and a man's life to be lived," where he was able to earn a name (Deadwood Dick) bestowed out of respect for his manly abilities at roping and shooting, and where he was able to become a man among men, "one of the leading cowboys of the West" (155, 118). Love represents the frontier as an environment free of racism against blacks, as a place where talent (at reading brands or shooting guns) and knowledge (especially of the various trails and geographies traversed by cattle herds) combine with a man's courage and work ethic to determine his status. Brackette Williams notes that Love becomes part of "a brotherhood of cowboys defined without regard to race or place" (viii), a color-blind society that makes the contemporary reader wonder what Love excludes from his construction of life in the American West.[1]

Love represents the frontier as an environment free of racism, whereas Henry O. Flipper's *Black Frontiersman: The Memoirs of Henry O. Flipper, First Black Graduate of West Point* (1916), which tells the story of his service with the Tenth Cavalry in Texas, Oklahoma, and along the Mexican border as the army's first commissioned black officer, begins with Flipper endangered by the potential of white racial violence. Sent with his white orderly "to the Wichita Indian Agency to inspect and receive cattle for issue to Indians," Flipper encounters white cowboys who "raved and swore when they knew a 'nigger officer' was there to inspect and receive the cattle and was occupying the only bed" (17). As it does for Love, the frontier represents for Flipper an opportunity to advance in his chosen career. Flipper's career, however, was ended "abruptly in 1882 by a court-martial conviction," one that Flipper claims was sparked by his friendship with a white woman, Mollie Dwyer (5–6).[2] Flipper's narrative calls into question Love's representation of African American life in the West by demonstrating the continuing effect of race and racism on his frontier experiences.

In his selection of cover art for his *Way Out West* (1957) album, musician Sonny Rollins presents a more contemporary response to the mythology of the frontier. The cover photograph depicts the jazz saxophonist posed in profile against a desert background—cactus, Joshua trees, the bleached skull of a steer. Rollins holds a saxophone in one hand and rests his other hand laconically against a gun belt. As Michael Jarrett points out, Rollins's clothing—a cowboy hat, a gun belt with an empty holster, a Brooks Brothers suit, a thin black tie—combines the iconography of the Hollywood Western with "the jazzman's air of urbanity" (237). Black texts, Henry Louis Gates writes, are "two-toned" or "double-voiced," and they "occupy spaces in at least two traditions," one European or American and "one of the several related but distinct black traditions" ("Criticism" 3-4). The *Way Out West* photograph points to just such an interplay between white and African American traditions, imagery, myths, histories, and fictions. While Rollins's appropriation of western imagery plays on a viewer's knowledge of the codes of the Hollywood western, the photograph also has another referent—to African American history, to the black army regiments (popularly known as the Buffalo Soldiers) of the nineteenth century, and to the black cowboys whose history has been unrepresented by mainstream adaptations of the frontier myth. For African American writers, I will argue, reference to frontier motifs often represents a similar double movement, a play on white mythology, a recuperation of black history and literary or artistic tradition.

I draw the term *frontier myth* from critic Richard Slotkin. His historical analysis of the development of the "myth of the frontier" in twentieth-century American culture starts in the year 1890, three years before Turner first presented his famous 1893 essay, and six years before the last volume of Theodore

Roosevelt's *The Winning of the West* appeared (1889–1896). Slotkin's *Gunfighter Nation* begins at the moment when "the landed frontier of the United States was officially declared 'closed,' the moment when 'Frontier' became primarily an ideological rather than a geographical reference" (4), and at the moment when the existence of this just "closed" frontier became of central importance to Turner's and Roosevelt's theories of American history, with both men arguing that the existence of a western frontier was central to the successful development of an American civilization.

Slotkin's *Gunfighter Nation* argues that repetitions of the frontier myth in twentieth-century culture are influenced most explicitly by these histories of Turner and Roosevelt. The structures of this myth, he argues, have been repeated throughout the twentieth century in various forms and genres. These various forms "conform precisely to the function we have ascribed to mythic narrative in modern culture: they deploy a language of traditional ideological symbols and narrative structures as a means to understanding a social/political crisis" (32). As a much repeated ideological narrative in American culture, the frontier myth has most often served the interests of the dominant race, class, and gender, providing a mythic justification for the positions of power held by middle-class white males. The myth is based on a racial opposition between the "civilized" (white) and the "savage" (non-white, usually American Indian but often African American or even lower-class whites or white immigrants) and tells the story of the evolutionary inevitability of the triumph of civilization over savagery and the dominance of the white race over all other races. The frontier myth is the narrative of the civilized individual's journey westward into the savage American wilderness. The process of conquering the wilderness (and often the native inhabitant of the wilderness) transforms the hero of the narrative, marking his transition from boy to man and establishing his independence from his

European ancestry. Although we traditionally locate the frontier in the American West, Slotkin argues that the place of the myth is a "moral landscape" that is "divided by significant borders, of which the wilderness/civilization, Indian/White border is most basic" (14). More generally, the frontier myth explores the border between Self and Other, especially as that boundary is marked by racial difference.

The savage/civilized dichotomy provides a structure through which cultural or political tensions can be played out, especially as those tensions occur across racial lines. As Fredric Jameson notes: "[I]f interpretation in terms of expressive causality or of allegorical master narratives remains a constant temptation, this is because such master narratives have inscribed themselves in texts as well as in our thinking about them; such allegorical narrative signifieds are a persistent dimension of literary and cultural texts precisely because they reflect a fundamental dimension of our collective thinking and our collective fantasies about history and reality" (34). The myth of the frontier provides a master narrative through which Americans engage in collective fantasies about history and reality, and through which various groups within American culture can articulate responses to historical events. This master narrative also provides a structure through which the dominant white culture can articulate its relationships to various groups of non-white peoples. While the frontier encounter between whites and American Indians might be described as the place where distinct human cultures first came into contact, that encounter is articulated in and through the master narrative of the frontier myth as a meeting between civilization and savagery, an articulation that serves an ideological purpose.[3] The dispossession of American Indians, for example, could be justified by imagining them not as representatives of distinct human cultures but as savages who must be eradicated to make room for the more advanced civilization.

In *The Frontier Experience and the American Dream,* David Mogen, Mark Busby, and Paul Bryant argue that "frontier mythology has created a symbolic vocabulary" that is "intrinsically *dialectical,* or, to use Mikhail Bakhtin's word, *dialogic,* insofar as traditionally Anglo, masculine purveyors of the American dream have called forth responses by women, minority writers, and others who write from different perspectives" (4). Understanding and examining the dialectical or dialogical nature of frontier mythology "will open up the canon, by revealing how different regions, ethnic groups, classes, and genders have adapted frontier archetypes and enriched the American dream" (5). In John A. Williams's *The Man Who Cried I Am* (1967), the protagonist, novelist Max Reddick, observes that he "wanted to do with the novel what Charlie Parker was doing to music—tearing it up and remaking it" (209). William L. Andrews points out that Henry Louis Gates identifies "signifyin(g)" as the dominant trope in African American "oral culture and written literature" (207). "Signifyin(g)," Gates writes, "in jazz performances and in the play of black language games is a mode of formal revision, it depends for its effects on troping, it is often characterized by pastiche, and, most crucially, it turns on repetition of formal structures and their differences" (*Signifying Monkey* 52). The processes of appropriation, improvisation, and revision that we associate with jazz as a musical form provide a valid metaphor for African American responses to the symbolic vocabulary of the frontier myth, to the remaking of or signifyin(g) on that myth in the work of writers such as John Marrant, Oscar Micheaux, Nat Love, Pauline Hopkins, Richard Wright, Chester Himes, William Gardner Smith, John A. Williams, and Toni Morrison.

As these writers engage frontier mythology, they also respond to ideologies of gender. In the *Way Out West* photograph, Rollins's substitution of one phallic signifier (saxophone) for another (pistol), playful and ironic as that substitution is, also points to one of the central problems common to frontier narratives. Specific definitions of masculine behavior shift during the nineteenth and twentieth centuries, but a patriarchal and very often violent masculine ideal remains central to articulations of the frontier myth. I will argue that individual writers vary in their acceptance or criticism of this ideal. Gail Bederman notes in *Manliness and Civilization* that individuals, although "inescapably defined" by the discourses in which they are immersed, are also "able to take advantage of the contradictions within and between these ideologies" in order to assert themselves as "pro-active historical agent[s]" (11). I will not locate in my examination of these narratives a "new frontier" where the cultural norms of masculinity have been completely remade, but I will map out a geography of accommodation and resistance to these norms. If the frontier serves as a physical terrain where writers set narratives of the construction of masculine subjectivity, we might argue that the frontier represents as well a space where the masculine ideal can be interrogated. By taking advantage of the contradictions within ideologies of gender as well as within the master narrative of the frontier myth, these writers create the potential for the production of new discursive positions and subjectivities—for remaking or resisting the ideologies of gender and race.

According to John Mack Faragher, "the theme that sparks the most debate today is the old Turnerian matter of West and frontier considered as place and process" (237), with the debate circling around whether we should regard the frontier as an actual and identifiable geographic region or whether we should examine the frontier experience as a process of change and transformation. Thus, for example, Slotkin's work focuses on the frontier as a mythic narrative not explicitly tied to the geography of the West. The landscape is moral and ideological rather than—or as well as—actual. Patricia Nelson Limerick's *The Legacy of Conquest,* on the other hand, argues for de-emphasizing the frontier-as-process in order to study the West as a "place undergoing conquest and never fully escaping its consequences"; by "rethinking Western history, we gain the freedom to think of the West as a place—as many complicated environments." Such an emphasis on the West-as-place "has a compensatory, down-to-earth clarity that the migratory, abstract frontier could never have" (26). Both Slotkin and Limerick, although approaching the topic from different angles, share a similar purpose—to critique the mythologies that have arisen about the American West.

Annette Kolodny's "Letting Go Our Grand Obsessions" engages two elements of the frontier (as an abstract meeting point between different cultures, as a specific geographic territory) in order to argue that an interrogation of both these elements is essential to a literary history of the frontier. According to Kolodny's formulation, the frontier always involves some physical terrain (including but not necessarily limited to the western United States) on which we can identify "some specifiable first moment in the evolving dialogue between different cultures and languages" (5). Although the geography of the frontier is important, she does not limit the terrain to a specific region of the country. Kolodny also critiques and dismisses the civilized/savage dichotomy of Turner's thesis by reformulating the term *frontier*, arguing that it is the place (real or imagined) where "distinct human cultures first encounter one another's 'otherness' and appropriate, accommodate, or domesticate it through language" (9). Revising Turner's civilized/savage dichotomy allows us to understand "the frontier as a specifiable first moment on that liminal borderland between distinct cultures" and allows us to "forever decenter what was previously a narrowly Eurocentric design" (11) that posits non-Europeans as inferior savages. Such a decentering enables "the literatures of the frontiers to stand—accurately, at last—as multilingual, polyvocal, and newly intertextual and multicultural" (12).

I will discuss the frontier in terms of the "down-to-earth clarity" of the specific geography of the American West. I will also examine the frontier (in terms drawn from Slotkin and Kolodny) as an ideological or mythic narrative or as a shifting physical terrain where a first contact takes place. Through readings of autobiographical narratives such as Nat Love's *Life and Adventures* (1907) and Oscar Micheaux's *The Conquest* (1913) and novels such as Pauline Hopkins's *Winona* (1902) and Chester Himes's *If He Hollers Let Him Go* (1945), I examine the small tradition of African American literature concerned directly with westward expansion and black experience in western territories and states. The last half of the book de-emphasizes the American West to focus on the way writers transform various geographies such as Mississippi, France, or Africa into frontier spaces where they set their narratives of constructing masculine subjectivities. William Gardner Smith's *The Stone Face* (1963) and John A. Williams's *The Man Who Cried I Am* (1967), for example, locate a new frontier in Africa. My approach, which begins with the American West and ends with Africa, is particularly appropriate as these two areas have long been linked in the African American imagination as frontiers potentially free from racial oppression. In the late 1870s, African American activist organizations proposed migration both to Africa (particularly Liberia) and into the American West. Henry Adams, a key organizer with the Colonization Council (which advocated African American migration to Liberia), became a proponent of black westward migration, and Benjamin "Pap" Singleton encouraged at various times migration to Kansas and to Africa (most notably when he was working with the Trans-Atlantic Society). "Liberia," Nell Irvin Painter writes, "was an American frontier for Americans of African descent" (102). For many African Americans, however, "migration to Kansas offered a more feasible" and affordable alternative (140).[4]

This study will begin with brief discussions of the histories of Frederick Jackson Turner and Theodore Roosevelt (U.S. president 1901–1909), to establish the relationship between the mythology of the American West and dominant constructions of American masculinity emerging at the end of the nineteenth century. Interdisciplinary readings of history and fiction such as James Fenimore Cooper's *The Deerslayer* (1841) and Owen Wister's *The Virginian* (1902) will demonstrate the mutual influence of different genres of writing in creating common frontier motifs and themes. Chapter 1 sets out the dominant cultural concepts of manhood and of the frontier that will be played out, resisted, and adapted in the work of African American writers. I also discuss works by two black writers—John Marrant's autobiographical *A Narrative of the Lord's Wonderful Dealings with John Marrant, a Black* (1785) and Toni Morrison's novel *Paradise* (1998). Through Marrant's eighteenth-century *Narrative* I establish an early connection between black literature and writing about frontier experience. Through *Paradise* I outline a critique of frontier mythology and patriarchal ideology by drawing on Morrison's black feminist perspective.

In chapter 2 I argue that in *The Conquest* Oscar Micheaux constructs the hero of his pioneer narrative, a fictionalized version of himself named Oscar Devereaux, as a figure whose behavior and work ethic counters widely disseminated stereotypes of the savage black man. The South Dakota frontier serves as a place where Micheaux hopes black manhood can be reconstituted, where the hard-working African American man can be free from the racism that restricts his ability to succeed. Micheaux's book joins together a Turnerian story of frontier transformation with a narrative of racial uplift inspired by both Booker T. Washington and a domestic fiction tradition primarily associated with women writers. I argue that Devereaux's inability to achieve his desired masculine identity implicitly critiques both narratives, as by the end of the book the myth of the West and the myth of racial uplift are both revealed to be "closed."

In chapter 3 I argue that Love and Hopkins (more so than the other writers discussed here) draw from the genre of the Western, which has its roots in Cooper's novels, in nineteenth-century dime novels, and in Wister's influential *The Virginian*.[5] *The Life and Adventures of Nat Love* is a narrative of assimilation influenced by both Booker T. Washington's *Up from Slavery* (1901) and the western tall tale and dime novel traditions. Love's concept of manhood is more aggressive than the civilized manliness of Micheaux's farmer, as he employs what Slotkin calls the myth of "regenerative violence" to explain his transformation from slave to cowboy. Violence is "central to both the historical development of the frontier and its mythic representation" (*Gunfighter* 11). As a repeated trope in frontier mythology, violence functions as a means to individual and often societal regeneration, renewal, and transformation. Pauline Hopkins's *Winona* is a historical novel set before the Civil War on the border between Kansas and Missouri. In contrast to Love she uses the frontier setting to promote a philosophy of agitation and protest rather than assimilation and accommodation as the appropriate response to racial oppression. Published the same year as Wister's *Virginian* Hopkins's story grapples with similar issues (the legitimacy of extralegal violence, constructions of manhood and womanhood at the turn of the century) and uses similar narrative sequences (a lynching, a scene of extended convalescence from wounds, a climactic showdown). *Winona* contests the better-known *Virginian*'s conservative vision of life in the American West from a feminist and politically progressive point of view.

Writers such as Micheaux and Love articulate their desire to be considered human, to be accepted as the subjects rather than the objectified others of contemporaneous racist discourse, through dominant constructions of masculinity. Although I primarily focus on male writers, my discussion of Pauline Hopkins's *Winona* in chapter 3 provides an important counterpoint to the constructions of masculinity we find in the other books, an indication of the way male writers might have (but for the most part have not) reimagined concepts of manhood. Although Hopkins does not completely alter ideologies of gender, she does rethink relationships between men and women, and she grants her main female character an agency and ability to transgress gender roles that we generally do not see in the work of the male writers. African American women who have used western settings in their writings have, like the male writers, seen the frontier as a place where black manhood can be reconstituted, although such writers as Hopkins, Era Bell Thompson, Pearl Cleage, and Toni Morrison are more likely than the male writers to use the frontier setting to question ideologies of masculinity. In my concluding chapter, I will look back at the work of the male writers through the lens provided by Thompson's *American Daughter* (1946), Cleage's *Flyin' West* (1995), and Morrison's *Paradise*.

Chapter 4 begins with a discussion of short stories by Richard Wright and William Faulkner. I compare how these influential writers adapt the structure of the ritual hunt (an important component of both Roosevelt's and Cooper's vision of the frontier) in the context of black and white rather than white and American Indian racial relations. Wright demonstrates that the rituals of masculinity and violence that Faulkner's Ike McCaslin participates in are denied the black man. In stories such as "Big Boy Leaves Home" from the collection *Uncle Tom's Children* (1940) and "The Man Who Was Almost a Man" from the collection *Eight Men* (1961), Wright situates the ritual hunt in the context of Jim Crow–era Mississippi, a closed frontier where his characters find little in terms of opportunity. While Big Boy's leaving home symbolizes the early twentieth-century Great Migration from the rural South to northern urban centers, Bob Jones's journey to California in Chester Himes's *If He Hollers Let Him Go* (1945) parallels the large-scale World War II–era migration of African Americans to West Coast states. Himes explores the contradictions of African American western experience, representing California as a place that simultaneously offers and restricts opportunities for blacks. Both Himes and Wright express an ambivalence about black men and the myth of regenerative violence, and both writers construct narratives that illustrate how the black man's participation in the archetypal ritual of the hunt is more likely to be as the hunted than as the hunter.

In chapter 5 I argue that Smith's novel *The Stone Face* rearticulates the frontier myth in a context informed by both black activism in America and nationalist independence movements in Africa. The significant action takes place not in the western United States but in Europe, primarily in Paris during the Algerian war for independence. If the frontier offers, as Turner argues, "a gate of escape from the bondage of the past" (59), the protagonist (Simeon Brown) of Smith's *Stone Face* leaves America behind for Europe in order to escape the past of white racism. Smith represents Paris as a frontier space, an urban wilderness where Simeon can be free from the deforming values of (American) civilization. As for Nat Love, Simeon's journey to the frontier results in an erasure of racial identity. His sense of freedom in Paris contrasts with the oppression of the Algerians, who refer to the African American Simeon as a white man. Through the evolving relationship between Simeon and the Algerians, Smith attempts to develop for his protagonist a new sense of identity that will bridge the gap between America and Africa.

I conclude with a study of John A. Williams's *The Man Who Cried I Am*. Like the characters of Wright and Himes, Williams's protagonist, Max Reddick, finds himself caught up in hunting rituals throughout the narrative. The primary hunt here, however, takes place in the wilderness of racial politics, and the object of Max's hunt is to uncover the history of those politics. As does Simeon Brown, Max experiences in Europe a first contact with whiteness in the form of an interracial romance. Europe functions also as frontier between America and Africa. For Simeon Brown, the most important first contact is with another man—one who is fighting racism in his own country and whose model informs Simeon's own decision to fight against racial oppression. Max's primary encounter is with the otherness of African culture or, more precisely, with African history. Africa offers Max something he cannot find in America or Europe—history from a black perspective, a potential counter discourse to white versions of history. The change in consciousness brought about by his journey to the African frontier enables Max's own intervention in the making and writing of the history of American racial relations.

The stories told by the writers discussed here are shaped by issues of particular concern to African Americans at various historical moments in the twentieth century as well as by the mythology of the frontier. The journey west for Micheaux and Love provides a narrative form for exploring Booker T. Washington's philosophy of assimilation. Writers such as Hopkins, Wright, and Himes use their stories to link frontier mythology with the tradition of the slave narrative. This linkage occurs in and is influenced by the development of social protest writing as a literary genre that is particularly amenable to the concerns of African American writers. Although Smith and Williams rearticulate the frontier experience in a new context, one informed by the emergence of a postcolonial world, their new frontiers provide a space for addressing themes similar to those of earlier writers—the hope of finding a frontier free of racial oppression, a tendency to represent subjectivity and identity through the concept of manhood, and an effort to employ the symbolic vocabulary of the frontier in a way that articulates a connection to African American literary tradition and to contemporaneous black thought and politics.

In her discussion of early black writing in America, Rafia Zafar points out that African American writers "adopted many of the ideas and genres of the white dominant culture in order to declare themselves a part of it" (7). Rather than being "witless imitators," these writers "changed permanently the meanings of the genres they appropriated" (7–10). Similarly, the writers I discuss here look both to a tradition of African American writing and to genres associated with the white dominant culture as a means to find models for their exercises in selfmaking. Micheaux's hero explicitly states his awareness of dominant cultural myths and assumptions when he looks toward his "white neighbors and friends who were doing what I admired, building an empire," as models for his own frontier enterprise (244). At the same time as his hero looks to white neighbors, Micheaux himself turns to Booker T. Washington as a model for constructing his own authorial voice. This duality, this consistent reference to two literary traditions, is part of what constitutes the richness of this body of literature.

An important strand of contemporary criticism examines the relationship between African American literature and either African or black vernacular cultural forms. Houston Baker's argument that the blues are at the root of authentic African American expression might exemplify this approach. Paul Gilroy's argument that contemporary black music fuses Caribbean, African, American, and European musical forms might exemplify another strand of literary criticism, one that emphasizes the "unashamedly hybrid character" of black cultures (99). My emphasis here on the interplay of EuroAmerican and African American forms—particularly the way the frontier narrative and the slave narrative come together or come into conflict in the work of the writers I examine—places my argument within this second strand of African American literary criticism. My methodology has much in common with the approach taken by a number of contemporary feminist critics of African American literature such as Rafia Zafar, Ann duCille, and Claudia Tate.

I will argue that black writers do not simply imitate dominant cultural forms but adapt and revise those forms. Each of the works I examine involves a migration to a frontier space on the edge of civilized (white) society, a place where the protagonist's identity, choices, and decisions will not be limited by race-based restrictions. By claiming as their own a narrative structure that is associated with the dominant white culture, black writers also claim as their own a place in a society that refuses to acknowledge African American participation in and contribution to that culture. Through juxtaposing novels such as Hopkins's *Winona* and Wister's *The Virginian,* for example, I demonstrate that a black writer not only writes within a EuroAmerican tradition but also alters and extends that tradition in ways unimagined by white writers. My approach helps us to expand our understanding of the way African American writers have participated in the creation of American literature in general and of the literature of the frontier in particular—as both agents and innovators.

CHAPTER 1

"My Dress Was Purely in the Indian Stile"

Transformation and Manhood on the American Frontier

The dominant concepts associated with the frontier are apparent in a variety of works by writers such as Frederick Jackson Turner, Theodore Roosevelt, John Marrant, James Fenimore Cooper, Owen Wister, and Toni Morrison. The idea of frontier entails both transformation and the emergence of the American hero as a hybrid of savagery and civilization. Violence plays a considerable role in this transformation. I place a good deal of importance here on histories written by Turner and Roosevelt, in part because of their importance in popularizing the frontier myth both in the field of academic history and in the larger field of American popular culture.[1] Wister's popular novel *The Virginian,* for example, clearly shows the influence of Turner and (particularly) Roosevelt in its representation of the American West. By noting the interplay between history and fiction I demonstrate the mutual influence of different genres of writing in the creation of common structures, archetypes, motifs—frontier mythology, to use Slotkin's phrase. I will also argue that Turner, Roosevelt, and Wister use the frontier setting to address anxieties that emerge in the context of a cultural reformation of concepts of white manhood at the end of the nineteenth century. Later I will emphasize the way these concepts, structures, and motifs are played out, resisted, and adapted in the work of African American writers.

As a counterpoint to my discussion of white novelists and historians, I will also discuss works by two black writers, John Marrant's autobiographical *A Narrative of the Lord's Wonderful Dealings with John Marrant, a Black* (1785) and Toni Morrison's novel *Paradise* (1998). Marrant's story of capture by Cherokees is not only one of the earliest examples of African American writing but also one of the most popular "captivity narratives" published, appearing in numerous editions in the eighteenth and nineteenth centuries. This work demonstrates an early relationship between black writing and writing about frontier life. The discussion of Marrant's *Narrative* will establish that a writer of African descent has had an originary role in the creation of the frontier mythology codified by late nineteenth- and early twentieth-century writers such as Turner, Roosevelt, and Wister—whose influence on that mythology has been more traditionally recognized. The study of Morrison's novel will establish a critique both of frontier mythology and of masculinity from a contemporary black and feminist perspective. *Paradise* interrogates the celebration of male violence and male bonding that is central to frontier mythology—even when that violence is committed in the name of protecting a black community.

L'Hommelette on the Range

> For a moment, at the frontier, the bonds of custom are broken and unrestraint is triumphant. There is not tabula rasa. The stubborn American environment is there with its

imperious summons to accept its conditions; the inherited ways of doing things are also there; and yet, in spite of environment, and in spite of custom, each frontier did indeed furnish a new field of opportunity, a gate of escape from the bondage of the past.   —Turner, "The Significance of the Frontier in American History"

In his 1893 essay Turner argues that in the development of the United States the availability of unsettled tracts of land—and the advance of a frontier of settlement across the American continent—marks the United States' difference from Europe and marks as well the difference between the American and the European, for "the advance of the frontier has meant a steady movement away from the influence of Europe, a steady growth of independence on American lines" (34). The availability of free land to the west encouraged immigration to those areas, and the "continuous touch with the simplicity of primitive society" (32) and with the primitive nature of that environment forced fundamental changes in the immigrant's character. American social development enjoys a perennial rebirth on the frontier that constantly renews (and improves) a political and democratic society. Self-reliant individuals in frontier communities work together to create a process of democratic decision-making in their local governments. Individual activism working toward the collective good of the community in local frontier governments is then reflected in the continual renewal of democratic forms of government at the national level. The existence of western land opened for settlement made property ownership available to large numbers of people. The availability of land on the frontier provided the opportunity to fulfill the promise of upward mobility and also provided a means for ensuring the continued distribution of property—and power—in American society.

The first steps in settling this land were accomplished by the trader, through whom "the disintegrating forces of civilization entered the wilderness" (Turner 40). Through the actions of the trader every river valley and Indian trail "became a fissure in Indian society, and so that society became honeycombed. Long before the pioneer farmer appeared on the scene, primitive Indian life had passed away." As the American Indian followed the buffalo trail into the wilderness, so the trader followed the Indian trail, and behind him "the trails widened into roads, and the roads into turnpikes, and these in turn were transformed into railroads" (40). On the former sites of American Indian villages, "which had been placed in positions suggested by nature," trading posts became established, "situated so as to command the water systems of the country" and thus developed into major cities. In this evolutionary process of development, the buffaloes forge a path for the American Indians, who provide a way for the traders, who are then followed by the settlers, who lead the way for more advanced forms of civilization. "Thus civilization in America has followed the arteries made by geology, pouring an ever richer tide through them, until at last the slender paths of aboriginal intercourse have been broadened and interwoven into the complex mazes of modern commercial lines; the wilderness has been interpenetrated by lines of civilization growing ever more numerous. It is like the steady growth of a complex nervous system for the originally simple, inert continent" (41). The development of civilization here is rendered biologically, with the metaphor of the human mind applied to the infrastructural development of the American nation. The "primitive" American Indian provides the original "simple" system, which is replaced by the evolutionary advance of the more "complex nervous system."

If Turner describes the continent in terms of a human nervous system, we might note other ways Americans have traditionally figured the landscape. As Henry Nash Smith has pointed out *(Virgin Land)* and as Annette Kolodny has argued *(The Lay of the Land)* in their examinations of writing about the American landscape from the time of the earliest settlers to the late twentieth century, those who have written about America have consistently personified the American landscape as feminine. "European men, institutions, and ideas were lodged in the American wilderness, and this great American West took them to her bosom" (Turner 99). Writers have described the landscape either as a mother "receiving and nurturing human children," taking them to her bosom, or as a virgin who "apparently invites sexual assertion and awaits impregnation" (Kolodny, *Lay of the Land* 5, 67). In Kolodny's analysis literature about the American landscape continually repeats the Freudian account of the development of sexuality and subjectivity: "The dynamic of almost every piece of writing examined here, in fact, appears to repeat a movement back into the realm of the Mother, in order to begin again, and then an attempted . . . movement out of that containment in order to experience the self as independent, assertive, and sexually active" (153). The landscape at first offers a return to a state of "undifferentiated desire," which is replaced by an initial object-choice (the mother/land), which leads to the desire for possession of that object. This directed desire transforms the image of the landscape from mother (who, because of the incest taboo, cannot be desired) to virgin.

In Turner's 1893 essay, the colonist is initially infantilized by his encounter with the American landscape, which strips him of his clothing: "The wilderness masters the colonist" (Turner 33), returning him to a state of nature from which he may be reborn and remade. On the frontier, where civilization meets "the primitive American environment," the individual (again and again) re-creates both himself and American democracy, a "perennial rebirth" out of the womb of the American frontier, or out of the womblike shape of "the crucible of the frontier"

(47). The infantilized colonist returns to the pre-oedipal status of what "Freud describes as an 'oceanic self,' or what Lacan punningly refers to as 'l'hommelette' (a human omelette) which spreads in all directions" (Silverman 155). Before the infant's body "undergoes a process of differentiation, whereby erotogenic zones are inscribed and libido is canalized" for participation in "the sexually differentiated scenarios into which it will later be accommodated," the child does not distinguish between its mother and itself, and "its libidinal flow is directed toward the complete assimilation of everything which is experienced as pleasurable, and there are no recognized boundaries" (155). If the colonist experiences the arrival to the new land as a return to this infantile state, when the mother, not he, is the master, then the movement across the symbolic space of the American continent transforms him, taking him from a state of infantile regression to manhood, from being mastered to being the master. If *l'hommelette* initially spreads in all directions, his libidinal flow and desire is soon pointed in one direction—westward—and he soon transforms both self and wilderness, emerging as "a new product that is American" (Turner 34).

If (as Kolodny argues) descriptions of the American landscape reflect psychological processes, we might make a similar argument concerning the other key encounter in Turner's essay—that of colonist and American Indian. Central to the frontier myth is the belief that an encounter with otherness transforms the subjectivity of the hero, an encounter that bears a striking resemblance to what psychoanalytical theorist Jacques Lacan calls the mirror stage, the phase in an infant's development when it learns to recognize its own image in the mirror. This stage, which marks the infant's realization of itself as a separate and individual entity, is the first step in the establishment of a sense of self. The mirror stage represents "*an identification.*" It is an example of "the transformation that takes place in the subject when he assumes an image" (Lacan 2).[2] In the infant's maturation and development of a sense of individual identity, this image in the mirror "becomes a totalizing ideal that organizes and orients the self" (Gallop 79). The mirror stage represents a turning point by providing for the infant "the first totalized image of the body" as a unified whole rather than as a body "in bits and pieces" (Gallop 79). That unified ideal image forms the basis for the development of a sense of self. The individual self "as an organized entity is actually an imitation of the cohesiveness of the mirror image," a cohesiveness that is a projection of the developing infant's own desires to possess the mastery that he or she sees in (and projects onto) the mirror (Gallop 17).

In the scenario outlined by Turner, the European colonist encounters another man in the wilderness/virgin land, the American Indian. Initially the European recognizes the mastery of the American Indian and imitates his actions. Turner's description of this encounter provides a summary of the experience of frontier transformation:

> The wilderness masters the colonist. It finds him a European in dress, industries, tools, modes of travel, and thought. . . . It strips off the garments of civilization and arrays him in the hunting shirt and the moccasin. It puts him in the log cabin of the Cherokee and Iroquois and runs an Indian palisade around him. Before long he has gone to planting Indian corn and plowing with a sharp stick; he shouts the war cry and takes the scalp in orthodox Indian fashion. In short, at the frontier the environment is at first too strong for the man. He must accept the conditions which it furnishes, or perish, and so he fits himself into the Indian clearings and follows the Indian trails. Little by little he transforms the wilderness, but the outcome is not the

old Europe, not simply the development of Germanic germs. . . . The fact is, that here is a new product that is American. (33–34)

In Turner's account of the transformation of the European subject into "a new product that is American," the colonist, after his initial infantilization, locates in the image of the American Indian a totalizing ideal that organizes his change in identity. The European imitates the American Indian, whether in shouting the war cry, fitting himself into the Indian clearings and following the Indian trails, or in plowing with a sharp stick and seeding the earth. In the Lacanian account of the development of subjectivity, the identification with the mirror image is the first in a series of such identifications (including, for the male child, the image of his father), through which the self is brought into relation to others. The American Indian in Turner's account serves as a kind of substitute father. The Indian models an image of masculine ability that the colonist feels to be lacking in himself and that he desires to assume as his own.

Wister's representation of the American West in *The Virginian* is influenced primarily by his friend Theodore Roosevelt (to whom the book is dedicated), and we might note in the novel elements of both Turner's and Roosevelt's arguments. Like Turner's colonist the narrator of the book arrives from the East arrayed in the garments of civilization and ill-equipped for frontier life. "I was justly styled a tenderfoot," he observes, and "I was inveterate in laying my inexperience of Western matters bare to all the world" (*Virginian* 52). Later in the novel, the narrator notes his transformation from "Eastern helplessness" into a man who "had come to be trusted," from an individual who needs an escort for something as minor as an afternoon ride into someone able to cross "unmapped spaces with no guidance. The man who could do this was scarce any longer a 'tenderfoot'" (294). As is Turner's colonist, Wister's tenderfoot is aided in his transformation by the figure of another man encountered in the wilderness of the American West—the title character of the book, the Virginian, who serves as the ideal of masculinity and mastery. "In the whole man," the narrator observes, "there dominated a something potent to be felt, I should think, by man or woman" (7). In contrast to Turner's brief scenario, the manly presence that facilitates transformation here is not an American Indian but another white man. *The Virginian,* in a sense, tells a post-frontier story, one in which the transformation Turner describes has already taken place, with the Virginian representing the evolution of that initial transformation, the new man who has supplanted the American Indian as the image of admired masculine ability.

The Lacanian account of the operation of the mirror stage provides a means to explain how mythology (whether articulated in history, fiction, or film) works to disseminate ideology—by providing ideal images that invite the reader's (or listener's or viewer's) identification. Images of manhood are disseminated through mythical figures and mythic narratives, through versions of the frontier myth in which we recognize ourselves (or what we want to be) in the hero of the narrative. Ideology, Louis Althusser observes, "is both a real and [an] imaginary relation to the world—real in that it is the way in which people really live their relationship to social relations, but imaginary in that it discourages a full understanding of those conditions of existence" (233). Turner's representation of the advance of civilization is similarly both real and imaginary. Although he notes the displacement of America's native inhabitants, he renders this displacement in a way that "discourages a full understanding" of the relationship between colonists and the various groups of American Indians they encountered. "The disintegrating force of civilization entered the wilderness," Turner argues, via the Indian trail, which "became a fissure in Indian society. . . . Long before the pioneer farmer appeared on the scene, primitive Indian life had passed away" (Turner 40). Although the real relationship between American Indians and European colonists is one of violence and dispossession, in Turner's account the native inhabitants pass away and/or disintegrate in the face of advancing civilization.

In Turner's brief scenario of transformation, something essential but unnamed as such is transferred to the colonist— in a sense, perhaps, knowledge about the American continent and the necessary character needed to master that continent. Transformed in this encounter, the colonist also learns to do what the American Indian (according to Turner) has not done, which is to transform the wilderness. Having served his purpose in Turner's account of American history, the American Indian simply disappears, passes away. As Leverenz notes, Turner's "new product that is American" is "a hybrid, both savage and civilized," a combination of traits typical of a new type of hero, the "beast/patrician," developing in the nineteenth century (29–32). We might argue that Turner's account represents an imaginary joining of self and other, an incorporation by the new American man of the old American Indian within his own consciousness. In Turner's scenario, the trope of transformation serves to conceal the violent reality behind the disappearance of the American Indians. For Turner, the essential element of the American Indian, his primitive masculinity, remains—incorporated into, and thereby enabling the evolution of, the white American man. The archetypal encounter with a savage other facilitates the colonist's emergence as a new man and the representative of a new manhood, American masculinity, which both Turner and Roosevelt represent as the ultimate achievement of civilization, superior to both the savagery of the American Indian and the overcivilized manliness of the European because American manhood combines the best elements of both.

John Marrant

> I went over the fence, about half a mile from our house,
> which divided the inhabited and cultivated parts of the
> country from the wilderness. I continued travelling in the
> desart all day without the least inclination of returning
> back. About evening I began to be surrounded with wolves;
> I took refuge from them on a tree, and remained there all
> night.
>
> —MARRANT, A Narrative

At the time of the first publication of *A Narrative of the
Lord's Wonderful Dealings with John Marrant, a Black,* the genre
of the Indian captivity narrative was already well established in
America. The more popular of these accounts include Mary
White Rowlandson, *The Soveraignty and Goodness of GOD,
Together With the Faithfulness of His Promises Displayed; Being
a Narrative of the Captivity and Restauration of Mrs. Mary Rowlandson* (1682), and Peter Williamson, *French and Indian Cruelty Exemplified in the Life and Various Vicissitudes of Fortune of
Peter Williamson* (1775). Given the popularity of the genre, it is
not surprising that two of the earliest examples of African
American literature adapt the form. Preceding Marrant's *Narrative* is Briton Hammon's *Narrative of the Uncommon Sufferings and Surprizing Deliverance of Briton Hammon, A Negro
Man* (1760). Like Hammon's *Narrative,* Marrant's work is an
as-told-to story, written down by the white Methodist minister
William Aldridge, who asserts in his preface: "I have always preserved Mr. Marrant's ideas, tho' I could not his language; no
more alterations, however, have been made, than were thought
necessary" (Marrant 76). Although both Marrant and Hammon
were men of African descent, Marrant was free and Hammon
enslaved. Marrant's work differs from Hammon's in other
ways, especially in its popularity. Adam Potkay and Sandra Burr

describe Marrant's *Narrative* as "one of the three most popular works of that genre during the eighteenth and nineteenth centuries" (71) surpassed in number of published editions only by Williamson's *French and Indian Cruelty* and Mary Jemison's *A Narrative of the Life of Mrs. Mary Jemison, Who Was Taken by the Indians, in the Year 1755, When Only About Twelve Years of Age*, published in 1824.

Because of its popularity, numerous editions of and variations on the story were printed, including an undated fourth edition, which differs from others in that Marrant rather than Aldridge had direct control over its publication.[3] Potkay and Burr speculate that Marrant "may have asked Aldridge for permission to have a personal edition printed, in which he could freely describe experiences and feelings that Aldridge, sensitive to the sensibilities of the reading public, would not include in his publications" (73). Those additions include a frank description of the resentment felt by American Indians Marrant encountered in his travels toward white settlers and a long discussion of his attempt to start a church school for a group of slaves on a plantation in South Carolina. Among the events that Aldridge apparently found unnecessary to the telling of Marrant's story is his description of the mistress of the plantation's response to this attempt. Unable to convince her husband to punish Marrant (a free man), she ordered that the enslaved men, women, and children participating in Christian instruction be "strip'd naked and tied, their feet to a stake, their hands to the arm of a tree, and so severely flogg'd that the blood ran from their backs and sides to the floor" (Marrant 91). The inclusion of the plantation incident represents a significant departure from the conventions of the Indian captivity narrative and looks forward to the moves made by later African American writers to alter frontier mythology so as to accommodate black experience.

Born in 1755 in New York, Marrant moved to Florida with his mother shortly after his father's death when Marrant was four, and then to Georgia. At age eleven he moved to "Charles-Town, where it was intended I should be put apprentice to some trade" (Marrant 77). Rather than practice a trade, however, Marrant was inspired to play music, and "in a twelve-month's time I became master both of the violin and of the French-horn," an accomplishment that earned invitations to play at balls and assemblies and that also "opened to me a large door of vanity and vice" (77). Early in the narrative, Marrant introduces a pattern of establishing and inverting oppositions that will eventually result in his overturning the central trope of white-authored frontier narratives, the essential dichotomy of the civilized white self and the savage racial other. Marrant's mastery of his musical instruments leads to its own inversion, a type of slavery: "I was now in my thirteenth year, devoted to pleasure and drinking in iniquity like water; a slave to every vice suited to my nature and to my years" (77). As Zafar observes, even though "the word 'slave' is wielded in a moral sense, as synonym for one helplessly trapped by things of this world . . . the history of African slavery lurks as a palimpsest behind this rhetorical trope" (Zafar 57–58). If we read Marrant's statement in context of his later experiences on the South Carolina plantation, his self-enslavement—his being mastered by rather than controlling the desires of his own body—contrasts with the forced enslavement of his fellows on the plantation whose bodies are not their own to control. The comparison seems to indicate a somewhat naïve narrator, as the only vice he confesses to is "fishing and hunting on the sabbath-day" (Marrant 77–78). However, like the plantation mistress (if different in degree), Marrant is a poor master, abusing the body under his control and neglecting the spirit. In contrast to the plantation mistress, Marrant learns to become a better master by opening himself to the word of God. The mistress remains, to her detriment, closed to Christian ideals and is divinely punished when her abuse of others is revisited on her own body in the form of a mortal illness.

In the first part of the narrative, Marrant's play on the term *master* refers ultimately to his search for his true master—God himself. Marrant works on a trial basis for a carpenter who offers to have him bound as his apprentice in spite of the boy's often staying out late playing music "so as to render me incapable of attending my master's business the next day" (Marrant 78). While still weighing the offer, Marrant passes by a meeting-house and is told by his companion that "a crazy man was hallooing there" (78). Curious and mischievous, Marrant decides to disrupt the service by loudly blowing his French horn. This proposed prank is circumvented when the speaker, George Whitefield, "looking round, as I thought, directly upon me, and pointing with his finger . . . uttered these words, 'PREPARE TO MEET THY GOD O ISRAEL.' The Lord accompanied the word with such power, that I was struck to the ground, and lay both speechless and senseless near half an hour" (78). Marrant's conversion experience follows to form, a physical illness that mirrors his spiritual distress ("The lad will surely die," his sister laments), a protracted dark night of the soul ("in this distress of soul I continued for three days without any food, only a little water now and then"), and finally the miraculous intervention of God's grace: "near the close of his [a minister sent by Whitefield] prayer, the Lord was pleased to set my soul at perfect liberty, and being filled with joy I began to praise the Lord immediately" (79). By receiving the Lord as his master, Marrant liberates his soul from its early enslavement to vice and ultimately declares himself free of all earthly masters. He refuses to go back to work for the carpenter and even rejects his own physical mastery over his musical instruments: "I continued with my sister about three weeks, during which time she often

asked me to play upon the violin for her, which I refused" (80).
Marrant exchanges one form of mastery for another, refusing
his instruments in order to himself become an instrument of
God. By so doing, he claims as his own the power with which
he has just become acquainted—the power that accompanies
the "word." In another inversion, Marrant, initially struck
speechless by his first encounter with this power, becomes quite
verbose, and his speech becomes a conduit through which
God's power is manifested on the earth. Praising the Lord
becomes the means by which Marrant establishes his own
empowering voice.

Marrant's newfound piety and verbal expression thereof do
not appear as a blessing to his family, and "they called me every
name but that which was good" (80). Ultimately, Marrant
reconsiders his position at home: "I thought it was better for
me to die than to live among such people. . . . I took up a small
pocket Bible and one of Dr. Watts's hymn books, and passing by
them went out without one word spoken by any of us. After
spending some time in the fields, I was persuaded to go from
our home altogether. Accordingly I went over the fence, about
half a mile from our house, which divided the inhabited and
cultivated parts of the country from the wilderness. I continued
travelling in the desart all day without the least inclination of
returning back" (80–81). Silence ("without one word spoken by
any of us") symbolizes his alienation from his family. Although
the wilderness is a place where human voices are initially
absent, it is also a place where he may speak freely without cen-
sure. Much of his time spent in solitary wandering through the
wilderness is spent in prayer and conversation with God. In the
wilderness, Marrant hones the skill that is the clearest sign of
his civilization—the verbal ability that informs the effectiveness of his ministry.

Marrant's *Narrative* looks both backward to such earlier
captivity narratives as that of Mary Rowlandson and forward

to such later narratives of frontier experience as Cooper's
novels and Turner's history. Although eventually held captive
by Cherokees Marrant decides to cross the border from civilization ("the inhabited and cultivated parts") into savagery by
his own free will. In contrast to Rowlandson's narrative, in
which civilization (the puritan town) is invaded by savagery
and Rowlandson taken captive, Marrant is more like Turner's
composite pioneer, journeying into the wilderness of his own
accord, initially finding himself mastered but ultimately
regaining mastery of himself and his surroundings. Unlike
Turner's pioneer farmer, Marrant does not set forth to colonize
and possess the wilderness. In keeping with the representation
of the landscape in earlier captivity narratives, Marrant's
wilderness is an allegorical or typological terrain, not a savage
wilderness waiting to be transformed into civilized private
property. Marrant sets forth to test his faith, and each incident
in his journey deeper into the wilderness represents either a
trial or an unexpected example of God's power and mercy.
Marrant wanders aimlessly for almost two weeks, "feeding
upon grass, and not knowing whither I was going; but the Lord
Jesus Christ was very present, and that comforted me through
the whole." Even an encounter with two bears causes "very little
fear." The bears walk away "without growling," and "I went and
returned God thanks for my escape, who had tamed the wild
beasts of the forest, and made them friendly to me" (82).

Immediately after this encounter with the bears, an Indian
hunter bolted out from his hiding place "and put his hands on
my breast, which surprized me a few moments" (82). Although
this juxtaposition implies a connection between two types of
forest savages, Marrant redirects that comparison. Whereas the
bears did not even growl, the hunter speaks (and in English,
even, as he trades in the town). He is puzzled by the solitary
Marrant carrying on a conversation with an invisible companion: "Having heard me praising God before I came up to

him, he enquired who I was talking to? . . . . He further enquired
what preserved me from being devoured by the wild beasts? I
replied, the Lord Jesus Christ kept me from them. He stood
astonished, and said, you say the Lord Jesus Christ do this, and
do that, and do every thing for you, he must be a very fine man,
where is he? I replied, he is here present. To this he made no
answer" (82–83). If Marrant's initial encounter with the hunter
implies a comparison to other beasts of the forest, he soon
regards his companion as fully human, and they spend several
months traveling together. Although Marrant states that the
bears were made friendly by God, he does not attribute the
hunter's amiability to such a divine source. Rather, the hunter's
actions seem to be his own and his interest in Marrant a sign of
his humanity (or human curiosity). Like Turner's colonist
Marrant initially adapts to a new environment by imitating and
learning the skills of the Indian hunter: "Our employment for
ten weeks and three days was killing deer, and taking off their
skins by day, which we afterwards hung on the trees to dry till
they were sent for" (83). Although Turner's colonist may behave
in orthodox Indian fashion, he does not act in concert with
American Indians. For Turner, any joining of civilized self and
savage other depends on the physical disappearance of the
American Indian and the corresponding incorporation within
the civilized white psyche of certain essential qualities of savagery. For Marrant, shared employment results in a shared
sense of identity—as symbolized by his shift here from the singular "I" to the first person plural, "we."

The sense of companionship established by Marrant and the
hunter is symbolized as well by the creation of a common language, a mixture of Cherokee and English. As the hunter
already speaks enough English to communicate, the task falls
on Marrant's shoulders to learn the other's language. Through
his companion, Marrant "acquired a fuller knowledge of the
Indian tongue: This, together with the sweet communion

I enjoyed with God, I have since considered as a preparation for the great trial I was soon after to pass through" (83). Language difference does not symbolize an essential opposition between civilization and savagery. Rather, Marrant associates his learning the Indian tongue with his enjoyment of "the sweet communion" with God. Through knowledge of the one, he is able to introduce his eventual captors to the knowledge of the other—and not incidentally save his own life in the process of saving the souls of the Cherokees who hold him captive.

At the end of hunting season, Marrant returns with his companion to "a large Indian town, belonging to the Cherokee nation," where, despite the assurances of the hunter, he is stopped by a guard and sentenced to death, a prospect that initially "made me very happy, as the near prospect of death made me hope for speedy deliverance from the body" (83–84). This sanguine attitude toward his own death changes "when the executioner shewed me a basket of turpentine wood, stuck full of small pieces like skewers; he told me I was to be stripped naked, and laid down on one side by the basket, and these sharp pegs were to be stuck into me, and then set on fire" (84). This description of the manner of his execution causes him to burst into tears and to ask for permission to pray (85). Although he initially prays in English, divine intervention sparks another strategy: "The Lord impressed a strong desire upon my mind to turn into their language, and pray in their tongue. I did so, and with remarkable liberty, which wonderfully affected the people. One circumstance was very singular, and strikingly displays the power and grace of God. I believe the executioner was savingly converted to God. He rose from his knees, and embracing me round the middle was unable to speak for about five minutes; the first words he expressed, when he had utterance, were, 'No man shall hurt thee till thou hast been to the king'" (85). Power in this scene shifts from the executioner to the condemned. That shift is represented linguistically in the contrast between

Marrant's bilingual eloquence and the executioner's inability to speak. By saving the executioner, Marrant saves himself, for once the man's powers of speech return, he speaks in Marrant's defense.

The Cherokee king proves a tougher case. While he is speaking with Marrant the king's daughter enters, takes Marrant's Bible from his hand, opens it, and kisses it. Although delighted with it, she states with much sorrow that "the book would not speak to her" (86). If the book will not speak, Marrant speaks in its stead, and in the midst of his prayer "some of them cried out, particularly the king's daughter" (86). The king, angered by this turn of events, orders Marrant's execution. When his daughter falls ill, the king offers Marrant one more chance—cure her or be killed. Marrant observes: "The Lord appeared most lovely and glorious; the king himself was awakened, and the others set at liberty. A great change took place among the people; the king's house became God's house; the soldiers were ordered away, and the poor condemned prisoner had perfect liberty, and was treated like a prince. Now the Lord made all my enemies to become my great friends" (87). The power may be God's, but the conduit is Marrant and the medium his skillful use of language. Through the power that accompanies the word of God, Marrant himself finds the power to overturn a whole series of oppositions. In the earlier wilderness scene, God makes the two bears friendly. As in the earlier miracle, agency belongs to God for it is he that makes enemies friends. If one scene echoes the other, there is nonetheless a great difference between becoming friendly and becoming friends (which the bears do not become). God acts upon the Cherokees as he acted upon Marrant himself, and the level of transformation that takes place depends on the inherent qualities of the affected. Savage wild beasts can be made friendly but only his fellow humans can be made "great friends."

Marrant is changed by his encounter with savagery, and he uses clothing to symbolize this transformation. Like Turner's colonist, Marrant is stripped of "the garments of civilization"—with the significant exceptions of his Bible and hymnal. As Turner's colonist is arrayed "in the hunting shirt and the moccasin," so Marrant assumes "the habit of the country, and was dressed much like the king" (87). Turner's colonist takes to planting Indian corn and plowing with a sharp stick, adopting primitive farming skills that will eventually evolve into more sophisticated agricultural techniques as savagery recedes before the advance of civilization. Marrant, on the other hand, emphasizes his growing knowledge of language: "Here I learnt to speak their tongue in the highest stile" (87). Through selective imitation of the other, Turner's colonist becomes master of the wilderness. Despite numerous hardships, Marrant is never entirely mastered by the wilderness because his (and the land's) true master is ever present. Although a precursor to Turner's account of wilderness transformation, Marrant's *Narrative* does not represent his journey in terms of an oedipal scenario. The landscape is not feminized but, rather, infused with the divine presence of God himself. Turner's oedipalization indicates a significant shift both in historical context and in rhetorical purpose. Marrant does not desire to possess the land he passes across. The "totalizing ideal" (Gallop 79) that facilitates his transformation is God, and his allegorical journey involves a process of progressively remaking the self in order to better approximate the divine image.

Turner retains many of the elements of frontier contact represented in Marrant's account, particularly the idea of transformation. The wilderness sojourn as an explicit religious allegory, however, has been emptied from his secular and political narrative. Turner's pioneer is reborn, not converted, and the end result of frontier transformation is not a man of God but a political creation, "a new product that is American." This product is both the independent and individualized citizen and the system of government ("American democracy") emerging from the complex interaction of civilization and savagery within the crucible of the frontier. Whereas Turner describes the encounter between colonists and American Indians in evolutionary terms (with savagery necessarily receding before civilization), Marrant describes a mutually transformative encounter from which both parties emerge changed. The American Indians in his account do not disintegrate but are converted and contribute to the further spread of Christianity to other tribes. Marrant's knowledge of their language and culture enables him to view the incursion of European settlers from the native's point of view: "When they recollect, that the white people drove them from the American shores, they are full of resentment" (88). In the midst of his travels among the different groups Marrant observes, "I had not much reason to believe any of these three nations were savingly wrought upon, and therefore I returned to the Cherokee nation" (88). The real barrier to conversion, Marrant implies, has more to do with this understandable resentment than with any natural inclinations of the nations he encounters.

After his sojourn with his captors-turned-companions, Marrant returns to civilization: "My dress was purely in the Indian stile; the skins of wild beasts composed my garments; my head was set out in the savage manner, with a long pendant down my back[,] a sash round my middle, without breeches, and a tomohawk by my side" (88). After several days of walking, he makes contact with a family on the outer edge of settlement: "As I was coming to the door the family saw me, were frightened, and ran away. I sat down to dinner alone, and eat very heartily" (88). Although the trappings of savagery obscure the Christian virtue of the man who wears the garments, he coaxes the family from their hiding place and stays with them for six weeks. When he reaches his uncle's house, "the singularity of my dress drew every body's eye upon me, yet none knew me" (89). When the family neglects to say a blessing at supper, Marrant reproved them: "this so affected the man, that I believe it ended in a sound conversion. Here is a wild man, says he, come out of the woods, to be witness for God, and to reprove our ingratitude and stupefaction" (89). Initially startling, Marrant's appearance contributes to the effectiveness of his ministry. Marrant walks out of the wilderness as the embodiment of civilization and savagery combined—his clothing that of the savage, his actions those of the civilized Christian man. Whatever direct influence his *Narrative* may have had on later writers, the strangely garbed Marrant who emerges at the end of his wilderness sojourn is clearly a precursor to the beast/patrician figure popularized as the heroic ideal in the work of such nineteenth-century writers as Cooper, Turner, and Roosevelt.

Henry Louis Gates focuses his interpretation of Marrant's book on the scene of the Cherokee king's conversion—a scene that must be reconsidered in light of Marrant's additions.[4] Of particular interest to Gates is Marrant's revision of "the trope of the talking book," which first appears in James Albert Ukawsaw Gronniosaw's *A Narrative of the Most Remarkable Particulars in the Life of James Albert Ukawsaw Gronniosaw, An African Prince, written by Himself* (1770). After observing his master in prayers over the Bible, the enslaved Gronniosaw places the book to his ear and hearing no voice comes to the conclusion that the book refuses to speak to him because he is black. Marrant inverts the trope of the talking book by placing the king's daughter in the position of the illiterate other. By so doing, Gates argues, he establishes his difference "in contrast with other people of color" and places "the perilous burdens of negation" upon the Cherokee (*Signifying Monkey* 145). Marrant, Gates asserts, "amounts to a substituted white man in the presence of the Cherokee," whose illiterate otherness provides the ground for Marrant's own self-definition (150). Through his relationship with his newfound friends, however, Marrant undermines any easy assertions of racial or cultural difference as evidence of an opposition between superior and inferior. Through the medium of Marrant's body, seeming opposites are conjoined, as the civilized God of Christianity speaks in a savage voice through the body of a black man. When Marrant returns to settled areas, he emerges as a sign of an equally complex fusion of different cultural identities: a bilingual Christian black man dressed in the savage manner.

The plantation mistress's violent efforts to halt Marrant's ministry undermine any association of civilized status exclusively with whiteness. Savagery, for Marrant, is behavioral rather than racial, a point that may be obscured in other editions of the *Narrative*. After his return from the wilderness, John Marrant joins his carpenter brother to do repair work on a plantation located outside Charleston and owned by a Mr. Jenkins. When finished with the day's work, "I used to spend my time in reading God's Word, singing Watts's Hymns and in Prayer, the little negro children would often come round the door with their pretty wishful looks" (Marrant 91). Finding them unable to recite the Lord's Prayer, Marrant tells them "if they would come every evening I would teach them." These lessons continued without interruption for three or four months and soon grew into a congregation of around thirty people including the parents of the children. However, "the old Lion began to roar, their mistress became acquainted with our proceedings, and was full of rage at it." When told that "the free Carpenter" was teaching the Lord's Prayer to the children, she "stirred up her husband against us" and told him "it was the ready way to have all his negroes ruin'd." Together with his overseer and several neighbors, Mr. Jenkins "Beset the place wherein we met, while we were at prayers; and as the poor creatures came out they caught them, and tied them together with cords, till the next morning, when all they caught, men, women, and children were strip'd naked and tied, their feet to a stake, their hands to the arm of a tree, and so severely flogg'd that the blood ran from their backs and sides to the floor, to make them promise they would leave off praying" (91). By including the plantation scene in a narrative of wilderness journey, Marrant inverts the central trope of frontier mythology. In the savage wilderness he discovers the essential humanity of the heathen Indians. In civilization he discovers the most reprehensible savagery—the behavior of "civilized" whites. Marrant's relocation of savagery initiates a strategy of revision that will be repeated by other black writers of frontier narratives.

Marrant draws our attention to the ironic interplay between events that take place with the Cherokee and on the plantation by repeating common elements. His comment that "the old Lion began to roar" echoes the encounter with the two bears in the wilderness. The beasts of the forest were made friendly by God and left without growling, but the savage rage of the white woman, the most celebrated symbol of white civilization, remains untamable. Marrant's attempts to calm her rage mirror his earlier encounter with the Cherokee king. Although he carefully translates for her ears the will of God, she (like the Cherokee king at first) refuses to listen. Marrant tells her husband that "the blood of those poor negroes which he had spilt that morning would be required by God at his hands" (92). Meeting with the mistress, Marrant told her the same, "but she laught at it, and was only sorry that she had not been able to get me flog'd with them" (92). Marrant gives no indication if the mistress is literate or illiterate, but whether the book speaks to her or not, she is as unwilling to listen to the word of God as she is to Marrant. When the Cherokee king refuses to hear God's will his daughter falls ill: "They used the skill of all their doctors that afternoon and night; but physical prescriptions were useless" (87). Similarly, when the mistress laughs rather than listens, "it pleased God to lay his hand upon" her, and "she was seized with a very violent fever" (92). Physical prescriptions are useless here as well, for "No medicine that they could produce would remove" the fever, and "she died in a very dreadful manner" (92). Although the Cherokees certainly indicate a propensity for extreme violence (the proposed manner of Marrant's death), they are nonetheless open to the redeeming word. The heaven-inspired restraint of the Cherokees contrasts sharply with the heaven-rejecting violence of the white slave-holders. In distinct contrast to the white narratives of the frontier (discussed in the next section), white violence against a racial other is divinely punished rather than celebrated.

Before leaving the plantation, Marrant encourages the enslaved blacks "to call upon God as well as they could" (92). The lesson that Marrant eventually teaches his students is that even if the body is controlled by white masters the spirit is not—and that spirit can be liberated even while the body remains enslaved. Although the mistress persecutes them until her death, they "nevertheless continued their meetings though in such imminent danger" (92). By liberating the soul, Marrant introduces into the enslaved community a physical as well as a spiritual resistance. As Marrant's conversion provides him with a means to establish his own empowering voice, so the captivity narrative provides him with a form through which to tell his story and be heard. That power was tempered by his having to tell his story through a white editor. When able to control the final product himself, Marrant uses the cultural authority provided by the Indian captivity narrative to deliver a political message about the treatment of slaves—and about the possibility of using Christianity as a tool for resisting oppression.

Regeneration through Violence

The agents of historical change in Turner's history are the independent yeoman farmers who made up what Turner sees as a democratic collective of individuals working to create and support a social order that emphasizes a widespread distribution of property and power. In *Gunfighter Nation*, Slotkin argues that in the nineteenth century the frontier myth "became the site of a cultural contest between two different schools of American ideology," the populist and the progressive schools, with each ideological position symbolized by the choice of an archetypal frontier hero, the farmer or the hunter (22). Both populists and progressives connected an economic crisis at the end of the nineteenth century with the closing of the frontier, and both groups also connected the end of the frontier with changes taking place in the American economy— the crisis of modernization resulting in the transformation of small farms, shops, and businesses into industrial farms, factories, and corporations, resulting as well in the concentration of wealth in the hands of a few.

Unlike the populist's vision of life on the frontier as producing a social order in which a democratic collective formed the primary agents of political life, the progressives read "the history of savage warfare and westward expansion as a Social Darwinian parable, explaining the emergence of a new managerial ruling class," which describes itself as a new race of men, one particularly suited for ruling over other Americans (Slotkin, *Gunfighter* 22). As Americans lamented the closing of the frontier that had produced this new race of men, they also began to search for new frontiers that would not only transform the American nation into the American empire but also provide a savage testing ground for the continued evolution of American manhood. We will see this crisis of modernization reflected as well by shifts in definitions of gender. As Amy Kaplan observes, "the republican quality of character based on self-control and social responsibility" associated with earlier ideals of American manhood (and with a less centralized economic system) shifts during this period to a definition of masculinity based on "a corporeal essence identified with the vigor and prowess of the individual male body" (662).

We might argue that, structurally, Roosevelt's multivolume history *The Winning of the West* (1889–1896) illustrates the emergence of this new manhood emphasizing vigor and prowess, and that Roosevelt's construction of masculinity responds to the rise to power of a new managerial ruling class. Through discussions of a series of types—ranging from the Backwoodsman (who initially entered the American wilderness individually or in small groups) to the Scout (who, as the settlements grew larger, mediated between the individualistic Backwoodsman and the army regulars, especially the more patrician officers) to the Military/Political Leader—Roosevelt shows a progressive evolution of the American type, from the individualistic loner represented by the Backwoodsman to the hero-chief, or natural aristocrat, the powerful individual who manages other men, both on and off the battlefield, whose vigor and prowess is necessary for controlling large groups of people. This military leader represents the culmination of a process of evolution, the highest achievement of civilization, who after proving his worth on the battlefield emerges at the end of the nineteenth century to take rightful control of political leadership as well as leadership in the business world.

Cooper's Natty Bumppo provides an important precursor and articulation of the "new man" who emerges in Roosevelt's history—the beast/patrician who combines the savage and the civilized in one body, and who will eventually develop in Roosevelt's history into the natural aristocrat. In an often quoted and explicated passage from Cooper's *The Deerslayer* (1841), we see Natty Bumppo move from boyhood to manhood through the slaying of an American Indian man:

> The black, ferocious eyes of the savage were glaring on him, like those of the crouching tiger, through a small opening in the bushes, and the muzzle of his rifle seemed already to be opening in a line with his own body.
>
> Then, indeed, the long practice of Deerslayer as a hunter did him good service. . . . To cock and poise his rifle were the acts of a single moment, and a single motion; then, aiming almost without sighting, he fired into the bushes where he knew the body ought to be, in order to sustain the appalling countenance which was alone visible. There was not time to raise the piece any higher, or to take a more deliberate aim. So rapid were his movements that both parties discharged their pieces at the same instant. (121)

Deerslayer is grazed by a rifle shot. His opponent is shot through the body, although not immediately killed, and before he dies he provides the Deerslayer with "a more manly title": "'That good name for boy—poor name for warrior. Get better quick. No fear *there*—' the savage had strength sufficient under the strong excitement he felt, to raise a hand and tap the young man on his breast—'eye, sartain—finger, lightning—aim, death. Great warrior, soon—No Deerslayer—Hawkeye—Hawkeye—Hawkeye—Shake hand.'" (124). Leverenz argues that this moment of violence leads to "mythic transformation" and a rebirth for the hero in which he receives a new identity, as "Deerslayer becomes Manslayer." However, Leverenz notes, "the name goes the other way, from Deerslayer to Hawkeye. A bird's soaring, predatory quickness dignifies and sharpens Natty's rightful yet brutal dominance" (29) with the new name emphasizing not the act of violence but the skill involved in that act.

Several of the individual encounters that Roosevelt describes in *The Winning of the West* replicate the crucial scene from *The

Deerslayer in some detail, especially in their emphasis on a mythic transformation through violent actions. For example, Roosevelt notes that a "favorite stratagem" of the American Indian was "to imitate the call of game" and thus lure an unsuspecting hunter to his fate, with the hunter becoming the hunted—although, Roosevelt tells us, the hunted often became again the hunter (149–50). Roosevelt narrates the specific story of a hunter named Castleman who, like Deerslayer, employs a "quick and certain eye" to discover and dispatch an enemy "glaring on him . . . through a small opening in the bushes" (Cooper 121). Roosevelt rewrites the scene: "Creeping cautiously up, and peering though the brush, [Castleman] saw something the height of a stump between two forked trees. It did not look natural; he aimed, pulled trigger, and killed an Indian" (Roosevelt 150).

In contrast to Turner, Roosevelt emphasizes that land was not free but had to be taken by force. Whereas Turner argues that the development of the United States is the history of European colonists slowly overcoming geographic obstacles, Roosevelt instead argues that the determining factor was the presence of the American Indians, a presence that caused "the process of settlement to go on at unequal rates of speed in different places" (Roosevelt 17). American history for Roosevelt is the history of a series of battles pitched against both native inhabitants and European countries such as England, France, and Spain over the possession of the American continent. These violent encounters—not the availability of free land—create the distinct, exceptional, masculine American character.[5]

For both Turner and Roosevelt, the colonist's encounter with a savage other facilitates his emergence as a new man. If Turner's colonist goes to planting Indian corn and plowing with a sharp stick, Roosevelt's frontiersman likewise transforms himself through imitation—and likewise invests the figure of the American Indian with all the qualities that the

frontiersman desires, the possession of which will distinguish
him from his European fellows. As a hunter soon learns to copy
the movements of his prey in order to become successful, the
whites soon "copied from the Indians their system of individual
and private warfare," rather than relying on the movement of
large divisions associated with European strategy (Roosevelt
150). Through imitation of the other, borrowing tactics of warfare rather than farming techniques, the white settler sheds his
civilized habits and begins his evolution into a new man. While
each historian notes the reality of the existence of various
groups of American Indians on the continent, each writer also
sees in the figure of the American Indian a reflection of his
own desires—great (if savage) warriors, efficient (if primitive)
farmers.

Roosevelt argues that "many noted border scouts and Indian
fighters—such men as Boon, Kenton, Wetzel, Brady, McCul-
loch, Mansker—grew to overmatch their Indian foes at their
own game" (127). Almost fooled by a game call, one Indian
fighter named Mansker "became suspicious, and 'placed' his
adversary behind a large tree. Having perfect confidence in his
rifle, and knowing that the Indians rarely fired except at close
range—partly because they were poor shots, partly because
they loaded their guns too lightly—he made no attempt to
hide.[6] Feigning to pass to the Indian's right, the latter, as he
expected, tried to follow him; reaching an opening in a glade,
Mansker suddenly wheeled and killed his foe" (151). Again,
Roosevelt draws on Cooper in his description. As are Deerslayer's, Mansker's actions are "the acts of a single moment, and
a single motion" (Cooper 121). Mansker next encounters two
foes. One he kills, and the other escapes only because "the gun
would not go off" (Roosevelt 152). Each act of killing increases
Mansker's abilities until Mansker becomes a leader of men and
continues to develop his ability on an increasing scale of violence. Mansker represents an example of the type who "was a

wonderful marksman and woodsman, and was afterwards made a colonel of the frontier militia," a movement from individual accomplishment to a managerial position consistent with many of Roosevelt's types (150). In the evolutionary story that Roosevelt advances, we see a line of descent from these individual Indian fighters to military leaders in the Indian wars to Roosevelt himself and his contemporaries.

According to Roosevelt, the early white settlers in America possessed latent in their blood the vigor and masculinity of a more primitive time. This masculinity, inherent though it was in what Roosevelt calls the "German stock," had lost potency in the civilized society of Europe. Leaving behind their European homes and venturing onto the American frontier placed the white settlers in a position where those latent qualities could be made manifest. The encounter with the American Indian became for Roosevelt the means of renewing the white settler's capacity for manhood. The savage had a virility and primitive masculinity that the representative of the German stock had lost, that had been civilized from his blood.[7] For Roosevelt the German stock could regain this lost manhood only by encountering—and defeating—the savage in his own domain. Essential to this wilderness encounter with the savage is what Slotkin calls the myth of "regeneration through violence" (*Gunfighter* 12). This act of violence, for Roosevelt, enables a "spiritual exchange" to take place between the white settler and the other while allowing "no admixture of blood" (*Gunfighter* 47). Only by killing the savage can the white settler acquire his savage, primitive masculinity and thus transform himself into a new man.

In his discussion of José Ortega y Gasset's *Meditations on Hunting,* Eric Sundquist notes the mythic and ritualistic elements of hunting. The strategy of the hunt in its various permutations and contexts, Sundquist argues, is to "obliterate distinctions between hunter and beast" primarily in order to "reassert those distinctions in an act of murderous violence"

(145). As the ritual of the hunt is played out, "the ascendancy of slayer and slain fluctuates, equalizing the respect for, and power over, the other that each has" (140). The equality between subject and object exists as part of "a ritual of mastery in which identities are collapsed only to be asserted more brutally than ever" (142). In a scene late in Cooper's *The Deerslayer,* Natty Bumppo is captured by Hurons and is offered, in exchange for his life, marriage to the wife of the man he killed earlier in the book. Bumppo's refusal to become her husband angers the woman's brother, named the Panther. Cooper writes, "the animal from which he got his name does not glare on his intended prey, with more frightful ferocity, than his eyes gleamed on the captive" (473). The Panther follows a yelled insult by tossing a tomahawk at Natty, but luckily, "the loud tones of the speaker had drawn the eye of Deerslayer towards him," and Natty catches the tomahawk in the air. "His eye kindled . . . and a small red spot appeared on each cheek, while he cast all his energy into the effort of his arm, and threw back the weapon at his assailant. . . . The keen little axe struck the victim in a perpendicular line with the nose, directly between the eyes" (473–74). Cooper's language here functions to "obliterate distinctions between hunter and beast" (Sundquist 145). Initially, Bumppo is assigned the status of beast, the intended prey of the hunter. The Indian's position as hunter, however, is undercut by his name, the Panther, and by his animal-like frightful ferocity. For a moment, Natty Bumppo and his opponent take on qualities associated with both hunter and beast. Bumppo's "kindled" eye matches the animal-like ferocity of the glare and gleam of his opponent's eyes. Such a blurring of distinctions serves primarily to "reassert those distinctions in an act of murderous violence" and to establish the unquestionable dominance of the white hero (145).

If the hunt Roosevelt describes in *The Winning of the West* is familiar to both European tradition and rural American culture (whatever the region), he nonetheless places this ritual in the context of the American West, where it takes on a particularly marked character—due, in large part, to the object of the hunt, a foe whose status as an opponent reflects greater glory on the white man capable of defeating him. The frontier version of this "universal" hunting ritual marks out two clear positions; the civilized white hunter and the savage object of the hunt, the American Indian. By enacting the ritual of the hunt, by defeating a formidable foe, the white American can regain the manhood that has been "civilized" from his blood. Engaging the savage other in battle enables the civilized white man to return to a savage state of being, to become like the beast he hunts but only in order to prove his superior status by emerging as the victor from the battle. The mythic transformation precipitated by the encounter with the other is also a transformation in class status that establishes the superior manhood of Roosevelt's hero and distinguishes him from the mass of men. By means of frontier violence, the hero establishes his natural entitlement to a position of power in American society. Roosevelt's history not only justifies the coming to power of a new managerial ruling class but also provides a heroic and attractive image of manhood in which the men of his class can recognize themselves.

We can see Roosevelt's ideas reflected quite clearly in Wister's *The Virginian*. The novel's main character, the Virginian, undergoes a process of maturation similar to Roosevelt's descriptions of the evolution of the frontiersman from individualistic, solitary hunter to leader and manager of men. In contrast to both Roosevelt's *The Winning of the West* and Turner's "The Significance of the Frontier in American History," the primary activity in *The Virginian* is ranching rather than either farming or fighting American Indians. Wister emphasizes the importance of frontier experience in developing management (of cattle, of men) skills. We see the

Virginian advancing from cowhand to temporary foreman to permanent foreman to landowner and full partner with Judge Henry in his ranching enterprise. Savagery in *The Virginian* resides not so much in American Indians as in what the novel terms the "equality"—the masses, the men and women of lower classes who refuse to submit to the authority of "natural aristocrats," or the "quality." The novel presents us with such examples of the "equality" as Trampas, the Virginian's nemesis, and the other cowboys—who at one point threaten to go chasing after gold rather than returning to Judge Henry's ranch and completing their duty. As temporary foreman, the Virginian must see to it that both cattle and hired men reach their respective destinations. He does so via a tall tale about frog ranching that puts Trampas, the instigator of the rebellion, in his place. For Wister, the frontier prepares the natural aristocrat for the task of controlling the "equality," through a well-told tall tale, if possible, or by other means if necessary—as symbolized by the Virginian's participation in the lynching of cattle rustlers and by his eventual killing of Trampas. This climactic act does not so much indicate a transfer of virility from the savage Trampas to the civilized Virginian as it provides evidence that the "quality" still maintains the masculine capacity for violence that is needed to control the unruly masses.

Although violence is a central element in the work of African American writers as well, they will generally (as does John Marrant) relocate the concept of savagery in terms of white behavior. In Pauline Hopkins's *Winona*, a historical novel set on the antebellum border between Missouri and Kansas, savagery is represented by the actions and philosophies of the proslavery Missouri Rangers. Novelist and filmmaker Oscar Micheaux's silent 1920 film *The Symbol of the Unconquered* (discussed in chapter 2) includes such staples of the Western as horse thieves, bar fights, and land grabs. The representatives of savage otherness, however, are not marauding Indians, outlaws, or even the "equality," but the Ku Klux Klan, whose members attempt to force Hugh Van Allen, the film's hero, off his oil-rich homestead.

Homosocial Desire and Frontier Manhood

> *I will be using "desire" in a way analogous to the psychoan-alytic use of "libido"—not for a particular affective state or emotion, but for the affective or social force, the glue, even when its manifestation is hostility or hatred or something less emotively charged, that shapes an important relation-ship.*
>
> —Sedgwick, *Between Men*

In *Between Men*, Eve Kosofsky Sedgwick argues that "homo-social desire" is part of "the *structure* of men's relations with other men" (2). According to Sedgwick, "there is a special rela-tionship between male homosocial (*including* homosexual) desire and the structures for maintaining and transmitting patriarchal power" (25). Essential to the maintaining of that structure of patriarchal power is the creation of bonds between men, and one of Sedgwick's main points is that such bonding almost always occurs in the form of "traffic in women" (25). That is, "it is the use of women as exchangeable, perhaps sym-bolic, property for the primary purpose of cementing bonds of men with men" (25–26). In Turner's version of the frontier myth, the American landscape provides the bond of a joint possession of that land between white male American individ-uals—the property-owning democratic collective. We might argue that what takes place in Turner's account is the homoso-cial bond between white men on the frontier, in a space per-sonified as feminine, and over the body of the American Indian whose dispossession is articulated as a disappearance.

If, to quote Leslie Fiedler's argument about the core scene of American literature, "there is a pure marriage of men" (211), one white, one non-white, in a wilderness place, that "marriage" for Turner is not primarily between the white man and his non-white other but between the white man and other white men. Homosocial desire for Turner involves the social force that binds white men into an important relationship—American democracy. For Turner the feminized American landscape serves as an object of exchange between (white) men. Turner locates the essential homosocial bond as taking place within the democratic collective of gentleman farmers. Roosevelt sees the necessity for a more limited set of bonds between men—that of an elite class of managers. Through his version of the frontier myth, Roosevelt provides a history of the development of a particular set of homosocial bonds seeking to justify and naturalize the position of power and privilege within American society held by this group of men. Whatever the differences between populists and progressives, both ideological schools advocate a social order that is distinctly patriarchal, that depends on the creation of bonds between men. Turner and Roosevelt, representatives of these ideological schools, articulate the frontier myth in ways that justify each writer's ideological position.

In Cooper's *The Deerslayer,* before he slays the Indian, Natty Bumppo arrives with his friend Henry March (nicknamed Hurry Harry) at Glimmerglass Lake. A Huron raiding party threatens March's friend Floating Tom, who lives with his two daughters, Judith and Hetty Hutter, in a cabin built on stilts in the middle of the lake—transforming the lake into a protective moat. March intends not only to help protect the two women but also to ask one of them (Judith) to marry him. The same Huron raiding party has captured the bride-to-be of Bumppo's Delaware friend Chingachgook, and Bumppo has joined with March primarily to rendezvous with Chingachgook in order to mount a rescue. Before the rendezvous, however, Bumppo finds himself involved in protecting the Hutter daughters. As he comments, "Men are'n't apt to see females in danger, and not come to their assistance" (Cooper 95). Assisting females in danger "shapes" the relationship established between Hurry Harry, Floating Tom, and Natty Bumppo. Woman, as a potential object of exchange between white men and American Indian men, also shapes the relationship between those two groups of men—as white men form alliances in opposition to American Indians in part to disrupt that potential.

The presence of women and Bumppo's manly need to provide protection facilitate his later slaying of the Huron warrior, an act of violence that represents an exchange between two men in which the virility of one is passed on to the other. Women in the novel function primarily as a means for cementing a bond between the civilized white man and his savage other, a bond based not on a political alliance but on the incorporation of savagery within the civilized white body. Bumppo's protection of white womanhood establishes his civilized status at the same time as it enables—indeed, necessitates—his act of savage violence. Woman-as-object-of-exchange in *The Deerslayer* facilitates, and conceals the contradictions inherent in, Bumppo's embodiment of aspects of manhood both savage (the capacity for violence) and civilized (the chivalrous protection of women).

Whereas the women in *The Deerslayer* mediate the relationships between men, Roosevelt's *Winning of the West* barely acknowledges the presence of women on the frontier. The history of America, Roosevelt argues, is continuous with European history in that the development of the United States continues the domination of the white race by selective breeding. The participation of women in this process disappears beneath the repetition of the names of male military leaders and the names of battles fought: "The fathers followed Boon or fought at King's Mountain; the sons marched south with Jackson to overcome the Creeks and beat back the British; the grandsons died at the

Alamo or charged to victory at San Jacinto. They were doing their share of a work that began with the conquest of Britain, that entered on its second and wider period after the defeat of the Spanish Armada, that culminated in the marvellous growth of the United States" (27). These movements represent "the past race-history" of the Germanic stock that reached its greatest heights in conquering and populating the American continent. They represent a specifically paternal legacy of whiteness passed down from father to son that seemingly dispenses with, and certainly marginalizes, the figure of woman.

For Roosevelt, women function as an implicit rather than explicit object of exchange between men. As did many "progressive" men of his era, Roosevelt believed that white Americans were obliged to push civilization toward evolutionary perfection, with "civilization" understood as "the achievement of a perfect race" (Bederman 27). To do otherwise would be to abandon the path of evolution to the savage races, to abandon the duty of the civilized peoples. Implicit in *The Winning of the West* as it is in *The Deerslayer* is the fear of miscegenation, necessitating the protection of white womanhood from sexual violation by the savage other. The very existence of savagery places females in danger, and this danger also threatens the perfection—and purity—of the white race. The figure of woman functions as an implicit (and textually nearly absent) object of exchange by necessitating a bond between white men established for the sake of protecting white womanhood—and necessitates as well the collective violence against the savage other who threatens not only the individual white woman but the racially pure civilization she represents. In *The Winning of the West*, the American Indian as an explicit textual figure substitutes for "woman" in Sedgwick's formulation as the exchanged object that cements "bonds of men with men" (Sedgwick 26). Roosevelt argues that the presence of the American Indian threat led the settlers to develop a system of gov-

ernment that adapted the need for representation to the specific conditions of frontier warfare. Shared acts of violence
create bonds between men that are racial as well as political.
Racial identity, whiteness, is itself homosocial, a paternal legacy
passed down from father to son.

∿

The writers I will discuss often articulate their desire to be
accepted as human through dominant concepts of what it
means to be a man. My approach builds on a critique of masculinity already initiated by black feminist critics and theorists
such as bell hooks, Joyce Hope Scott, Claudia Tate, and Hazel V.
Carby and by black women writers such as Alice Walker, Pearl
Cleage, and Toni Morrison. My argument draws on and is
influenced by this rich tradition of feminist and feminist-
influenced thought and writing. In particular, I follow these
critics in their willingness to approach critically the construction of gender in the writing of African American men, especially when male writers promote conservative notions of
appropriate masculine and feminine behavior.

In her novel *Paradise* (1998), Toni Morrison critiques frontier mythology as well as patriarchal masculinity, and especially
the uncritical acceptance of both by the black community. *Paradise* is the story of two towns, Haven and Ruby, in Oklahoma.
Haven is the name of the initial settlement in Oklahoma Territory, established by the Old Fathers. A "dreamtown in Oklahoma Territory" in the 1890s, it becomes, however, "a ghost-
town in Oklahoma State" in the 1930s (5). Faced with the fading
away of the dream of Haven, the sons of the men who established Haven pick up the town and move further west, establishing a new town (Ruby) and establishing themselves as the
New Fathers.[8] On the outskirts of Ruby is another "haven," a
house known as the Convent, where there lives a racially mixed
group of women (Consolata, Mavis, Gigi, Seneca, Pallas) who

have also sought refuge. The house, Pallas observes, "felt permeated with a blessed malelessness, like a protected domain, free of hunters" (177). The conflict in the novel involves these two protected domains, Ruby and the Convent, in close proximity to each other.

Although sympathetic with the desire to establish a space protected from white violence, Morrison is critical of excesses committed in the name of black solidarity. Central to the town's official story is the legendary journey of the original nine families ("Blackhorse, Morgan, Poole, Fleetwood, Beauchamp, Cato, Flood, and both DuPres families") from Mississippi and Louisiana across Texas to "unassigned land" in the interior of the Oklahoma Territory where Haven is eventually established in 1890 (188). Although anti-black sentiment and violence initiates the journey west, essential to the particular social development of Haven is an event referred to as the "Disallowing," an encounter with an all-black settlement in Fairly, Oklahoma. The settlers in this town refuse to accept the migrants, and "everything anybody wanted to know about the citizens of Haven or Ruby lay in the ramifications of that one rebuff out of many" (189).

Whereas "their horror of whites was convulsive but abstract," this rejection by other black people causes them to save "the clarity of their hatred for the men who had insulted them in ways too confounding for language" (189). The Disallowing causes a new realization: "Now they saw a new separation: light-skinned against black. Oh, they knew there was difference in the minds of whites, but it had not struck them before that it was of consequence, serious consequence, to Negroes themselves. Serious enough that their daughters would be shunned as brides; their sons chosen last; that colored men would be embarrassed to be seen socially with their sisters. The sign of racial purity they had taken for granted had become a stain" (194). The story of the Disallowing is retold in the form of the annual Christmas pageant. Rather than one Mary and one Joseph, several couples go from inn to inn seeking shelter only to be rebuffed, their search and rejection a reenactment of both the story of the birth of Christ and the legendary journey of the original nine families that established Haven. Rejected because of the dark skin that symbolizes their racial purity, the citizens of Haven respond by banding more closely together in proud defense of that purity. This defense involves keeping out of Haven anyone that might dilute the blood of the original families—white people, certainly, but also lighter-skinned African Americans.

The social structure of Haven and Ruby, observes the Reverend Richard Misner (an outsider who comes to Ruby as pastor of the Baptist church), was "born out of an old hatred, one that began when one kind of black man scorned another kind and that kind took the hatred to another level" (306). This hatred results in an increasing isolation not only from white society but also from other African Americans. In the novel's present in the 1970s, the social turmoil in the United States around issues of race threatens the stability of Ruby, as the New Fathers (led by the twins Deacon and Steward Morgan, who control most of the town's assets) reject efforts by Misner to organize the town's citizens in support of the civil rights movement. Many of the members of the younger generation of Ruby follow Misner's lead and argue that "there was a new and more manly way to deal with whites" than the town's isolationism (104). This generational conflict boils over into open argument over the meaning of the town's central symbol of identity—the brick oven that originally served for Haven as a communal cooking place and functions in the novel's present as a monument to the New Fathers' ability to replicate the Old Fathers' accomplishment.

Even though "what was needed back in Haven's early days had never been needed in Ruby," the New Fathers "took the

Oven apart, packed, moved and reassembled it," much to the unstated disapproval of the women who "resented the truck space given over to it" and "resented also the hours spent putting it back together" (103). Like *The Virginian, Paradise* is a post-frontier story, one in which the manly presence that facilitates transformation is not an American Indian but a man of the same race—another black man. For the men of Ruby, the towering legendary figures of the Old Fathers function as the "totalizing ideal that organizes and orients the self" (Gallop 79). The men of Ruby identify so strongly with the ideology and actions of the Old Fathers that they try to replicate rather than imitate their ancestors' accomplishments, establishing Ruby on the model of Haven, painstakingly rebuilding the Oven. The Oven itself is a female symbol taken over and controlled by men, a womblike monument whose meaning is anchored by "the words in the Oven's black mouth," put there in iron letters by the most prominent of the Old Fathers, Zechariah Morgan, grandfather to Deacon and Steward (Morrison 13). The reconstruction of this jointly possessed feminine object symbolizes the renewal in Ruby of the bonds between men originally established in Haven.

In the novel's present, the New Fathers are losing control both of the Oven itself (which has become a hangout for teenagers) and of the meaning of Zechariah's inscription. The young people in the town argue that the motto should read "Be the Furrow of His Brow" rather than (as the New Fathers insist is the scriptural truth) "Beware the Furrow of His Brow." As Reverend Misner observes, "It's not clear as daylight . . . It says '. . . the Furrow of His Brow.' There is no 'Beware' on it" (86). The New Fathers view this questioning of (what is understood to be) the clarity of the motto as a defilement of the Oven and an attack on the town's foundational ideals. Harper Jury asserts, "It says 'Beware.' Not 'Be.' Beware means 'Look out. The Power is mine. Get used to it'" (87). Although the New Fathers defer to

God, they realize that it is their power and not his that is being challenged. In the angry response to the young people's revisionist interpretation, Harper Jury speaks not only for God but for the New Fathers: "The Power is mine. Get used to it." The real battle, one of the women citizens of Ruby, Billie Delia, observes, was "about disobedience, which meant, of course, the stallions were fighting about who controlled the mares and their foals" (150). The battle for control over the symbolism of the Oven is viewed, if not as an attack on the women of Ruby, then certainly as an assault on the ideal of womanhood the New Fathers see it as their destiny to protect. The women being protected—the mares and their foals, to quote Billie Delia—seemingly have little say in this battle between two generations of "stallions."

In their isolation from white society and from other African Americans, the citizens of Ruby have unwittingly replicated the ideology of the dominant culture they reject. They have established the same kind of racially pure homosocial bonds as were celebrated by Roosevelt in *The Winning of the West*. As Reverend Misner contemplates the isolationism of Ruby and the attack on the Convent, he observes: "They think they have outfoxed the whiteman when in fact they imitate him. They think they are protecting their wives and children, when in fact they are maiming them" (Morrison 306). In *Paradise*, as in other works representing black frontier experience, the racial opposition between savagery and civilization is inverted. The actions of white men constitute the savagery that the black women of Ruby must be protected from. The fear of miscegenation implicit in *The Winning of the West* and *The Deerslayer* also shapes the social structure of Haven and Ruby. From the perspective of African American history this fear is certainly reasonable—resulting in a large degree from the reality of the sexual abuse black women suffered under slavery. But in Ruby, reasonable concerns lead to excessive and unreasonable actions. In Ruby, as one of the Morgan twins observes, a "sleepless woman" could walk anywhere in town during the night "without fear," for "nothing for ninety miles around thought she was prey" (8). The men of Ruby devote themselves to the ideal of the black woman as a racially pure figure who must be protected both from white men and from other (impure) African American men. The necessity of protecting the "sleepless woman" justifies the establishment of homosocial bonds—and justifies as well whatever action the men must take to ensure that protection. What, Morrison asks, does being so protected cost the "sleepless woman"?

The ideal of black womanhood is exemplified by a memory shared by both Deacon and Steward of "nineteen Negro ladies" posing for a photograph on the steps of a town hall in Oklahoma (109). Morrison writes that this shared image "was unlike the photographer's" for their "remembrance was pastel colored and eternal" (110). These idealized women are beautiful, inaccessible, posed on the steps as on a pedestal, forever unchanging as they are held in memory. For Steward in particular the women living at the Convent—who drink, dance, listen to popular music, and (most damningly) live without any men around—mock and desecrate this "vision that carried him and his brother through a war, that imbued their marriages and strengthened their efforts to build a town where the vision could flourish" (279). The danger that the men of Ruby act to eradicate is not so much a threat to the real women of Ruby as it is to their idealized vision of racially pure black womanhood. Ruby is a place where the women are "free and protected," as long as they conform to the ideals of femininity as established by the men who protect—or imprison—them (8).

Morrison does not attack the idea of racial solidarity in the book but rather critiques an extreme philosophy of purity that in fact prevents such solidarity and that ultimately expresses itself in the form of misogyny—for if the purity of blood is to be maintained, then the women must be controlled. As Patricia

(Pat) Best, the town's tolerated but not entirely accepted schoolteacher, observes, "everything that worries them must come from women" (217). Pat refers to the descendants of the nine families, their African ancestry undiluted by racial mixing, as "eight-rocks" because of their blue-black skin, the color of coal from "a deep deep level in the coal mines" (193). Her own quasi-outsider status in the town results from her lighter skin color. Her father, Roger Best, "was the first to violate the blood rule," marrying a fair-skinned African American woman who has passed down her impure blood to her daughter, Pat, and granddaughter, Billie Delia, who is even more of an outsider than her mother (195). As Steward Morgan states when he sees for the first time the woman Roger Best has chosen as his wife, "He's bringing along the dung we leaving behind" (201).

Punishment for that violation occurs in various ways. As Pat watches the annual Christmas pageant performed in 1974, she realizes that what were originally nine couples have become seven. Two of the original families have been erased from the official story, including her own ancestors, and she observes that in the eyes of the community she was "not good enough to be represented by eight-year-olds on a stage" (216). The mirror image of Haven and Ruby is Pura Sangre, an all-white town that Deacon and Steward's father encounters in 1920. On a journey to bring back supplies to Haven, he is told by three Sac and Fox men that "at its northern edge was a sign: No Niggers. At its southern edge a cross" (153-54). Ruby has also become Pura Sangre—a town that keeps out not only whites but also other African Americans whose skin color reveals their impure blood. Pat realizes that her own internalization of the town's ideology not only prevents her from being outraged that her family has been erased from town history but also influences her deteriorating relationship with her daughter. Thinking back over a quarrel between the two that turned physical, Pat realizes that her fight was with "the young girl that lived in the minds of the 8-Rocks, not the girl her daughter was" (204). Whatever the differences between mother and daughter, Pat and Billie (often with an ironic detachment appropriate to their quasi-outsider status) both appear in the narrative as critical voices whose interpretations of events contest the official story of things espoused by the New Fathers.

Consolata, the oldest of the women living at the Convent, observes that it was getting harder and harder to tell one female refugee from the other "because the timbre of each of their voices told the same tale: disorder, deception and . . . drift" (221–22). Through a ritual invented by Consolata called the loud dreaming, a creative combination of improvisational story-telling and painting, the women (as Anna Flood realizes after seeing their drawings on the Convent floor) find a way "to bridle, without being trampled, the monsters that slavered them" (264, 303). "It was never important," Morrison writes, "to know who said the dream or whether it had meaning" (264). The improvisational ever-changing nature of the ritual of the loud dreaming contrasts with the New Fathers' efforts to control and limit interpretation. Deacon and Steward (who forget nothing) in particular always carefully establish who (usually one of the revered Old Fathers) said what, when they said it, and exactly what it means. Through the loud dreaming, the women take control of the ghosts that haunt their lives. A customer driving back from the Convent to Ruby (with a bag of their famous hot peppers at her side) might realize that "the Convent women were no longer haunted" (266). But, as Morrison writes, the customer might also think that the women were not "hunted either . . . but there she would have been wrong" (266).

If the Convent represents a haven for women, the men of Ruby view it differently, and the women in the Convent become the scapegoats for the town's crisis of identity. The house "free of hunters" becomes filled with hunters, as a group of men from Ruby (some of the New Fathers and a few men from the younger generation) begin tracking down and shooting the women who live there. For the twin Morgan brothers, the Convent women represent the uncontrollably feminine—as evidenced by the drawings on the cellar floor, which the men view as "perversions beyond the imagination" (287). For Steward, the Convent women are a "new and obscene breed of female," a "flaunting parody" of the ideal womanhood represented in the twins' memory by the "nineteen Negro ladies" (279). Morrison views the hunting ritual we have seen elsewhere from a different perspective. The beast of this hunt is the female object of male violence. Fearing that the tensions in the town will result in the death of Ruby, as Haven had once died out, the New Fathers hope that violence will cleanse the town, that their actions inside the Convent will "make sure it never happens again. That nothing inside or out rots the one all-black town worth the pain" (5). The hunters, all descendants of the Old Fathers, include Deacon and Steward Morgan, their nephew K. D., Jeff and Arnold Fleetwood, Harper Jury and his son Menus Jury, Sergeant Person, and Wisdom Poole. The number of hunters replicates the original number of intact families that settled in Haven, and their violent actions are meant to renew and repeat the homosocial bond between nine men that originally established the settlement. In an example of circular reasoning, the men ultimately decide to protect women by killing women. Or, rather, they decide to protect their ideal of womanhood by murdering real women who do not live in accordance with that ideal.

Lone DuPres, having overheard the men planning the raid at the Oven, leads a rescue mission that arrives too late. Although Lone later "became unhinged by the way the story was being retold," by the efforts the family and friends of the nine Ruby men make toward "enhancing, recasting, inventing misinformation," she succeeds in bringing witnesses to the crime, "Luther Beauchamp—who told the most damning story—and

Pious, Deed Sands and Aaron—who corroborated much of Lone's version" (297–98). If not for these voices, "the whole thing might have been sanitized out of existence" (298). Complicating the effort to establish a true story of the attack, the bodies of the five women simply disappear, presumably through a mysterious "door" or "window" that Misner and Anna Flood discover (or sense) in the Convent garden. The attack also changes Deacon Morgan, whose remorse, Misner observes, "was at having become what the Old Fathers cursed: the kind of man who set himself up to judge, rout and even destroy the needy, the defenseless, the different" (302). Misner, appalled by what has happened and on the verge of leaving the town at the end of the novel, decides to stay "because there was no better battle to fight, no better place to be than among these outrageously beautiful, flawed and proud people" (306).

If Misner envisions the possibility of hopeful change in the aftermath of the attack, Morrison gives Billie Delia the last word. At the end of the novel, she observes that Ruby had become a "backward noplace ruled by men whose power to control was out of control and who had the nerve to say who could live and who not and where; who had seen in lively, free, unarmed females the mutiny of the mares and so got rid of them" (308). While such works as Roosevelt's *The Winning of the West* and Cooper's *The Deerslayer* justify acts of violence by linking them to the protection of womanhood, Morrison reveals that male violence, which the frontier narrative so often celebrates, is more likely to be employed against (rather than in protection of) women. Through the attack on the Convent, Morrison makes visible the contradiction usually concealed in the trope of transformative violence—the irony of trying to achieve a civilized goal (protecting womanhood) through savage (violent) actions.

Chapter 2

Civilized Manliness on the South Dakota Frontier

Oscar Micheaux's *The Conquest: The Story of a Negro Pioneer* (1913) presents an ambivalent representation of African American western experience. The journey westward of Micheaux's protagonist moves him further away from an African American community at the same time that it enables his economic success, making him "a stranger in a strange land, inhabited wholly by people not my own race" (77). Although the frontier symbolizes freedom from white racism for Micheaux, it also represents escape from a black community that he represents as having as great a detrimental effect on individual African American achievement as race-based restrictions. Joseph Young argues in *Black Novelist as White Racist* that Micheaux's writings express a philosophy of assimilationist imitation of a white worldview, advocating that blacks adopt "Anglo-Saxon myths, Anglo-Saxon values" (1) as a means of overcoming their inferiority to whites. Micheaux represents his narrator as a black man who has not been denied the frontier but who has rather availed himself of opportunities other African Americans (who lack ambition, according to Micheaux) have failed to exploit. In *The Conquest* Micheaux's attempt to define himself via the frontier success story is undermined by his hero's inability (unlike Nat

Love) to achieve his desired masculine identity, his inability to adopt completely "Anglo-Saxon myths."

In *The Conquest*, Micheaux engages with a contemporaneous cultural discourse on the nature of black manhood. The South Dakota frontier serves as a place where Micheaux hopes black manhood can be reconstituted, where the hard-working African American man can be free from the racism that restricts his ability to succeed. Using Booker T. Washington as a model he constructs the hero of his pioneer narrative, a fictionalized version of himself named Oscar Devereaux, as a figure whose behavior and work ethic counter widely disseminated stereotypes of the savage black man. Two of Micheaux's primary goals in the book—to prove that the legends of the West can also be the legends of black America, and to refute a racist discourse that defines the black man as primitive—come into conflict as he attempts to prove the African American man's civilized status by adapting a narrative that traditionally involves a journey away from civilization and into savagery. He tries to resolve this conflict by bringing together frontier mythology with elements drawn from the African American literary tradition, from the domestic fiction and "racial uplift" narratives of such turn-of-the-century writers as Booker T. Washington, Pauline Hopkins, and Frances E. W. Harper.

The first half of *The Conquest* tells the story of a black man making the most of frontier opportunity homesteading in South Dakota.[1] The second half of the book is concerned with Devereaux's attempts to find a wife, his subsequent troubled married life, and the collapse of his homesteading effort. Micheaux splits his story into two parts, one an account of a determined individual conquering his environment, the other a domestic tale reminiscent of the novels of Hopkins and Harper. The feminist critique of masculinity often found in domestic fiction conflicts with Micheaux's attempt to reconstitute manhood via the frontier myth, and rather than coming to a successful resolution *The Conquest* ends with a failed marriage (and a stillborn child) and a failed attempt at conquering the wilderness as the hero's marriage and his pioneering enterprise collapse simultaneously—as each plot seemingly undermines the other. *The Conquest* seems to call into question Baker's observation (*Long Black Song* 2) that the tales of pioneers are not those of black America. The book nonetheless demonstrates the difficulty involved when an African American writer attempts to engage the mythology of the American West.

The Conquest *and the Myth of the Frontier*

Writer and filmmaker Oscar Micheaux (1884–1951) was the author of seven books, ranging from *The Conquest* (1913) to *The Masquerade: An Historical Novel* (1947). In his writing, Micheaux draws from such generic sources as the melodrama, the frontier story, and the detective story.[2] While the action in his books takes place in a variety of geographies, Micheaux is perhaps best known for the books that draw from his own experiences as a black homesteader in South Dakota. As a pioneering black filmmaker, Micheaux directed and produced around forty films, including his first silent feature produced in 1919, *The Homesteader* (based on his 1917 novel of the same name); a sound version of the same book entitled *The Exile* (1931); and such features as *Within Our Gates* (1920), *The Symbol of the Unconquered* (1920), *Ten Minutes to Live* (1932), *God's Step Children* (1938), and *The Betrayal* (1948).[3] While his films have garnered an increasing amount of critical attention, James W. Byrd notes that Micheaux is one of the most neglected African American writers of the first half of the twentieth century (1141).

The first half of *The Conquest*, an autobiographical narrative written "By the Pioneer," is the Turnerian story of an individual entrepreneur/farmer going west to avail himself of the

opportunity to purchase cheap land and, through the investment of his labor and initial capital, develop that land into a
profitable enterprise. Micheaux writes: "I concluded on one
thing, and that was, if one whose capital was under eight or ten
thousand dollars, desired to own a good farm in the great central west he must go where the land was new or raw and undeveloped. He must begin with the beginning and develop with
the development of the country. By the proper and accepted
methods of conservation of the natural resources and close
application to his work, his chances for success are good" (53).
At the same time that Micheaux provides a detailed and factual
description of frontier life, the book also operates in the realm
of myth, as Devereaux is quite clearly presented as a larger-
than-life figure, exemplary, a hero for others to admire and imitate. Although Devereaux journeys to pioneer South Dakota
several years after Turner declared the frontier closed,
Micheaux's hero undergoes a Turnerian transformation. Devereaux enters into a "raw and undeveloped" country raw and
undeveloped himself, an innocent who is taken in by every
horse trader in the West, but one who, as he develops his land
and increases his capital, transforms both self and land and
emergs as a new and competent man in the process.

Although property ownership is an important component
of masculine identity in general, such ownership has particular
resonance for a descendent of slaves. The first few chapters of
The Conquest provide a little information about Devereaux's
family history (he was the fifth child in a family of thirteen, his
grandfather a slave who was sold in Kentucky to somewhere in
Texas where contact was lost) in order to demonstrate how far
he has risen. The early chapters follow Devereaux from his
birth near the Ohio River in Illinois, through his brief sojourn
in the city of Chicago and his time spent as a Pullman porter
earning the money he would later use to stake his claim in
South Dakota, to his steady movement westward. Four years

after buying his relinquishment and seven years after leaving his family in southern Illinois, Devereaux "had put two hundred eighty acres under cultivation, with eight head of horses—I had done a little better in my later horse deals". At the midpoint of the story, Devereaux claims "ownership of land and stock to the value of twenty thousand dollars" (153). Because of his hero's ability to succeed, Micheaux notes he "had been referred to in the local papers in the most complimentary terms, and was regarded as one of the Little Crow's best citizens" (155). Devereaux's acquisition of land marks his difference from his ancestors who as slaves were themselves property rather than property owners. The frontier offers him the opportunity to own his own labor as well, to employ the actions of his body in order to increase his own wealth and status.

In the traditional form, the frontier narrative includes an opposition between two places—the East and the West, the Metropolis and the Wilderness (see Slotkin, *Fatal Environment*). The process of conquering the Wilderness (and often its native inhabitants) transforms the hero of the narrative, marking his transition from boy to man and establishing his independence from his European ancestry. The hero leaves behind the Metropolis in order to rid himself of its corrupting civilized values and return to a more natural state of being on the frontier, where, as Turner states, "the bonds of custom are broken and unrestraint is triumphant" (59). If the frontier provides an escape from the corrupting values of civilization and of the Metropolis, Micheaux rearticulates this basic element of the frontier myth from an African American perspective. If, for Turner, "each frontier did indeed furnish a new field of opportunity, a gate of escape from the bondage of the past" (59), for the African American pioneer the escape from the bondage of the past takes a particular form, an escape from the past of slavery and an escape from the present of racial restrictions and discrimination existing in the Metropolis.

Frontier is an alien word to black America both because blacks were excluded from participation in frontier opportunity and because the role African Americans have played in the history of the American West has been erased. In the wake of the Civil War, movement westward marked the first mass migration by free African Americans. Between 1870 and 1910 the black population increased in the western mountain states by thirteenfold and in Washington, Oregon, and California by fivefold (Katz 183). Between 1870 and 1880 the black population of Kansas grew by 26,000 people, with 6,000 of those people arriving during the Kansas Fever Exodus of 1879. Painter argues that both fear and hope sparked this exodus westward—the fear that the outbreak of anti-black violence in southern states during the 1877 elections would only worsen, and the hope that blacks would find in the West a way around the barriers that prevented or limited black landownership in the South (146–47, 184–201). African Americans soon discovered, however, that restricting laws and anti-black terrorism migrated west as well.

Devereaux's own hopes parallel those of other African Americans who went west, although Micheaux indicates little interest in the collective black movements contemporaneous with his hero's adventures. Between 1890 and 1910, Oklahoma's black population increased by 537 percent, with 137,000 people living mostly in thirty newly established black communities (Katz 249). In spite of political efforts on behalf of African Americans in Oklahoma (including Booker T. Washington's lobbying President Theodore Roosevelt not to admit Oklahoma until blacks were guaranteed that the new state would not pass Jim Crow laws), Oklahoma's statehood in 1907 was followed in 1910 by a grandfather clause in the state constitution "that disfranchised its black citizens on the basis that their grandfathers, as slaves, had not voted," and by a 1914 Supreme Court ruling that segregation was legal in Oklahoma (Katz

252). The midpoint of Devereaux's story is 1907, the moment of his greatest success and of the first step in the collapse of African American hopes for establishing Oklahoma as a black state. While the chronology of the collapse of Devereaux's enterprise parallels the disintegration of conditions in Oklahoma for blacks, Micheaux draws no explicit connection between the two, as his interest is in promoting individual—not collective—black achievement, in constructing a mythology as much as a history.

As does the white hero of the frontier myth, Devereaux crosses into Indian country, for it is on reservation land newly opened for settlement that he buys his homestead. For Micheaux ownership and development of property indicate the difference between civilization and savagery. He depicts American Indians as particularly savage in their inability to understand civilized economic matters. Although the Sioux Indians "owned at one time the larger part of southern South Dakota and northern Nebraska," they "were always selling" rather than developing their property. Far from being practical and conservative in economic matters, they indiscriminately spent the money they earned from selling property on "fine horses, buggies, whiskey, and what-not" (178). While Micheaux argues that the racial distinctions detrimental to success in the East are absent on the frontier, which represents a new field of opportunity for African Americans, his utopia free from racial distinctions is itself built on racial difference—as Devereaux (like Nat Love) aligns himself with white settlers in opposition to native inhabitants, adopting white stereotypes of American Indians as his own.

Micheaux's utopia involves other racial distinctions as well. If the Metropolis represents the place where racial prejudice exists, the city is also the place of racial identity and of the African American community—a community that Devereaux leaves behind and that he represents negatively. Devereaux's movement westward is also a movement away from, as Chester J. Fontenot describes it, "the vices of black urban life" (115). Micheaux renders those "vices" as a greater detriment to racial equality than the "prejudice and hatred of the white race," which, according to Devereaux, is merely an "excuse for the negro's lack of ambition" (Micheaux 17). Devereaux's travels represent a double journey—away from racial restrictions, certainly, but also away from what Micheaux sees as the restrictions of race.

Civilized Manliness and Its Discontents

Although the men of Roosevelt's class and era viewed masculine passion as essential to male identity, they also believed that such passion had to be kept in check lest it devolve into savagery. White Americans believed that all men, whatever their race or class, possessed "primitive" passions, but only white middle-class men also possessed the strength of character or civilized manliness to check those urges, an ability that had been developed over generations of white manhood. Wister's Virginian, rather than symbolizing only primitive (but masculine) savagery, for example, represents the necessary balance of restraint and passion. As the Virginian observes to the narrator in apology for an uncharacteristic outburst, "A man . . . ought to own a big lot of temper. And like all his valuable possessions, he'd ought to keep it and not lose any" (Wister 170). While the Virginian demonstrates his ability to act violently, his various displays of manly restraint indicate his equal ability to contain passion until the need for justice calls for its release.

A great deal of anxiety accompanied the shift in the late nineteenth century from an emphasis on civilized manly self-restraint to an ideal of a "balanced" masculinity that placed as much importance on "vigor" as control. This anxiety became

focused on the middle-class man's body and led to the discovery of two new diseases (no longer recognized by medical
science as diseases), homosexuality and neurasthenia, a bodily
disorder that "resulted when a highly evolved person seriously
overtaxed his body's finite supply of nerve force" (Bederman
85). Wister himself was diagnosed with neurasthenia and was
advised by nerve doctor Silas Weir Mitchell to seek a cure in the
outdoor life of the American West—his experiences there providing background material for his novels.[4] The transformation of *The Virginian*'s narrator represents the curative powers
of the American West for the overtaxed male body—although,
we might note, his relationship with the Virginian acknowledges the ambiguity of seeking a cure for neurasthenia (and the
figure of homosexuality the disease also evokes) in a context
that also invites intense bonds between men.

The narrator's admiration of the Virginian certainly treads
the line between appropriate and inappropriate desire. When
the Tenderfoot sees in the Virginian "something potent to be
felt, I should think, by man or woman," he seems to identify
(here and elsewhere) with the desiring gazes of both sexes
(Wister 7). While indicating his appreciation of a manly image
that he would like to model himself after, his admiration of the
Virginian's "potency" (which can be "felt" as well as seen) also
demonstrates his ability to imagine how the Virginian might be
seen from the point of view of feminine sexual desire. "Had I
been a woman," he later states, observing a particularly
engaging smile from the Virginian, "it would have made me his
to do what he pleased with on the spot" (195). Blake Allmendinger argues that the Virginian's relationship with Steve,
his close friend who turns to cattle rustling, not only pushes the
boundaries of acceptable homosocial partnerships but also
represents a "potentially dangerous transgressive love" (*Ten
Most Wanted* 154). The eventual lynching of Steve (in which the

Virginian participates) is ambiguous, for it "precipitates—and also resolves—the crisis at the center of the same-sex relationship," evoking in the Virginian an uncharacteristic emotional response at the same time removing from the narrative the unacceptable object of his emotions (158).

Although Wister may acknowledge the potential for "dangerous love," the novel primarily represents the American West as a wilderness space where those characters who behave in ways inappropriate to their gender (the feminist Molly, the neurasthenic narrator) may escape the deformative influence of civilization and return to natural (and sharply divided) masculine and feminine roles. Analogous to the suspension of the categories of hunter and beast in the hunting ritual, we might argue that the novel's gender transgressions represent momentary fluctuations, which serve as a prelude only to the inevitable reestablishment of categories of difference. One of the novel's most important homosocial relationships is between the Virginian and his employer, Judge Henry. If the central narrative of *The Virginian* is the wooing of Molly, that courtship is paralleled by the Virginian's efforts to win the favor of Judge Henry, to whom he remarks upon being named foreman, "I'll try to please yu" (Wister 198). Marriage represents the Virginian's willingness to accept responsibility—another step in his maturation that further pleases Judge Henry. As indicated by the Judge's wedding present, his offering the Virginian partnership in the ranch, the Virginian's entry into the bonds of matrimony with Molly is a prelude to the further development of his homosocial bond with the judge (392). Already a landowner, the Virginian uses this initial partnership to generate other homosocial bonds: "the railroad came, and built a branch to that land of the Virginian's where the coal was. By that time he was an important man, with a strong grip on many various enterprises" (392). If the novel explores the possibility of transgressive male relationships, the Virginian's marriage to Molly channels male desire back into acceptable forms, homosocial rather than homosexual bonds.

The African American writer, and African Americans in general, encountered in the public discourse at the beginning of the twentieth century an identity already constructed, one that associated people of African descent with animal passion, savage sexuality, laziness, a lack of morality. The dominant discourse of the period classified African Americans as primitive, savage, as a less-evolved race, as children in the progressive scale of humanity who had not yet developed to the higher status of civilized white people—and some argued that black people would never reach that status, that they were naturally primitive and would always remain so. African American men were positioned "as the antithesis of both the white man and civilization itself. As such, black men embodied whatever was most unmanly and uncivilized" (Bederman 49). The Victorian era's achievement of an evolutionarily superior manhood provided evidence as well of the achievement of a superior civilization. African American men understood that their supposed lack of manliness "legitimized their social and political disfranchisement," and, given this context, they realized as well the importance of trying to obtain political and civic power "through gender—by proving that they, too, were men" (Bederman 20–21). In Micheaux's *The Conquest*, he uses the figure of Devereaux and the narrative of frontier conquest to reconfigure the dominant imagery of black manhood.

In this context, Micheaux embraces a definition of manhood more in keeping with the Victorian notion of civilized manliness than with the balanced masculinity we see celebrated by Wister and Roosevelt. Unlike the white hero's, Devereaux's journey is, in a sense, away from savagery and into civilization, a transformation achieved ironically by leaving behind the Metropolis for the Wilderness. Micheaux is ultimately unable to resolve the contradiction of engaging a narrative that traditionally involves a journey into savagery as a means of refuting the stereotype of the savage black man, although he introduces various strategies for doing so. Devereaux's work ethic, his good sense and practicality, mark out a place for him in the discourse of civilized manliness. Micheaux does not, however, completely refute the stereotype of black savagery. Rather, he employs that stereotype to demonstrate Devereaux's exceptional status, creating a contrast between his hero's manly behavior and the unmanly behavior of other black men. This contrast is most clearly figured in a relationship between Devereaux and the man who will become his father-in-law, the Reverend N. J. McCraline, an older, established male figure who should be (but to our hero's dismay is not) *The Conquest*'s version of Wister's Judge Henry. Any hope of establishing a productive homosocial bond between Devereaux and McCraline is doomed from the start by the reverend's unmanliness.

Devereaux observes that although he lives among people "not my own race," he nonetheless "had been treated with every courtesy and respect," in part because "I had kept my place as regards custom" (Micheaux 155). On the one hand, *The Conquest* addresses a white audience, providing evidence that a black man on the frontier can take advantage of that opportunity and earn courtesy and respect according to white values. At the same time Micheaux addresses an explicitly black audience—or at least he imagines that he addresses a particular segment of the black audience: "There are two very distinct types or classes, among the American negroes," those like himself "who are quick to think, practical, conservative as well as progressive" and those who "do not realize what it takes to succeed" (142–43). Unlike Devereaux, many other African Americans suffer from a "love of luxury" reminiscent of the Sioux Indians and their love of fine horses, buggies, whiskey, a "savage" vice detrimental to the hard work required to become a civilized and respected landowner (146). Micheaux addresses himself to the latter class of blacks, stating that "the idea is prevalent among this class that all white people should be rich, and regardless of how ideal the success has been, I learned that no white person could be accepted as an example for this class to follow. . . . One of the greatest tasks of my life has been to convince a certain class of my racial acquaintances that a colored man can be anything" (145).

Here, as elsewhere in the book, Micheaux aligns himself philosophically with Booker T. Washington, who also provides a general model for Micheaux's construction of manliness. Micheaux's language closely follows Washington's observations in "The Intellectuals and the Boston Mob" chapter of *My Larger Education* (1911). Washington begins the chapter with a discussion of the importance of reading, noting the satisfaction he found as a boy when reading about "the lives of men who had risen by their own efforts from poverty to success" (Washington 102). While such stories could inspire the young reader "to do something and make something of his life," Washington notes that the stories he and his friends read in school "were all concerned with the success and achievements of white boys and men" (102–3). When Washington argues that "what others had done some of us might also be able to do," his schoolmates respond that "because of our colour and because we carried in our faces the brand of a race that had been in slavery, white people did not want us to succeed" (103).

Washington's ideas about success, Maurice Wallace argues, "depend fundamentally on one's demonstrating virility sufficient 'to do something' that presumably the impotent (the boy) cannot do" (263). Washington's schoolmates, like Micheaux's "certain class of my racial acquaintances," blame the hatred of the white race for their impotence. If "no white person could be accepted as an example" Micheaux, following Washington, constructs a manly image that provides an example for other black men to follow, a demonstration of virility ("doing something") that counters stereotyped beliefs about black manhood (Micheaux 145). At the same time, Micheaux deploys stereotypical images of other African Americans as a means of marking his hero's achievement, his manliness, as contrasted to the impotence of the members of that "certain class." If, as some have argued, Micheaux is guilty of race hatred, he is also guilty of "self-hatred," or hatred of that masculine identity constructed for him by the racist discourse of the period.[5] His resistance to that image of self is played out and displaced in his relationship with other African Americans. The cost of his resistance is a separation of himself from that image and a consonant projection of that image onto the bodies of other African Americans, who come to represent the image of "black inferiority" and black manhood that he himself has transcended and left behind in his journey westward.

Marriage, Fatherhood, and Masculine Identity

In his most famous autobiographical narrative, *Up from Slavery* (1901), Booker T. Washington notes that more than once he had tried to imagine himself "in the position of a boy or a man with an honoured and distinguished ancestry ... who had not only inherited a name, but fortune and a proud family homestead" (21). Because he has no such ancestry, Washington resolves to "leave a record of which my children would be proud, and which might encourage them to still higher effort" (21). Washington moves from uncertainty about his patrimony (not knowing the identity of his biological father) to the discovery of a symbolic father figure in the white general Samuel C. Armstrong (head of Hampton Institute where Washington goes to school), and ultimately to his attaining status as a father himself—both biologically and symbolically—when he becomes head of Tuskegee Institute and marries shortly thereafter Fannie N. Smith, who gives birth to Washington's first

child, Portia. Washington's performance of a masculine identity is complicated by his lack of a patrilineal past in terms of
property to pass down as well as black examples of success—an
absence of fathers both in economic (property) and symbolic
(role models) terms, an absence that Washington compensates
for in part by adopting a symbolic white father. Raymond
Hedin argues that as Washington establishes himself in the role
of biological father to his own children, so does he also try to
establish himself through his efforts at Tuskegee and elsewhere
as the "unencumbered father that neither he nor any other
blacks in America had previously enjoyed" (97). Through his
success, Washington could "leave a record of which" not only
his own children but all African Americans could be proud and
by so doing "encourage them to still higher effort" (*Up from
Slavery* 21).

Although not fatherless in the same sense as Washington,
Devereaux likewise looks outside his biological family for a
symbolic father. Devereaux notes that his "parents and grand-
parents had been slaves, honest, but ignorant. My father could
neither read nor write, had not succeeded in a large way, and
had nothing to give me as a start, not even practical knowledge"
(Micheaux 244). His biological father's lack of property to pass
down and his failure to provide Devereaux with either an economic or a symbolic patrimony erase his status as masculine
head of the family. Although there is no single symbolic white
such as General Armstrong in the novel, Devereaux follows
Washington by looking toward "white neighbors and friends
who were doing what I admired, building an empire," as
models for behavior (244). Devereaux's desired goal recalls the
achievements of the Virginian in Wister's novel, his steady
accumulation of property and respect and his emergence at the
end of the book as "an important man, with a strong grip on
many various enterprises" (Wister 392). Devereaux's success in
becoming a property owner, however, does not provide him

with a sense of completion. Once he has established his homestead, the narrative turns to Devereaux's search for a suitable wife. He desires to become a father as well as a property owner, and by so doing to become the initiator of a patrimony that begins with his name and that symbolically establishes Devereaux (like Washington before him) as a Black Father, an image of African American manhood for others to imitate.

In her discussion of black women's writing in *The Coupling Convention*, Ann duCille notes that for African Americans "recently released from slavery and its dramatic disruption of marital and family life, marriage rites were a long-denied basic human right—signs of liberation and entitlement to both democracy and desire" (14). In novels such as William Wells Brown, *Clotel* (1853), Frances E. W. Harper, *Iola Leroy, or Shadows Uplifted* (1892), and Pauline Hopkins, *Contending Forces* (1900), "marriage rites and the right to marry—rather than such 'manhood rights' as suffrage, property ownership, or literacy—function as the primary signifiers of freedom and humanity" (duCille 19). In earlier African American writing by men, marriage also serves as an important sign of both liberation and manhood achieved. In the autobiographies *The Life of Olaudah Equiano, or Gustavus Vassa, the African. Written by Himself* (1789) and the *Narrative of the Life of Frederick Douglass, An American Slave. Written by Himself* (1845), both Equiano and Douglass view marriage as an important component of their transformations from slaves to free men. Douglass even went so far as to print his marriage certificate as part of the narrative.[6]

Micheaux's text in part responds to the literature produced by these African American writers. He follows them in representing the right to marry as a signifier of freedom, humanity, and civilization at the same time as he also asserts the importance of the traditional manhood right of property ownership as a signifier of the achievement of a masculine identity: "Usually in the story of a man's life, or in fiction, when he gets the girl's consent to marry, first admitting the love, the story ends" (241). In the story of a *man's life,* as Micheaux puts it, that life is made complete with marriage and the assumption of the iden-tity offered by the role of the patriarch. For Micheaux's hero, the assumption of that identity is essential to the completion of the story, to the making of a man's life, as it is for the heroes of the slave narrative. Micheaux adapts the Turnerian vision of the frontier, but the masculine identity he forms by acquiring and developing land seems to him incomplete.

Micheaux mainly represents opportunity in economic terms, but he also articulates frontier freedom in the form of an interracial romance. Devereaux falls in love with a woman whose family had immigrated to South Dakota from Scotland, although he notes, "I became in a way frightened, for I did not by any means want to fall in love with a white girl" (155). This romance is a frontier experience, for such a love is accompanied by "the knowledge that custom, tradition, and the dignity of both races are against it" (156). Their love, however, is only momentary and cannot flourish even on the frontier. Dev-ereaux's frontier freedom is circumscribed along racial lines that he will not cross. Micheaux writes that Devereaux wanted not only to succeed but also to "hold the respect and good will of the community, and there are few communities that will sanction a marriage with a white girl, hence, the sacrifice" (168). On the frontier, the African American pioneer must still con-front the racial distinctions supposedly left behind.

Complicating the decision to sacrifice his love for the white girl is his race loyalty, his sense that he can do more good for African Americans by marrying within racial lines, a sensibility often expressed in black women's writing of the period. In Harper's *Iola Leroy,* for example, her heroine decides to refuse the marriage proposal of the white Dr. Gresham. Like Dev-ereaux, Iola Leroy names race loyalty as the primary factor in rejecting an interracial marriage: "No, Doctor, I don't think that I could best serve my race by forsaking them and marrying you" (235). Ultimately, Iola meets the African American doctor Frank Latimer, whose proposal she accepts. As "kindred hopes and tastes had knit" the hearts of Iola and Frank, their union also represents a joining of "grand and noble purposes" as they plan a future in which they "labor for those who had passed from the old oligarchy of slavery into the new commonwealth of freedom" (271). Even if he has moved westward away from the African American community Devereaux's sacrifice, like Iola's choice, indicates a similar sense of responsibility for the uplift of that community. For turn-of-the-century African American women writers such as Harper, matrimony often means "not submission and domesticity but partnership in race work" (duCille 42). Although Micheaux likewise links matrimony to racial uplift, his approach to "race work" is through providing an uplifting and exemplary figure for emulation, not through the social activism in the black communities of the South as envisioned by Frank and Iola.

As Devereaux has transformed undeveloped land into a profitable enterprise, he also looks to transform his intended wife, the timid and obedient Orlean McCraline, into someone who is practical and hard-working like himself and who can provide a feminine counterpart to his own uplifting image. Devereaux applies lessons learned from farming to courtship, demonstrating a similar work ethic in both his courting and his farming, applying "accepted methods of conservation" in balancing the investment of time and money in land development and in trips to Chicago to visit Orlean. Whereas partnership may be essential to Harper's definition of marriage, Micheaux represents marriage almost in terms of ownership. Devereaux certainly views Orlean as a project that, like his farmland, needs to be developed. The link between land and wife is further revealed when one of Devereaux's first actions after his engagement is to use Orlean to increase his property—by filing a claim on her behalf.

Micheaux also represents marriage as a type of employer/employee relationship, keeping in place a hierarchy of gender roles that the domestic novel often seeks to undermine. Orlean has certain tasks assigned her to perform, and these tasks are clearly gendered—housekeeping, cooking, and ultimately reproduction. Although Devereaux sees their arrangement as practical, Orlean insists on a more romantic relationship, expecting (to Devereaux's dismay) an engagement ring, a wedding in Chicago, and also signs of affection from her husband. Once in South Dakota, Devereaux finds that Orlean's weeping makes him "cross," that he begins "to neglect kissing her as much as I had been doing," which leads to more crying (Micheaux 245). In her novel Harper describes Iola's "heart quietly throbbing with a delicious sense of joy and love" after receiving Frank's proposal (Harper 271). As duCille notes, Harper uses images such as the throbbing heart and the sensations of joy and love as "sexual signifiers" that "suggest a controlled passion, about to be properly positioned within and satisfied by the institution of marriage" (duCille 46). Micheaux's vision of marriage indicates little use for affection or passion, as such sensations interfere with the practical concerns of business. The clearly unhappy Orlean "could only be made to stop crying when I would spend an hour or two petting and assuring her I still loved her, and this when I should have been in the fields" (Micheaux 245). Devereaux has trouble tending to both land and wife, and we might argue that his inability to redefine marriage (as the domestic novel often does) and view Orlean more in terms of partnership than ownership contributes to the ultimate failure of both enterprises. We should place that failure in the context of a racist discourse that emphasizes the "unmanliness" of the African American man. Within that context, Micheaux preserves a conservative definition of gender and gender roles, emphasizing Devereaux's desire to achieve a traditionally defined masculine identity rather than reimagining the concept of manhood.

When Orlean gives birth to their child, Devereaux is away in the fields. Although the narrative does not explicitly blame his absence for what occurs, their first child, "the first colored child born on the Little Crow, and we thought we were going to make history," is stillborn (262). At this point the story diverges sharply from the narrative of frontier success. Whereas for Turner the frontier is the place of perennial rebirth, Micheaux instead leaves the reader with the image of Devereaux's dead son. Devereaux observes, "As he lay stiff and cold I could see the image of myself in his features" (263). Orlean notices Devereaux's gaze and comments, "It is just like you, dear" (263). Devereaux's own attempt at self-making, at being reborn on the frontier, is figured in the end of the narrative in the form of his dead son—a failed attempt at both birth and rebirth. If, in the "story of a man's life," that story is completed by fathering and supporting a family, the child's death prevents Devereaux from assuming that desired masculine identity and from achieving the symbolic position of race leader, of an exemplary figure whose success demands imitation.

The story of a man's life that usually ends when he gets the girl's consent to marry is for Devereaux "much to the contrary," as he endures a series of tragedies and misfortunes in the wake of his marriage (241). Following the death of the child, the weather turns bad, drying out the land, and Devereaux observes that his "two hundred and eighty-five acres of flax was a brown, sickly-looking mess, and I was badly discouraged, for outside of my family trouble, I had borrowed my limit at the bank" (289). In a "year of coincidences," Devereaux suffers from "the greatest drouth known for years, followed by the coldest winter and the heaviest snows," and from the exhaustion of his capital and his general "dismal prospect" (295). Reverend

McCraline arrives to rescue his daughter "from the heartless man, that was killing her in his efforts to get rich" (293). Micheaux writes that the reverend deprives his hero of (as the title of a poem Devereaux cites over and over again to himself sums it up) "the right to love" (296). After McCraline removes Orlean from South Dakota, Devereaux is reduced to living in a sort of stupor: "I had looked forward joyfully to the time when I should be a husband and father, with a wife to love, and a home of my own. This had been so dominant in my mind, that when I thought it over, I could not clearly realize the present situation. . . . I would at times rouse myself, pinch the flesh, and move about, to see if it was my real self" (295–96). Devereaux's "real self" is in a sense his imagined self, the self he wants to become, the husband and father whose image has been "so dominant in my mind," an image of self that he desires but is unable to attain.

Micheaux does not attribute Devereaux's failure to a racist social system. The fault belongs to forces within the African American community set on destroying the successful black individual—symbolized by the figure of Devereaux's father-in-law, who embodies most of the negative characteristics and philosophies of that class of blacks who "do not realize what it takes to succeed" (143). McCraline represents the corrupting values of the Metropolis arrayed in opposition to the hard-working pioneer. Young argues that Micheaux uses Devereaux and McCraline in order to comment on a contemporaneous debate "between assimilationists and cultural nationalists," between the ideologies most often associated with Washington on the one hand and W. E. B. Du Bois on the other (3).Washington de-emphasized political action and asserted the importance of practical education, of earning respect from whites by demonstrating African Americans' abilities to succeed economically in spite of race-based limitations. Du Bois argued for the importance of higher education in establishing a positive black self-consciousness and for political agitation in support of securing full civil rights for African Americans. Du Bois emphasized asserting the distinctiveness of African American cultural life and history. McCraline draws his ideas, Devereaux asserts, from a misreading of Du Bois's *The Souls of Black Folk* as filtered through "radical" newspapers. Although Micheaux does not directly criticize Du Bois, noting that he "was far too broad minded and intelligent in every way . . . to lead a lot of reckless people," he does represent the "professor in a colored university in Georgia" as the source of McCraline's bitter opposition to anyone who professes Washington's ideas (Micheaux 253). Micheaux exaggerates and caricatures rather than directly or specifically engaging criticisms of Washington. The uneducated McCraline, whose "eye was not the eye of an intelligent or deep thinking man" but reminiscent "of the eyes of pig" (225), is hardly the most flattering or accurate representation of the views of cultural nationalists.

Rather than directly reflecting the ideas of Du Bois or his followers, McCraline symbolizes more generally savagery and unmanliness, the black character traits that threaten to destroy the accomplishments of civilized blacks. While Devereaux advances reasoned and logical arguments concerning Washington's ideas, the reverend loses all composure at the very mention of his name (253). When Devereaux discovers McCraline and Orlean at the train station ready to leave him for Chicago, he also discovers that the reverend has coerced Orlean into cashing a bad check. Caught in an unmanly act, McCraline responds in an unmanly way, stammering that he "didn't do it" and appearing "a weak, shame-faced creature" (271). McCraline's unmanliness is further revealed by his inability to control his own passionate outbursts or appetites. He is said to be having sexual affairs with numerous women in the congregations on his circuit. At one point, Devereaux enters into the reverend's Chicago household to discover him "standing like a jungle king . . . pouring a storm of abuse upon his wife and shouting orders while the wife was trotting to and fro like a frightened lamb" (233). To Devereaux, he seems "more of a brute than a pious minister" (233). Instead of being a paternal protector, he operates as a despot who controls and manipulates his family. His relationship with his daughter, if not explicitly incestuous, is certainly represented by Micheaux as unseemly and unnatural. At one point, McCraline enters a room where Devereaux and Orlean are arguing, and Devereaux observes that she "kissed him—she had not kissed me" (310).

In the final scene of the book, Devereaux has come to Chicago to try to win back Orlean. They meet in the apartment of a mutual friend, and Devereaux seems on the way to a reconciliation when McCraline phones the apartment:

> The next moment I had taken the receiver from her hand, and called, "Hello, Rev. McCraline," "Hello, Rev. McCraline," in a savage tone. When he had answered, I continued in a more savage voice, "You ask my wife why she did not bring me to the house?"
>
> "Yes," he answered. His voice had changed from the commanding tone, and now appeared solicitous. "Yes, why don't you come to the house?" I seemed to hear it as an insult. (308–309)

Devereaux continues the conversation with "anger burning [his] voice" until he is crazed with anger, screaming and furious and finally "viciously" hanging up on McCraline (309). If McCraline represents the image of self that Devereaux is arrayed against, the double he must fight against becoming, this scene represents the final conquest as Devereaux is undone and unmanned, his efforts at achieving civilized manliness collapsing into a savage tone and voice, and uncontrolled, angry, vicious actions. Devereaux's increasing anger at McCraline may also represent a displacement of the anger he cannot (or is unwilling to) assert against racial restrictions imposed by white society. Whatever the cause (or causes), his outburst so upsets Orlean that she refuses to reconcile. McCraline arrives and takes his daughter away, closing the door behind him and ending Devereaux's marriage. *The Conquest* begins with a poem to "Opportunity" and ends with the image of a closed door and with the statement "That was the last time I saw my wife" (311). The conclusion of the book implies a closed frontier and a lost opportunity, represented by a series of events and images: a landscape caught in a drought, a dead child, dying crops, a failed marriage, the final loss of Orlean, a closed door.

By the end of the narrative, the book's title seems increasingly ironic. *The Conquest: The Story of a Negro Pioneer*, like the title *Up from Slavery*, implies the story of an African American individual overcoming the odds, and the first half of the book details just such a story of uplift. While Washington ends *Up from Slavery* with the observation that "there was never a time when I felt more hopeful for the race than I do at the present" (145), such optimism is absent from the last half of Micheaux's book. As a filmmaker, bell hooks argues, Micheaux draws material from "white 'master' narratives of cinema" in order to address "the black public's need to have race movies reproduce aspects of white mainstream cinema that denied their presence" (hooks 135). In *The Conquest*, Micheaux inserts a black presence into the "master narrative" of the frontier myth in part by weaving elements of African American literary tradition into his story, by joining together a Turnerian story of frontier transformation with a narrative of racial uplift inspired by both Washington and the domestic fiction tradition. Devereaux's inability to achieve his desired masculine identity implicitly critiques both narratives, as the myth of the West and the myth of racial uplift both seem closed.

The Symbol of the Unconquered

In *The Conquest,* Micheaux first tells a story that he will repeat and revise throughout his long career as a writer and filmmaker. Oscar Devereaux serves as the prototype for such later Micheaux heroes as Jean Baptiste in *The Homesteader* (1917), Hugh Van Allen in the film *The Symbol of the Unconquered* (1920), and Martin Eden in the film *The Betrayal* (1948).[7] I want to discuss briefly the silent movie *The Symbol of the Unconquered,* produced in 1920, which is the earliest existing feature-length film of black frontier life.[8] The difference between the two titles, *The Conquest* and *The Symbol of the Unconquered,* signals the most significant plot change. If Devereaux is more the conquered than the conquering hero, Hugh Van Allen emerges by the end of the film as the unambivalent symbol of the unconquered.

Micheaux alters the basic plot first set down in *The Conquest* as early as his third novel, *The Homesteader.* Although Jean Baptiste's adventure repeats many of Devereaux's South Dakota experiences, the novel continues the story past the ending of *The Conquest.* Jean Baptiste ultimately triumphs over the minister, and the Orlean / Rev. McCraline (renamed McCarthy in *The Homesteader*) plot culminates in a murder-suicide that sends father and daughter to their graves. The white girl that Devereaux falls in love with returns in *The Homesteader,* but the barrier to their relationship is erased in the final pages of the novel with the revelation that she is not white after all but, rather, a light-skinned woman of mixed ancestry. *The Symbol of the Unconquered* dispenses with the Orlean plot in order to focus on the relationship between the hero and the mixed-race light-skinned heroine (Eve Mason, played by actress Iris Hall). The movie also demonstrates a far more critical attitude toward white society. White individuals are no longer models of good behavior, and most of the primary white characters are either members of the Ku Klux Klan or otherwise associated with the vigilante group. The celebration of the Klan in D. W. Griffith's film *The Birth of a Nation* (1915) angered many African Americans, including Micheaux, and *The Symbol of the Unconquered* can be interpreted as a response to that film. Micheaux also certainly realized that the controversy created by such a negative portrayal of the Ku Klux Klan and of unscrupulous white characters in general would undoubtedly result in an increased take at the box office. Although Micheaux throughout his career continues to indicate his admiration for Booker T. Washington, we might also interpret *The Symbol of the Unconquered* as signaling a shift in his political philosophies.

As is clear in *The Conquest,* one of Micheaux's deeply held values is the idea of race loyalty. While Hugh Van Allen (Walker Thompson) and Eve Mason remain loyal to their racial heritage, the antagonist, the light-skinned Arthur Driscoll (Lawrence Chenault), passes as white. The effort he expends to repress his own ancestral past reemerges in the form of the violent oppression of other African Americans. He attacks his dark-skinned mother. He gleefully operates a segregated hotel and takes great pleasure in forcing his black patrons to sleep in the barn. And he is more than willing to join with his fellow conspirators and employ the Ku Klux Klan to force Hugh Van Allen off his land.

The film includes such conventions of the Western as a frontier setting (the town of Oristown), horse thieves, a bar fight, an attempted land grab, and a climactic showdown between the good guy and the bad guys. The representatives of savage otherness, however, are the Ku Klux Klan, whose members attempt to force Hugh Van Allen off his oil-rich homestead. The most prominent "Indian" in the film is actually from India, a bizarre character known as Tugi, the Indian fakir who is a member of the group trying to swindle our hero. The use of opposing male characters to represent manly and unmanly behavior that we saw in *The Conquest* appears here through Van Allen and Driscoll. Van Allen embodies many of the same characteristics of civilized manliness as Devereaux: he's self-sufficient, rugged but courteous, practical, kindhearted, and well mannered. However, the film recontextualizes and cautiously celebrates the uncontrolled outburst of temper that defeats Devereaux's efforts to restrain his passion. More in keeping with the model of manhood provided by the Virginian, Van Allen knows when to keep his temper and when to allow his masculine passion a freer rein. After he discovers that he has been conned into purchasing a stolen horse from Driscoll, Van Allen tracks the villain down to the local saloon and satisfies his honor by pummeling him in a fistfight scene that would seem extraordinarily out of place in *The Conquest.*

Infuriated by his defeat at the hands of our black hero, Driscoll vows to have vengeance. Driscoll's actions and gestures thoroughly establish his unmanliness. In a flashback scene, we see his proposal to a white woman interrupted by the appearance of his dark-skinned mother. Outraged that his mother has destroyed his attempt to pass, he loses control and chokes her (a most unmanly thing to do). Early in the movie Eve Mason neither claims nor denies her racial heritage. Van Allen mistakenly believes she is white, but Micheaux informs the audience of her ancestry via a scene showing her at the deathbed of her dark-skinned grandfather. Driscoll initially thinks she is white when she arrives at his hotel, but he soon deduces the truth and marches her out to the barn. Frightened during a storm, she rushes out into the rain. Driscoll, observing from his bedroom window, takes elaborate delight in the spectacle. As Bowser and Spence note, "Surrounded by an aura of shimmering whiteness (in white nightshirt and sheets, lit as if he were aglow), he thrashes his arms in triumph" (166). Driscoll, in fact, thrashes his entire body in this scene, his inability to restrain his passions

symbolized by his uncontrollable and excessive physical movements. In contrast Van Allen moves with calm deliberation
throughout.

If Eve does not advertise her African ancestry, she symbolizes her acceptance of herself as a black woman and her acceptance of other black people by taking in Driscoll's rejected
mother as a guest in her own cabin. It is interesting that the civilized easterner who undergoes frontier transformation is in
fact Eve. Early in the movie, she is easily frightened and needs
Hugh's neighborly reassurance. Her attempt to establish a
garden is hampered by her inability to shovel. She is too weak
and easily exhausted—her shoes (which we see in close-up)
would be better suited for a stroll down city streets. When word
arrives of the coming Klan attack, however, Eve rushes into her
cabin and reemerges wearing a fringed buckskin outfit and
hops onto her horse, which rears up dramatically on its hind
legs. Eve salutes her houseguest and rides off to seek help. Much
of the climactic attack of the Ku Klux Klan has unfortunately
been lost. We know the Klan is vanquished, and movie reviews
indicate that a brick-throwing black man is key to that defeat
(perhaps a reference to Washington's long discussion of brick-
making at Tuskegee Institute in *Up from Slavery*?).

The final scene of the movie recalls Harper's *Iola Leroy*. Eve
and Hugh reunite after a separation of two years (a result,
somehow, of the Klan attack). Hugh, like the Virginian, has tri-
umphed and developed into a man with his hand in many
industries—the oil business in particular. Eve has taken a position in a racial uplift organization, the Committee for the
Defense of the Colored Race, and she brings to Hugh a letter
informing him that he may give her his contribution without
fear because she also is a member of the black race. The barrier
separating them dissolved, they embrace. Their rapidly flut-
tering eyelids and accelerated breathing function as visible
signs of the sort of passion seemingly missing from the Deve-

reaux/Orlean relationship. Transformed by their frontier experiences Hugh and Eve join together romantically and politically, as committed to each other as they are to the cause of racial uplift. In the final image of the film, the two kiss, and as their lips meet, Micheaux cuts to the final title: The End. Hugh Van Allen, the symbol of the unconquered, enjoys the happy ending that eludes Oscar Devereaux in *The Conquest.*

CHAPTER 3

"You Have Got to Be the Man All Through This Mess"

Performing Gender in The Life and Adventures of Nat Love, Winona, *and* The Virginian

Both Nat Love's *The Life and Adventures of Nat Love* (1907) and Pauline Hopkins's *Winona: A Tale of Negro Life in the South and Southwest* (1902) use the regional setting of the American West to address a contemporaneous national debate among African Americans concerning appropriate responses to racial oppression. Love's *Life and Adventures* is the autobiographical story of his life as a black cowboy as well as a narrative of assimilation influenced by Booker T. Washington's *Up from Slavery*. Hopkins's *Winona* is a historical novel set before the Civil War on the border between Kansas and Missouri.[1] Hopkins draws from a more radical African American tradition in order to tell a story that uses the mythology of the American West to promote a philosophy of agitation and protest. Both Love and Hopkins also imagine the American West as a place for remaking a gendered black identity. Whereas Love uses his western setting to demonstrate that a black man can achieve the dominant culture's masculine ideal, Hopkins attempts to rethink constructions of both masculinity and femininity, and she represents the American West as a place where the potential for both racial and gender equity exists.

Love and Hopkins, more so than the other writers discussed here, draw from the genre of the Western, which has its roots in the fiction of Cooper as well as in the mass-produced dime novels of the nineteenth century. Love in particular satisfies the expectations evoked by the Western, incorporating into his autobiography such familiar elements of fiction as Indian attacks, outlaws, gunslingers, six-gun justice, cattle roundups, and cowboy contests. Although the early sections of Love's book rely heavily on Washington's *Up from Slavery*, his successful assimilation into the frontier community of white cowboys is paralleled in his storytelling by the submergence of elements drawn from African American literary tradition and the corresponding textual dominance of Western motifs. Hopkins, on the other hand, emphasizes throughout her novel the interplay between motifs specific to African American literary tradition and motifs common to the dominant-culture genre of the Western.

Although some critics feel that Hopkins's use of Western conventions results in the book's failure, I argue that *Winona* provides a number of moments when the juxtaposition of generic forms works particularly well, as the disjunction between what we expect to happen in a Western and what actually happens reveals vividly the disparity between black and white possibilities of self-making and self-representation.[2] At times the book seems to comment specifically on incidents in Wister's *The Virginian*—revising Wister's conservative Wyoming tale from the perspective of turn-of-the-century

African American feminism. Trying to reconcile seemingly unreconcilable genres, Hopkins attempts to criticize frontier mythology while at the same time appropriating the possibilities of western transfiguration for her characters.[3]

Up from Slavery

> To see me now you would not recognize the bronze hardened dare devil cow boy, the slave boy who a few years ago hunted rabbits in his shirt tail on the old plantation in Tennessee, or the tenderfoot who shrank shaking all over at the sight of a band of painted Indians. I had long since felt the hot sting of the leaden bullet as it plowed its way through some portion of my anatomy. Likewise I had lost all sense of fear, and while I was not the wild blood thirsty savage and all around bad man many writers have pictured me in their romances, yet I was wild, reckless and free, afraid of nothing, that is nothing that I ever saw, with a wide knowledge of the cattle country and the cattle business and of my guns.
>
> —Love, *Life and Adventures*

In his *Life and Adventures of Nat Love, Better Known in the Cattle Country as "Deadwood Dick"* (1907), Nat Love represents the frontier as a place where "a man's work was to be done, and a man's life to be lived" (155), where he was able to earn a name ("Deadwood Dick") bestowed out of respect for his manly abilities at roping and shooting, and where race did not restrict him from becoming "one of the leading cowboys of the West" (118). Love's descriptions of his experiences certainly contain an element of truth about the lives of black cowboys. Katz notes that "black cowboys probably suffered less because of discrimination than almost any other occupation open equally to black and white at the time anywhere in the nation" (147).[4] Although Love's experiences may in some ways reflect the experiences of black cowboys, largely absent from his *Life and Adventures* are descriptions of the lives of most African Americans in the West, the stories not of rugged cowboys but of communities. In his study of the American West, Quintard Taylor argues that the influence of cowboys in western history, black or white, has been exaggerated and overly mythologized. Instead of focusing on the rugged, mythic, solitary cowboy "loosened from moorings of family, home, and community," Taylor examines the way African Americans in the West went about "developing supportive community institutions and attempting, as much as possible, to integrate themselves into both the larger social and political lives of their cities and the cultural and political life of the national African American community" (22–23). Love emphasizes instead the mythic story of "a stranger in strange land, inhabited wholly by people not my own race" (Micheaux 77). Love, unlike Devereaux in *The Conquest,* finds a satisfying place both within the "strange" landscape of the American West and among his white associates—the "brotherhood" of cowboys on the frontier.

Love's success as a cowboy, his overcoming of racial barriers, is represented as an erasure of racial marking, as Love drops textual references to his race or skin color after journeying west. That crossing over from racially marked to racially unmarked has proved a problem for literary criticism of the book. Allmendinger observes that the autobiography is rarely referred to in studies of black literature primarily because "no critical strategy for making sense of black texts seems to work when discussing Love's memoirs" ("Deadwood" 79). The reader who searches for a black viewpoint in *The Life and Adventures* labors "fruitlessly" (79). What Brackette Williams calls Love's "western voice," his use of braggadocio, hyperbole, and humor, so predominates that his story "does not prove easily recognizable as an African-American one" (vii), leaving the contemporary reader to "wonder why he decided to write his life in the voice of a generic cowboy" (xiv). If we have difficulty locating a black voice beneath the concealing western voice, we should examine more closely how Love accomplishes this feat of ventriloquism, what textual strategies he employs that enable him to "pass," to cross over racial barriers and boundaries. We should also open our definitions of what makes a black text. Stories of assimilation and accommodation are as much a part of African American literary tradition as those of protest. Neither Love's failure to protest explicitly against white oppression nor his attempt to represent himself as raceless necessarily makes him an anomaly among black writers.

Love transforms frontier mythology into a tale of black America by bringing elements of African American literary tradition to his western narrative. He aligns his story with Washington's philosophies of integration through useful work and of racial uplift through individual effort. Washington observes that "Every persecuted individual and race should get much consolation out of the great human law, which is universal and eternal, that merit, no matter under what skin found, is, in the long run, recognized and rewarded" (*Up from Slavery* 24). Although Love's adventures may draw on the mythology of the American West, he uses these adventures to prove (to use Washington's phrase) that "he possesses [the] intrinsic, individual merit" that enables him to transcend race and become recognized and rewarded for that merit (24). Unlike Micheaux's Devereaux, Love succeeds (by his own account) in achieving his desired masculine identity—and achieves a successful integration into the society of cowboys. He does not do so without cost, however. It is clear he leaves gaps in the account of his experiences. His "useful work" involves violent actions, and as Allmendinger points out, Love achieves success and acceptance "by terrorizing members of minority racial and ethnic groups" ("Deadwood" 86). Love's bond with his fellow cowboys is cemented by shared acts of violence, and his transformation from slave to cowboy hinges on the myth of "regenerative violence."

Although Love places the greatest emphasis on his time in the "cattle country," his *Life and Adventures* begin with his childhood under slavery in Tennessee: "In an old log cabin, on my Master's plantation in Davidson County in Tennessee in June, 1854, I first saw the light of day. The exact date of my birth I never knew, because in those days no count was kept of such trivial matters as the birth of a slave baby. They were born and died and the account was balanced in the gains and losses of the Master's chattels" (7). Love clearly borrows from Washington (who borrows from Frederick Douglass and other slave narrative authors) in constructing this opening paragraph. Washington begins his autobiography with the statement, "I was born a slave on a plantation in Franklin County, Virginia. I am not quite sure of the exact place or exact date of my birth" (7). Love alters the syntax of the opening sentence, and he uses the phrase "I first saw light of day" rather than "I was born," but he retains Washington's emphasis on noting the county and state and the fact that he was born on a plantation. He repeats the phrase "exact date of my birth" in the second sentence before diverging from Washington's language. Other bits and pieces of Washington's phrasings and observations appear in Love's account. Of his owner, Love states, "He was in his way and in comparison with many other slave owners of those days a kind and indulgent Master" (7), echoing Washington's observation that his owners were not "especially cruel . . . as compared with many others" (7).

Although Love and Washington note the exceptional status of their specific owners, both writers nonetheless condemn slavery as an institution. Love notes that his "kind and indulgent Master," upon returning from the Civil War, "did not tell us we were free. And instead of letting us go he made us work for him the same as before" (15). Love's account of the cruelty of slavery is particularly scathing, although he condenses his criticism into an "I have seen" paragraph detailing events he witnessed growing up. "I have seen men beaten to the ground," he writes (13). Of the treatment of female slaves, he observes, "I have seen the long, cruel lash curl around the shoulders of women who refused to comply with the licentious wishes of the men who owned them" (13). Having given witness to the treatment of African Americans under slavery, he suggests that the reader "Go and see the play of 'Uncle Tom's Cabin,' and you will see the black man's life as I saw it when a child" (13). But this is not the primary story either Washington or Love wants to tell. Love uses the slave narrative tradition primarily to set up his own story, one that emphasizes individual achievement in a post-emancipation society. Like Washington he begins his autobiography in slavery not to condemn an institution already declared illegal but to demonstrate the low from which he has risen—and to demonstrate by example the ability of meritorious individual blacks to overcome racial barriers.

Although Love borrows phrases and observations from *Up from Slavery*, the primary parallels between the two books are structural and philosophical. An important initiation scene takes place within the first quarter of each book. Both autobiographies contain a climactic public event that signifies the narrator's achievement of success—Washington's Atlanta Cotton Exposition speech, Love's winning a cowboy contest in South Dakota. Both autobiographies are narratives of education in which Washington and Love carefully note lessons learned—either moral or in terms of developing skills and abilities—from events described. As Washington's lessons (learning to read, learning the habits of cleanliness while working for Mrs. Ruffner) are specific to his own particular education and eventual field of endeavor, so are Love's lessons consistent with his later career. His first experience with drunkenness (on his mother's homemade wine) gives him his "taste for strong

drink" and certainly contributes to the fact "that I could out-
drink any man I ever met in the cattle country" (11); the "rock
battles" of childhood prepare him for later gun battles; his
youthful experiences breaking colts for a dime per animal
"stood me in good stead in after years during my wild life on
the western plains" (32). The early death of Love's father forces
him as a teenager into a position of responsibility as "the head
of the family," which teaches him "lessons in self-dependence"
(21, 25). The death of Love's father enables him to take his
father's place and share his status and responsibilities—but
without having the encumbrance of becoming a biological
father to his own children. Although the desire to become a
father is a driving force in both *The Conquest* and *Up from
Slavery*, Love achieves symbolic status as a father at an early age.
This achievement for Love is not a goal in and of itself but one
step in developing the strength of character that enables his
later success.

Armed with these lessons in self-dependence and with such
nascent cowboy skills as horse-breaking and drinking (and
freed of familial responsibilities by the arrival of an uncle),
Love eventually sets out "to see more of the world," winding up
in Dodge City, Kansas, in 1869 at around the age of fifteen (37).
As is the case for Washington upon his arrival at Hampton
Institute, Love must complete an initiation/examination before
he can continue his education. While Love's demonstration of
horse-riding abilities in Kansas may remind us, as Allmendinger points out, of the conventional western scene of a
"tenderfoot" freshly arrived from the East who surprises a
group of experienced cowboys with his skills ("Deadwood" 81),
this scene also recalls Washington's description of his first experiences at Hampton. As a test of his readiness, Washington is
instructed to clean a recitation room. He observes that "the
sweeping of that room was my college examination," one that
he emerges from by impressing the head teacher, Miss Mary F.

Mackie, "a 'Yankee' woman who knew just where to look for dirt" (28–29). As a test of cowboy ability, Love is mounted on a horse known as "old Good Eye," which "proved the worst horse to ride I had ever mounted in my life, but I stayed with him and the cow boys were the most surprised outfit you ever saw, as they had taken me for a tenderfoot, pure and simple" (41). As a reward, he is praised by the cowboys and offered a job by the head of the outfit. Both Washington and Love turn the tables on the observers' expectations, putting into practice during their initiation scenes the skills they have already begun to develop.

Having passed the test, ex-slave Nat Love becomes the owner of "a new saddle, bridle and spurs, chaps, a pair of blankets and a fine 45 Colt revolver" and of a new name, "Red River Dick," all supplied by his new employer (41). Love's initiation begins his education in earnest. As Allmendinger notes, *The Life and Adventures* conforms to an often repeated narrative structure in African American autobiographies in which a physical journey also involves a quest for literacy and for freedom ("Deadwood" 85).[5] Love knows how to read and write before going west, and his representation of literacy is filtered through Washington's concept of industrial education, as an acquisition of such job skills as learning to read the landscape or cattle brands. Love's growing ability at distinguishing brands causes "the cattle men . . . to recognize my worth" and eventually leads to a lucrative position with the Gallinger company as "their chief brand reader" (Love 47).

In my discussion of Turner's summary of frontier transformation, I argued that the colonist projects onto the figure of the American Indian an image of masculinity that the colonist desires to assume as his own. His subsequent transformation is facilitated by his identification with the ideal image he sees in the "mirror" of the American Indian. The image of identity that Love assumes as his own is reflected back to him by the approval of the watching cowboys. What Love describes here is, in a sense, his experience of being "hailed," of the process that Louis Althusser calls "interpellation."[6] He is "addressed" by representatives of "society" who offer him a new image of self—as symbolized by his new name, "Red River Dick." Love recognizes himself in that new name. He recognizes his new identity in the mirror of the cowboys' collective approval of his actions, which attaches signified to signifier, verifying his sense of his own merit, and enables him to represent his experiences as evidence of Washington's great law—that merit demonstrated through useful work will enable individual blacks to transcend racial barriers. Whereas Washington's transformation proceeds at a slow but steady pace, Love undergoes a series of rapid changes, his identity shifts symbolized by changes in name and clothing, and by another initiation scene—his baptism by fire and blood during an Indian attack.

Regeneration through Violence

> *We only had fifteen men in our outfit, but nothing daunted we stood our ground and fought the Indians to a stand. . . . During this fight we lost all but six of our horses, our entire packing outfit and our extra saddle horses. . . . As we only had six horses left us, we were unable to follow them, although we had the satisfaction of knowing we had made several good Indians out of bad ones.*
>
> —LOVE, *Life and Adventures*

Middle-class white men at the turn of the century began to react negatively to the constructions of civilized manliness promoted as the masculine ideal during the Victorian period. They feared that too much manly self-restraint put them in danger of becoming "overcivilized" and thus unable to uphold a perfect civilization against the degenerating effects of the savagery of the non-white races. Middle-class white men wanted to find a way to balance civilized self-restraint (which defined their superior manliness) with the exercise of "primitive" or "natural" passions (which they also began to see as an essential part of masculine identity). We might argue that Turner's frontiersman renews his capacity for natural masculine behavior by journeying to the frontier. He indicates that he still retains his civilized manliness by then transforming the wilderness into civil society—by changing unowned land into property. In order to contradict contemporary constructions of black savagery, Micheaux represents Oscar Devereaux's journey as a means of demonstrating his civilized manliness, not as a means of returning to a state of primitive masculinity. The contradiction that Devereaux cannot overcome (escaping black savagery by journeying into the wilderness) seems to present no problem for Love as he easily imagines himself the embodiment of both savagery and civilization: "while I was not the wild blood thirsty savage and all around bad man many writers have pictured me in their romances, yet I was wild, reckless and free, afraid of nothing" (70). How, we might ask, is Love able to assert a vigorous and natural masculine identity without fear of being read in terms of black savagery, which would undercut his assertions of subjectivity and humanity?

One strategy he uses is his erasure of racial identity. Love's character and identity undergo a transformation as the narrative progresses, and so does his physical body: "To see me now you would not recognize the bronze hardened dare devil cow boy, the slave boy who a few years ago hunted rabbits in his shirt tail" (70). Allmendinger observes, "Written self-portraits . . . make Love seem toughened ('hardened') by riding horses and herding cattle outside and, hence, tanned (made 'bronze') by the blazing overhead sun" ("Deadwood" 80). Love's race is displaced by these descriptions, as "Love represents himself as being like any white ranch hand whose skin slowly weathers"

(80). Rather than representing himself as if he were "any white ranch hand," I would argue that Love displaces color, black, white, or bronze, as a significant marker of identity as his narrative progresses.

In his verbal descriptions of himself, Love emphasizes the marks he has earned as a cowboy, his scarred body serving as evidence of his manhood and achievements. He tells of adroitly surviving Indian attacks ("My nose had been nearly cut off, also one of my fingers had been nearly cut off. These wounds I received when I was fighting my captors with my empty gun" [99]); natural disasters ("when the blizzard had passed they noticed an object out on the prairie in the snow, with one hand frozen, clenched around my Winchester and the other around the horn of my saddle. . . . the marks of that storm I will carry with me always" [115]); and various gun battles. ("I am naturally tough," Love writes, "as I carry the marks of fourteen bullet wounds on different part of my body, most any one of which would be sufficient to kill an ordinary man, but I am not even crippled" [103]). As Love's construction of himself as a masculine cowboy progresses, the importance of skin pigmentation—which marked his identity as a slave—as a signifier and as a synecdochic representation of the whole man recedes. The significant physical marker of identity is the scar, for such a marking (like the name Red River Dick) must be earned through manly action. Although Love may note the damage done to individual body parts, his survival indicates that he is blessed with toughness of body and strength of character, that he is superior to an ordinary man both in his physique and in his will to survive. Each part reveals the whole man, and his whole body, naturally tough, emerges as the primary signifier of masculine identity.

We might argue that Love's primary strategy for addressing the contradiction of a black man engaging with the frontier myth involves the trope of regenerative violence, a strategy that

Micheaux's farming narrative does not employ. Shortly after his successful ride of "old Good Eye," Love leaves town with the other cowboys. Joined up with "as jolly a set of fellows as on [*sic*] could find," Love sets out "on a journey which was to prove the most eventful of my life up to now" (41–42). Love completes the transformation signaled by his name and clothing change by entering into battle: "This was my first Indian fight and likewise the first Indians I had ever seen. . . . I was too badly scared to run." His companions instruct him to shoot, and "their words brought me back to earth." After firing the first shot, "I lost all fear and fought like a veteran" (42). This act (and other acts) of violence facilitates Love's assimilation into the brotherhood of cowboys and into the dominant culture this brotherhood represents. By participating in white violence against the other, Love divests himself of a black identity as he earlier shed his eastern clothes. The presence of an enemy, an object of exchange, facilitates a homosocial bond between Love and the other men; violence enables him to enjoy an identity usually reserved for white men, to take part in (to paraphrase Eve Sedgwick) "[white] men's relations with other [white] men" (2). Being "cool, observant and ready for what might turn up, made me liked and respected by my employers," Love observes later, and "among my own companions my position was as high as a king, enjoying the trust and confidence of my employers and the homage of the men" (70).

Such bonding is missing from *The Conquest,* and we might read that narrative as consisting of a series of failed attempts to initiate homosocial bonds. Although Devereaux observes he "was regarded as one of the Little Crow's best citizens," he also realizes that he has "been treated with every courtesy and respect" in part because he has "kept [his] place as regards custom" (Micheaux 155). Marriage to a white woman—and the subsequent bond with white men—is not an option for Devereaux, as such an action would go against custom and might result not in courtesy and respect from his fellow landowners but ostracism. Because of the prohibition against interracial marriage, Devereaux is put in the contradictory position of earning courtesy and respect by refusing to participate in the exchange of women between men that would make him part of men's relations with other men and thus integrate him further into the community. Because he is excluded from this system of exchange, he attempts to rearticulate a system of homosocial bonds with black men, an attempt that likewise fails, as McCraline not only seems incapable of enacting such a civilized compact with Devereaux but also actively disrupts any hope of such a bond. In contrast to Toni Morrison's critique of patriarchy in *Paradise,* in *The Conquest* homosocial bonding is viewed as a lost opportunity.

The climax of Love's story occurs in 1876 when he wins a cowboy contest in South Dakota as well as "the name of 'Deadwood Dick,' a name I made even better known than 'Red River Dick.' And a name I was proud to carry and defend, if necessary, with my life" (77). Unlike "Red River Dick," this new name signifies a specific accomplishment that marks Love as more than simply good enough to be a cowboy, for he must defeat "the best men of the West" to win the contest (97). Whereas "Red River" was given to him by the boss of a cowboy outfit, "Deadwood" has more populist connotations, as it "was given to me by the people of Deadwood, South Dakota, July 4, 1876, after I had proven myself worthy to carry it" (97). If Cooper's Natty Bumppo is provided with "a more manly title" by the man he has fatally shot, Love's new names come from his comrades rather than his enemies, and his being named Red River precedes the violence that proves him worthy of the new identity. Between being named Red River Dick and being renamed Deadwood Dick, he proves himself to the brotherhood of cowboys through a series of violent acts. His worthiness to carry a new name, one that signifies his manhood, has already been established before the cowboy contest—by his victories on the various battlefields that precede the contest. The people of South Dakota formalize a victory already won, and their accolades symbolize Love's successful assimilation into the dominant culture, an assimilation facilitated by his willingness and ability to commit acts of violence in the name of that culture.

Love's new name connects him to Edward Wheeler's famous dime novel hero, and he refers to that series (involving thirty-three novels published between 1877 and 1884) when he comments, "I was not the wild blood thirsty savage and all around bad man many writers have pictured me in their romances" (70). Love's rebirth as Deadwood Dick on July 4, 1876 (a nicely symbolic date for an All-American hero), precedes the first appearance of Wheeler's hero, and Nicole Tonkovich argues in her discussion of *Deadwood Dick on Deck* (1878) that Wheeler draws on the life of Nat Love for his inspiration. As Tonkovich points out, however, Wheeler's Deadwood Dick's adventures "had to be attributed to a white man" in order to be accepted by the book's readers (243).

In *Deadwood Dick, The Prince of the Road* (1877), Wheeler's initial description of a white hero hidden by a "thick black vail" recalls the masking used by black-faced minstrel actors. The description begins conventionally enough. Deadwood Dick is "trim and compactly build, with a preponderance of muscular development and animal spirits" (280). With "limbs small yet like bars of steel, and with grace of position in the saddle rarely equaled," Deadwood Dick indeed "made a fine picture for an artist's brush or a poet's pen." However, "one thing marred the captivating beauty of the picture":

> His form was clothed in a tight-fitting habit of buck-skin, which was colored a jetty black, and presented a striking contrast to anything one sees as a garment in the wild far West. And this was not all, either.

A broad black hat was slouched down over his eyes; he wore a thick black vail over the upper portion of his face, through the eye-holes of which there gleamed a pair of orbs of piercing intensity, and his hands, large and knotted, were hidden in a pair of kid gloves of a light color.

The "Black Rider" he might have been justly termed, for his thoroughbred steed was as black as coal, but we have not seen fit to call him such—his name is Deadwood Dick, and let that suffice for the present. (280)

We might wonder here if the "thing" that "marred the captivating beauty of the picture" is the race of the figure who inspired Wheeler's hero. The tight-fitting black (buck-)skin that creates such a striking visual contrast certainly points (if not to Love himself) to a black cowboy, whose true racial identity must be both overtly referred to (he is black from head to toe) and hidden away (even his hands are covered by gloves).

Nat Love and Ownership

As in Turner's essay and Micheaux's narrative, the cornerstone to civilization in Love's *Life and Adventures* is an understanding of individual property ownership. Savage actions that end in civilized results (transforming wilderness into property) enable a man to exercise his aggressive instincts without devolving into savagery. The relationship between African Americans and property is complicated by a history of slavery, which designates the black individual as the object not the subject of property. In such eighteenth- and nineteenth-century slave narratives as *The Life of Olaudah Equiano, or Gustavus Vassa, the African* (1789) and the *Narrative of the Life of Frederick Douglass* (1845), the negotiation of that economic status is particularly marked and may be relevant to Micheaux's and

Love's constructions of subjectivity. Equiano earns enough money eventually to purchase himself, to become literally the owner of his own body and thereby the agent of his own freedom.[7] Douglass likewise realizes the importance of becoming a property owner and enters into an agreement with his master that allows him to hire himself out for pay. In Micheaux's narrative, Devereaux similarly attempts to transform self via property ownership. Love enters into the economic system as an agent by hiring himself out and receiving wages and thereby indicating his ownership of his body and his labor.

South Dakota remains for Devereaux a strange land. As property ownership is central to Micheaux's concept of manliness, his hero's failure to retain his property at the end of the narrative parallels the collapse of his sense of a civilized identity. For Nat Love, transforming a strange land into a symbolic extension of the self results not from ownership but from possessing knowledge and understanding of that territory: "Naturally I became very well acquainted with all the many different trails and grazing ranges located in the stretch of country between the north of Montana and the Gulf of Mexico, and between the Missouri state line and the Pacific ocean. This whole territory I have covered many times in the saddle, sometimes at the rate of eighty or one hundred miles a day" (46). Love demonstrates little interest in owning his own land or cattle. Knowing rather than owning land signifies his identity, for that education makes him employable.

Love signals his transformation from slave to human not through acquiring property rights but through protecting the property rights of others. The cowboys' job, Love notes, "is to protect themselves and their employer's cattle from the Indian thiefs and the white desperadoes who infested the cattle country" (51). Love aligns himself with the forces of civilization not by imitating white property owners but by acting violently to protect white property. Although Love "passes" by joining the cowboys, he achieves more accurately a state of racelessness, neither white nor black. Becoming a cowboy erases all racial distinctions, both whiteness as well as blackness. "White," in fact, functions as a racial marker within the narrative—assigned to the white outlaws, whose racially marked identity signifies their difference from the equally white but racially unmarked cowboys. *White, Indian,* and *Mexican* are all marked terms representing an inferior, savage identity. By enacting violence that is unlike the savagery of white outlaws and American Indians, Love represents the law itself—the protection of property in opposition to the savages who attempt to ignore property rights, the cornerstone of civilization.

Whereas Love's actions may be savage, his intent is civilized. If the "need to protect white womanhood" functions to justify violence for Cooper and for Roosevelt (and thereby protect the purity of the system of exchange of women between white men), for Love, traffic not in women but in another form of property—cattle—facilitates a bond between men. Love does not lay claim himself to objects of exchange, whether in the form of land, white women, or cattle. His homosocial bonds are based on sharing in labor with his fellow workers, the cowboys who, like him, facilitate the exchange of transportable property between various members of a white landowning class of wealthy men. Love may represent the law of the land (the protection of white property), but he does not threaten the system of exclusions on which the law rests; he does not try, as does Devereaux, to become a property owner himself.

Violence functions as a rhetorical figure that conceals Love's process of interpellation, the work of ideology, the creation of homosocial bonds that ultimately reinforces the consolidation of power and property in the hands of a ruling class of white men. Unlike many of the other black protagonists discussed in this study, Love's assertion of masculinity is indeed recognized and valued by the dominant culture. Because he acts to protect white ownership of property, his sense of manhood serves rather than threatens the dominant culture. In exchange for this sense of identity, Love forfeits access to other signifiers of manhood, such as full participation in political process or property ownership for himself. He also sacrifices an identity based in the black community in order to support a white power structure that enables his sense of individual freedom while collectively denying such freedom to most African Americans.

If marriage is crucial for Micheaux, Love marries only after the closing of the frontier dissolves the homosocial bond between himself and the other "boys"—a bond that is starkly absent from the last quarter of the book, which details his post-frontier life as a Pullman porter. Although he does not comment explicitly on the difference between porter and cowboy, he does provide a narrative that makes those differences hard to miss. The train service keeps Love in motion, moving from place to place and seeing the country, but he is no longer in control of his own movement, no longer guiding his own horse. The knowledge of the landscape is no longer essential to his job, and his perspective is reduced to that of a tourist. Love still emphasizes the importance of a job well done, and he describes his education in learning how to provide service to passengers that results in good tips and choice assignments from his supervisors. Although he may earn the "confidence of [his] employers" as a porter, we do not get the sense that he enjoys "the homage of the men," his fellow porters (70). He seems, in fact, alienated from them.

At the end of the autobiography, there is a strong sense of regret, not only for the loss of his frontier freedom but also for the loss of his relationship with his former comrades, the "ever decreasing band of men under whose blue and buckskin shirts there lives a soul as great and beats a heart as true as ever human breast contained" (1). The coming of the railroad—and civilization—disrupts Love's ability to enjoy his life's work and brings to an end his identity as Deadwood Dick. Once his usefulness in protecting white property has ended, he must return to a subordinate position (as a porter) and identity. If Love follows Roosevelt in depicting warfare on the frontier as a means of unification, the cessation of the battle dissolves the bonds forged by that violence. Love's successful assimilation on the frontier is undone by civilized society's color line, as revealed most clearly by his meetings with former frontier comrades—ex-cowboys or railroad friends made during his cowboy days such as William Blood and E. W. Gillett who work as conductors and passenger agents, not porters (149). Love's narrative laments the passing of a time gone by, but he does not explicitly comment on or protest against the racial politics that contribute as much to his loss of freedom and identity as the closing of the frontier.

Manhood and Womanhood in Winona

Pauline Hopkins's *Winona* indicates frustration with the ideas of Washington that Love embraces. Hopkins, Martha Patterson writes, believed in "more vehement public protests against the escalating mob violence endorsed by Jim Crow culture" (446).[8] Hopkins uses the historical setting of Kansas in 1856 "to justify the need in 1902 for the kind of organized resistance to racist violence led by the anti-slavery leader John Brown" before the Civil War (Patterson 445). Brown and his followers symbolize the efficacy of organized resistance to racial oppression. The proslavery forces represent as well a more general example of racist ideology, as the savagery of the Missouri Rangers and slaveholders symbolizes the actions of post-Reconstruction lynch mob violence. Such extreme racial oppression, Hopkins argues, calls for an equally strong response. She struggles, however, with the contradiction inherent in employing violence to advance civilized purposes. As Winona accuses her adopted brother Judah, "You make yourself as vile as the vilest of them—our enemies" (*Winona* 422). If one must act savagely to counter savagery, what prevents one from becoming the very thing opposed?

Such moral quandaries, however, seem reserved for the book's black characters, particularly Judah, who asks: "But how is a man to distinguish between right and wrong? What moral responsibility rests upon him from whom all good things are taken?" (379). Through Judah, whose innate nobility, good heart, and physical superiority are emphasized throughout, Hopkins hopes to refute the dehumanizing stereotypes of savage black manhood often deployed to justify lynch mob behavior. This effort, however, conflicts with the book's political purpose—to assert the necessity of radical, even violent, action to protest against oppression of blacks. Her attempt to reconcile these contradictory purposes results in an ambivalent portrayal of Judah's character that, Patterson argues, "invokes the very racist rationale for Jim Crow culture she seeks to refute" (451). While acknowledging the ambiguity of Judah's representation, I argue that Hopkins achieves a greater complexity in her portrayal than the simple repetition of a stereotype.

The question of what justifies violence, especially violent acts by individuals or groups that take place outside a structured legal system, provides a point of contact between *Winona* and Wister's *The Virginian*. *Winona* originally appeared serially in six parts in *Colored American Magazine*, running from May to October of 1902, with the first installment appearing a month after the initial publication of *The Virginian*.[9] Both books include a scene of sanctioned group violence (John Brown's execution of captured Missouri Rangers in *Winona*, the hanging of Steve and Ed in *The Virginian*), and both books culminate in scenes of individual violence, the celebrated

Western showdown. Judah finally faces man-to-man his tor-
menter from a Missouri plantation, and the Virginian on his
wedding day confronts Trampas, who has been his nemesis
throughout the book. Whereas Love accepts as a given, if not a
condition of his employment, the justice of his violent acts,
both Wister and Hopkins include several scenes wherein characters debate and question the legitimacy of extralegal violence.
Winona and *The Virginian* also foreground debates about the
roles men and women play in society and examine from quite
different perspectives the interplay between gender and sanctioned violence.

   Winona begins just outside Buffalo, New York, in a setting of
natural beauty, "white clouds" and "dazzling sunshine," and
social intermingling, a "mixed community of Anglo-Saxons,
Indians and Negroes," a place seemingly outside the racist ideologies of slavery and segregation (287–90). Winona, a light-
skinned African American woman of mixed ancestry, represents this intermingling of peoples. She is the daughter of
White Eagle, a white man adopted by the Seneca Indians. Her
mother is a fugitive slave, "a handsome well-educated mulat-
tress" who arrives on the island where White Eagle lives seeking
refuge for herself and an infant boy, the child of another female
slave who died during the escape (290). After crossing into
Canada together, the two marry, return to the island, and adopt
the infant boy, Judah. After giving birth to Winona, the mother
dies, leaving White Eagle and an elderly Seneca woman, "old
Nokomis," with care of the two children (290).[10] In the middle
of Lake Erie, White Eagle's small island is an ideal space,
belonging to neither Canada nor the United States, a place of
harmony between individual and the environment and
between one racial group and another.

   The plot of the novel is enormously complicated. The mysterious White Eagle is really a British subject, heir to the Carlingford estate, in hiding because he has been falsely accused of

murder. Seeking out the Carlingford heir is aristocrat Warren Maxwell, a young British lawyer who enters the narrative on a rainy night and, by chance, becomes acquainted with Winona and Judah. Although Warren himself observes that "there must have been some dark shadow in White Eagle's past life to cause him to bury himself here in a wilderness," he does not think to connect his quest to the mystery of White Eagle's past and does not realize his true identity until the end of the novel (313). In the background is the Fugitive Slave Act of 1850, which has effectively shifted the border between freedom and slavery as the northern United States no longer represents a safe refuge. A hotel owner in northern New York who befriends the two children (and who will eventually join Brown's abolitionist cause), Ebeneezer Maybee, comments that Judah and Winona fall victim to "the new act for the rendition of fugitive slaves jes' passed by Congress" (314). Representing the ideology of the South are Colonel Titus and Bill Thomson, whose menacing entry into the story is foreshadowed by the sound of a gunshot, the shooting and killing of an eagle whose flight Winona and Judah observe from their island paradise. Titus and Thomson, we eventually discover (but immediately suspect), are behind the subsequent murder of White Eagle, which sets the plot events in motion. Their motive in part is to capture Winona and Judah as fugitive slaves. Control of Winona is particularly important, as with the death of White Eagle she has become the true heir to Carlingford, an estate that both Titus and Thomson have a stake in securing for themselves.

Homosocial bonds in *Winona* are associated with slavery and with the southerners who benefit from and oversee that system of exchange. We see few women in the proslavery camp, only Thomson's wife (who is as cruel in her treatment of slaves as her husband is) and Colonel Titus's daughter (whose sickliness symbolizes a divine punishment inflicted on Titus). Only the antislavery forces include women in their group, and this female presence works a civilizing presence on the men who bear arms, preventing them from losing their spiritual purpose to the savagery of masculine passion and desire for revenge. As a slave Winona is a piece of property whose status as an object of exchange is essential to the cementing of the bonds between men that make the ideology of the South into a brutal reality. As the female heir to the Carlingford estate, Winona's existence as a free woman disrupts the patriarchal tradition of inheritance from father to male heir. As property owner rather than property, Winona destabilizes the division between black and white, and by evading her racial designation as object of exchange, she represents a symbolic threat to the maintenance of the homosocial bonds that constitute the slavery system.

With the murder of White Eagle and the capture of Judah and Winona, the setting shifts from the Canadian border to the novel's most significant frontier setting, the Kansas/Missouri border. Like White Eagle's island, Kansas represents a potential utopia of interracial harmony, but this potentiality is threatened by the proslavery forces' efforts to extend the ideology of the South from border to border, from south to north, from east to west. "It's the destiny of the South," Colonel Titus observes, "to rule in this glorious country" (331). Magnolia Farm, Titus's Missouri plantation, is a dystopia ruled by the southern ideology of racial subjugation and exploitation of resources. The land has been harnessed for cotton production, a contrast to the still wild western landscape across the river in Kansas. Missouri, with its functioning (if corrupt) legal system and well-established system of property ownership and exchange, represents the Metropolis, or civilization, whereas Kansas represents the Wilderness, where law has not been extended. In civilized Missouri, though, the law is unjust and the emphasis on individual property rights the greatest evidence of savagery. As does Marrant in his *Narrative,* Hopkins inverts the frontier myth's savage/civilized dichotomy by revealing the savagery of white civilization.

The novel takes up the story two years after the capture of Winona and Judah, a period of time that "seemed centuries long to the helpless captives, reared in the perfect freedom of Nature's woods and streams" (320). If Love's journey west symbolizes his change from slave boy to free, wage-earning man, Winona and Judah's westward travel represents the opposite, a shift from freedom to enslavement. As does Love, Hopkins adapts a particular convention of the Western—the seeming greenhorn/tenderfoot character freshly arrived from the East who surprises and wins over the crowd by riding a horse that supposedly cannot be ridden—to represent the change in status brought about by her male protagonist's westward journey. Love's horse-breaking abilities demonstrate his merit and result in an elevation in his status. After a similar display of horsemanship on Judah's part, Bill Thomson, the overseer for Magnolia Farms, responds, "Breaking hosses in ain't wuth a cent to a nigger" (328), and Judah's reward for his accomplishment is his "first experience of slave discipline," a severe beating designed by Thomson to teach him "a nigger's place" (321, 328).

Judah, we are told, has been taught by White Eagle "to speak like a senator, ride bareback like a hull circus; he can shoot a bird on the wing and hunt and fish like all natur' " (310). His capture, though, interrupts the natural evolution of his character. Even though he has "developed into a lion of a man," he has also "lost his sunny disposition and buoyant spirits" and become "stern, silent" (320). When given the opportunity to act according to his "natur," Judah breaks his silence and drops the mask of servility he has learned to adopt as a slave. After observing Thomson attempt and fail to ride a horse that he has bet he can break, Judah intervenes, saying, "Don't shoot him yet, sir; I can tame that horse and win your bet for you" (322). Hopkins writes: "A murmur of approval broke from the crowd.

... Judah stepped forward and began giving his orders without a shade of servility, seeming to forget in the excitement of the moment his position as a slave. Once more he moved as a free man amidst his fellows and for the time being forgot all else" (323). The horse "plunged forward, reared wildly, pawed the air, and whirled around," and in response to the horse's "furious attempt to throw the rider," Judah provides the gathered crowd with "an exhibition of the most daring horsemanship ever witnessed in Kansas City" (325–26).

The acknowledgment of his manhood achieved by Love through a similar display of skills is denied Judah. Although Judah receives an ovation from the gathered men, the result of his ride is not acceptance as it was for Nat Love but an order to report to a Kansas City prison where slaves are taken to be beaten (326). He is a free man amidst his fellows only for a moment. After his feat, Love is clothed in the proper costume to reflect his accomplishment. Judah's display of skill and masculine ability is rewarded with an order to "strip yourself," his nakedness a humiliating counterpoint to Love's acquisition of the manly accoutrements of a cowboy (327). He is "strung by his thumbs to the cross-beams" and whipped, and each "merciless lash was engraved on his heart in bleeding stripes that called for vengeance" (327–28). For Love, the conventions of the Western provide him with a structure for articulating his sense of worth and humanity, as doing the things a cowboy is meant to do—riding wild horses, using his six-gun in battle, driving cattle, and so on—serve as proof of his manhood. Although Judah, like Love, has demonstrated that he has intrinsic, individual merit, Hopkins uses this scene to draw a different conclusion about the reward for that merit. As the South attempts to invade the West, so does the existence of slavery alter and invert Western conventions. As a representative of the dominant culture of the South and as a figure of authority in that culture, Bill Thomson has the power to refuse to recognize

Judah's assumption of identity, to deny his assertion of manhood and humanity. Whereas Love's identity is recognized
by an act of naming (as he is given a new name by the outfit
boss), Thomson uses his authority to ascertain that Judah
assumes the name ("nigger") and identity assigned to him in
the South.

If this horse-riding scene belongs to the Western, Thomson's
actions punish Judah's generic transgression by placing him in
a scenario familiar to African American tradition—the beating
of a slave at the hands of a particularly cruel overseer. As in the
eighteenth- and nineteenth-century narratives written by
former and escaped slaves, Hopkins uses this scene to protest
the abuses of slavery and racial oppression. Punishment of the
male body, however, is not uncommon to the Western where,
Mitchell observes, we find an "almost obsessive recurrence of
scenes of men being beaten—or knifed and whipped, propped
up, knocked down, kicked in the side, punched in the face, or
otherwise lacerated, clubbed, battered, and tortured into
unconsciousness" (169). In Wister's *The Virginian,* for example,
Molly Wood discovers the Virginian, wounded in an Indian
attack, with "his face . . . sunk downward against the shelving
rock, so that she saw only his black, tangled hair" (255). When
she moves closer, she discovers a "patch of blood at his
shoulder" and observes that "the man's whole strong body lay
slack and pitifully helpless" (255). While the rhetorical purpose
of beatings in the slave narrative is to reveal the savagery of the
plantation system, punishment functions in the Western primarily to test the quality of the protagonist's manhood. If manhood is proved by violent actions against an other, Mitchell
argues, "one also becomes a man by being punished" and by
demonstrating one's ability to recover from that punishment
(170); the Western reduces men's strong bodies to a state of
helplessness primarily "so that we can *see* men recover, regaining their strength and resources in the process of once again

making themselves into men" (Mitchell 174). Thus, in the Western the period of recovery is as important to the narrative as the eruption of violence that damages the body.

Love finds in the beating and recovery scenario yet another means of representing his successful achievement of the dominant culture's masculine ideal. At one point, he takes on a "large party of Indians," firing with deadly aim until out of ammunition despite numerous wounds (Love 98). His attackers, impressed by "a man whose fighting powers were [so] out of the ordinary," capture Love, dress his wounds, adopt him as a member of the tribe, and arrange for him to marry the chief's daughter (99). "I had other notions just then," Love observes, "and did not want to get married under such circumstances" (101). Love's emphasis here is action, a showcase for his extraordinary fighting abilities displayed in the initial attack, and his captivity primarily a prelude to his subsequent daring escape from the tribe and unwanted marriage. Between these two action scenes, Love describes a recovery aided by a "salve made from herbs . . . placed on my wounds" and by "the good attention the Indians gave me" (101–4). While he notes the efficacy of native healing techniques, the toughness of his body primarily accounts for the surprisingly short time of his recovery, a brief period of convalescence (a matter of days) as out of the ordinary as his fighting powers (101). As in other descriptions of his uncanny ability to take physical damage, Love again demonstrates his strength of both character and body, his superior combination of both the will to survive and the physical stamina capable of enduring numerous wounds, "most any one of which would be sufficient to kill an ordinary man" (103).

Whereas both Love and Hopkins focus on the scene of punishment, Wister takes the opposite approach, showing the result of the Indian attack (the Virginian's wounded body) but not the attack itself, which takes place offstage. Rather, Wister devotes page after page to the Virginian's physical recovery and the parallel restoration of his manhood. With much effort, Molly gets the barely conscious Virginian onto a horse and leads him back to her home, where we see each slow step of the Virginian's progress back to health under her care. This scenario, in which an injured man is nursed by a character whose feminine presence functions as a catalyst for recovery, appears repeatedly in twentieth-century Westerns (Mitchell 178). In *The Virginian*, the hero's physical illness is accompanied by mental and emotional maladies, hallucinations, rambling speech, a "deep inward tide of feeling which he could no longer conceal, being himself no longer" (Wister 263). As the Virginian's wounding and recovery demonstrate his ability to take physical punishment, so do his loss and subsequent recovery of emotional restraint provide evidence of his achievement of civilized manliness. If frontier narratives often foreground the idea that too much civilization and too much control endangers manhood, the beating scenario explores the opposite danger—the loss of control of body, mind, emotion, and the subsequent inability to check passions. A "restorative female 'gaze' at the male body" is necessary not only "to the re-creation of that body" but also to ensure the return of masculine restraint, of control over emotion and passion, the quality of manliness that enables the frontier hero to embody aspects of masculinity both civilized and savage (Mitchell 179).

For Love punishment provides a means of further proving his manhood—his unmanning only momentary and representing no real threat to his sense of his own humanity. The beating of Judah is not only an unmanning (the reduction of a "whole strong body" to a state of helplessness) but also a dehumanization. Like the horse Judah must be "broken in" and reminded that "a nigger's place" is closer to livestock than humanity (*Winona* 326). Judah's beating precipitates a crisis both existential and physical, as he must recover not only his bodily strength but also his humanity, must struggle to redraw the boundary between man and beast that slavery seeks to erase. The Virginian's temporary surrender to a "deep inward tide of feeling" does not cause such a categorical crisis. Even at his most delirious, in fact, the Virginian demonstrates an innate, almost unconscious, ability to remain civil. When referring to Molly Wood in his ramblings, "nothing less respectful came out" than "Miss Wood," and while he occasionally breaks into "the language of the round-up," his "inmost habitual thoughts were clean, and came from the untamed but unstained mind of a man" (Wister 262–64).

As Judah is denied manhood by the dominant culture, so does Hopkins's storytelling reflect his inability to make Western conventions his own—she refuses to represent one moment of his recovery from his wounds. In her narration of the adventures of the white Warren Maxwell (whose experiences parallel Judah's), Hopkins follows the expected pattern of beating and recovery, an indication of her awareness either specifically of Wister's *The Virginian* or of the general expectations evoked by the Western. Maxwell's physical recovery is granted both narrative space and the presence of the "restorative female gaze," that of Winona. If Hopkins adapts the Western beating scene for her black male protagonist, Judah's recuperation consists primarily of overcoming not the punishment to his body but the damage to his nature. As Winona observes, concerning his later behavior, "It is not like you—you who are generally so generous and true-hearted" (379). Judah's beating initiates a passionate desire for revenge that almost consumes all other aspects of his being. Although Hopkins does not dismiss Judah's physical suffering, she emphasizes the damage to his character—to his heart, where each "merciless lash was engraved . . . in bleeding stripes that called for vengeance"—over the damage to his body (328). That recovery of character, of manly control over violent emotions, will be visibly represented and will be nurtured by a female presence—Winona.

The Pluck of a Man

Winona, the title character of the book, is described as having "the pluck of a man," but she seems a conventional and passive heroine early in the story (348). Our first sight of the two main African American characters as they travel by canoe to White Eagle's island sharply distinguishes them by gender. Hopkins describes Judah in terms of masculine power, skill, and agency, as a "lad who handled the paddle so skilfully [he] might have been mistaken for an Indian at first glance, for his lithe brown body lacked nothing of the suppleness and grace which constant exercise in the open air alone imparts" (289). Winona is described in terms of femininity, passivity, beauty, and she is first viewed "as she leaned idly over the side trailing a slim brown hand through the blue water" (289). On land, Judah observes her admiring a group of flowers, and he notices a comparison between the two: "the beautifully chiselled features, the olive complexion with a hint of pink like that which suffused the fragile flowers before them" (292). Later, Winona is described in terms of the "soft curve of her waist and supple body" (341), "the noble lines and graceful pose of [her] neck and shoulders" (352), and as a "living picture" with a "graceful form" (356).

She faints at the news of her father's death while the others scurry to uncover the details of the crime: "The girl gave one quick, heart-breaking cry, and would have fallen had not Warren caught her in his arms" (305). Her movements are those of an object at the mercy of the actions of others—captors or rescuers. In a daring escape from a riverboat on the Missouri, Warren Maxwell "grasped the girl about the waist, swung her clear of the railing and held her suspended by the wrists over the black, boiling flood" (344). Judah, standing beneath them in the boat, "caught Winona in his arms as deftly as a ball is caught and tossed from one player to another" (344). Hopkins's strategy in this portrayal is to establish for Winona early in the narrative such aspects of "true womanhood" as virtue, passionlessness, beauty, and passivity. In response to a dominant discourse that stereotypes black women as lascivious, primitive, unable to control their passions, Hopkins realizes the necessity of claiming for her heroine a traditionally passive, delicate, civilized feminine identity. At the same time, Hopkins recognizes that such a claim to traditional femininity threatens to erase the active identity she wishes to construct. Thus, as Tonkovich argues, we see in the novel a "struggle to find new configurations of domesticity that would not subsume women to invisibility" (246). In Kansas, Winona will be transformed from passive object to player in her own right, a participant in the novel's action, a rescuer, and a leader within the John Brown camp, while still retaining distinctively feminine duties and values.

Both *Winona* and *The Virginian* appear in a context of uncertainty about gender roles, sparked in part by women's activism in the public sphere. Although *Winona* represents the West as a place for collapsing rigid gender roles, *The Virginian* conceives of the West as a place where the "natural" division of the sexes can be reestablished. The social as well as the natural aspects of *The Virginian*'s Wyoming setting (the only state that had extended suffrage to women) are particularly important to the novel's argument about gender relations: "At a time when the suffrage movement was regaining strength, Wister offered an elegy for the old West that was also a defense of male hegemony. Indeed, more important than any action performed in the novel is the Virginian's careful rationale for women's subordination" (Mitchell 98). In *The Virginian*, the humorous story of the ill-fated hen, Emily, serves as a cautionary tale about proper gender behavior: "With an instinct of maternity as undiscriminating as it was reckless," Emily tries to adopt potatoes, turkeys, puppies, and other hens' chicks (Wister 59). The Virginian observes that the "manly-lookin" hen who "does hate the roosters so" would "be just the schoolmarm for Bear Creek" (56–58). Unable to escape natural instinct but also unwilling to reproduce with her own kind, Emily ends up dying from terror when she hatches a chick from an egg the Virginian has placed beneath her.

Molly Wood, the woman who does become the Bear Creek schoolteacher, like Emily fails to practice proper gender behavior. We are told that Molly "can be very independent and unconventional," and she herself reveals to the Virginian that "I've always wanted to be a man" (Wister 103–7). In a letter written after his proposal of marriage to Molly, the Virginian uses the story of Emily to criticize Molly's reticence: "Did I ever tell you about a hen Emily we had here? She was venturesome to an extent I have not seen in other hens only she had poor judgement and would make no family ties" (218). Like a schoolteacher overseeing other people's children Emily "would keep trying to get interest in the ties of others taking charge of little chicks and bantams" (218). In case Molly has not yet seen the analogy, the Virginian concludes the letter by noting: "She died without family ties one day while I was building a house for her to teach school in" (218). Molly turns "deep pink" as she reads the letter, recognizing herself in the Virginian's story and crying out, "The outrageous wretch!" (218). As Tompkins observes in *West of Everything*, Molly ultimately becomes "society's 'happy' version of Em'ly; she is the hen who doesn't refuse the rooster, and so can assume her rightful place in the social order" (141–42). If Molly begins as an independent and unconventional character, she eventually accepts and submits to the Virginian's masculine superiority.

Winona's transformation will be in the other direction. Although her journey to Kansas has been a passive one, we see Winona's agency begin to emerge in the context of the Brown camp, where the fugitive slaves gather and prepare for the journey to Canada. Unlike the racial subjugation on Magnolia Farm, we find in Brown's camp "one soul of harmony and love [that] was infused into each individual dweller" (*Winona* 373). In the Brown camp, Winona returns to the "primal life" she had led with White Eagle, a natural existence where there was "not a thought of racial or social barriers" (376). The western landscape reflects this shift in social environment: "And to Winona all the land had changed. The red-golden light that rested upon it near the evening hour was now as the light of heaven" (375). In Kansas the woods "calmed her, their grays and greens and interlacing density of stems" (376). In this wilderness home Winona finds a room of her own, a cave close to the camp, a space that is both natural and female (womblike), a comfortable, private place where she may fling herself down at full length to think (376). Judah also finds the freedom and manhood denied him as a slave, and after various heroic actions, "his name was heralded with that of Brown as a brave and fearless man" (376). Love's home on the range is the constantly shifting, exclusively male, almost entirely white enclave of the cowboy camp. The frontier home that Hopkins locates in the Brown encampment is also temporary, but it differs sharply from the cowboy camp by being gender-balanced, more racially mixed, and both a natural and a domestic space.

Even in the Brown camp, activities are divided by gender, and when word is brought of the British lawyer Warren Maxwell's capture, "the women listened but did not intrude their opinions upon the men" (380). Winona "crept into the woods not to weep, but to think," and after contemplating Maxwell's situation and the need to "spy out the jail where he was confined," she emerges as if reborn, sure of herself and intent on implementing a plan of action (380). Although gender may be a dividing line under the "patriarchal care" of Brown, he is willing to allow Winona to cross that line, both figuratively and literally, for Winona's plan for saving Maxwell involves her masquerading as male to infiltrate the Missouri prison (373).

Hopkins plays out the difference between African American and dominant culture generic forms through the separate but intersecting stories of the black Judah and the white Warren Maxwell, the two central male characters. As the civilized white hero of the book, Maxwell journeys west, which results in his expected transformation, similar to that of the tenderfoot narrator of *The Virginian*. Whereas Judah's story follows in many ways the pattern of the slave narrative and Maxwell's that of the Western, elements of each appear in the other. Judah's exemplary horsemanship associates him with the Western hero; Maxwell's encounter with the "justice" of southern lynch mob violence provides him with firsthand experience of the brutality of slavery. The savage wilderness that Maxwell learns to negotiate is more social system, the institution of slavery, than natural landscape. His journey through that wilderness will involve several guides—Judah, Maybee, Brown, even Bill Thomson. During a clandestine meeting at Magnolia Farm, Judah tells Maxwell of his experiences on the plantation, a key moment in his education. "To emphasize his story," Hopkins writes, "Judah stripped up his shirt and seizing the young white man's hand pressed it gently over the scars and seams stamped upon his back" (334). Following this presentation of tactile evidence of the cruelty of slavery, Maxwell agrees to help them escape. Despite all he has seen, heard, and felt Maxwell still fails to understand, as Maybee puts it, "that the South is a horned hornet on the nigger question" (351). Maxwell continues to hope that "the South well [*sic*] see its error and the Negroes will be granted freedom by peaceful means" (351). As Maybee observes, "there's nothin' so convincin' as ex-perience," and Maxwell's further experiences indeed convince him that peaceful means will not prevail (402).

Ambushed by Rangers, Maxwell is shot, captured, and in a sequence that echoes the hanging of Steve and Ed in *The Virginian*, handed over to a mob. While the lynching in *The Virginian* represents frontier justice as necessary, civil, even polite (prisoners and captors exchange pleasantries and sit together at the breakfast table before the execution), Hopkins emphasizes the savage ferocity of the participants in such justice. We see in *Winona*'s lynchers "the brute latent in every human being coming out from his lair to blot out the man" (368). Their "faces distorted like demons with evil passions," they come at Maxwell, their voices inhuman, "like the cries of wild animals, the screaming of enraged hyenas, the snarling of tigers, the angry, inarticulate cries of thousands of wild beasts" (367). Wister, through the voice of Judge Henry, goes to great and convoluted lengths to distinguish between southern lynch mob violence and the Wyoming hanging of rustlers, but Hopkins collapses these distinctions. Like the rustlers in *The Virginian*, Maxwell is guilty of theft—of helping human beings escape from bondage rather than stealing cattle but nonetheless acting contrary to the law of the land. In contrast to Wister and Love, Hopkins represents violence in protection of property not as a civil act but as evidence of savagery.

Maxwell's lynching also recalls Judah's whipping. Bill Thomson oversees both acts of violence. Like Judah, Maxwell is stripped, as Thomson and his ruffians take his money belt, guns, boots, coat, "his hat and so on" (362). As Judah in the earlier scene "bore his punishment without a murmur," Maxwell demonstrates a similar manly control, determining "to die and make no moan to please and gratify the crowd" (327, 370). In both cases the civilized control of the victim contrasts with the unleashed passions of the victimizers. Colonel Titus, concerned that the lynching will be a public relations fiasco for the southerners ("How are we to impress the world with our fair and impartial dealing with all mankind, and the slavery question in particular, if you and a lot more hot-headed galoots go to work and call us liars by breaking the slate?"), saves the partially burned Maxwell from death (372). He is subsequently delivered to a Missouri court, where a "farcical mockery of justice" condemns him to a year in prison to be followed by execution by hanging (382).

In the sequence of events that follows, Hopkins's use of two different genres of writing—the Western and the fugitive slave narrative—is played out in the architecture of the jail. Maxwell is confined in "a room sixteen feet square," under which "was another [room] of the same size, used as a lock-up for slaves" (384). A hole in the floor, originally intended for the pipe of a stove that had been removed, provides a means of intersection between the two rooms, and this hole "afforded diversion for the invalid who could observe the full operation of the slave system" (384). In the upper room, Maxwell's visible recovery from his beating (as does the Virginian's) will take place beneath a restorative female gaze. In the lower room, the unnarrated experiences of the captured slaves rise up through the hole in the floor and enter into the narrative of Maxwell's recovery. Before his sight, "many heart-rending scenes were enacted," and "one horror followed another in the crowded cage where a frightful number of human beings were herded together" (384). The experience of slavery comes to Maxwell in fragments, through the scars on Judah's back, through the stories of abolitionists Brown and Maybee, through his own experience of torture at the hands of the southerners, and finally through the scenes that pass before his eyes and the voices that rise up disembodied through the hole in the floor, culminating in his viewing of a scene that causes him to fall "fainting with terror and nausea upon the floor. He had seen a Negro undergoing the shameful outrage, so denounced in the Scriptures, and which must not be described in the interests of decency and humanity" (385). Maxwell's vicarious experience of the rape of an African American man completes his education in the reality of slavery and results in his falling ill again, "delirious—requiring the care of two physicians and a slave who was detailed to nurse him" (385).

In a remarkable sequence, Winona, a light-skinned African American woman and a fugitive slave, stains her face dark and puts on men's clothes in order to pass as an African American male. The female fugitive slave plays the part of a male fugitive slave and has herself recaptured in order to infiltrate the prison. In his cell, in a "delirium of pain and weariness," Maxwell becomes "conscious of the tender care of his nurse" (386). He is somewhat surprised when at one point the nurse kisses the patient, and he observes that not only is Allen Pinks "the prettiest specimen of boyhood he had ever met" with his "beautiful large dark eyes" but also that there is something familiar about him, as he evokes in Maxwell "an evasive but haunting memory" (387–89).[11] Aided by Winona's knowledge of the jail, Brown's group arrives to rescue Maxwell. As the semi-conscious Maxwell is borne away in the bottom of a cart, he marvels at "his own stupidity in not recognizing Winona; beneath the stain with which she had darkened her own exquisite complexion, he could now plainly trace the linaments [sic] that had so charmed him" (396).

In *The Virginian*, the beating scenario calls into question the male hero's masculinity, unmans him in a way that forces the female heroine into an active role. Molly, if only briefly, takes charge of the Virginian's gun, and he responds, "You have got to be the man all through this mess" (Wister 259). Playing out this manly role is only temporary, for being the man makes her aware of the necessity of becoming the woman, of nursing the Virginian back to health. But such nursing will only go so far. As Mrs. Taylor harshly informs her, "A year of nursing don't equal a day of sweetheart" (265). Wister parallels the slow process of the Virginian's recuperation with the dissolution of

Molly's resolve not to marry. As the Virginian recovers his manhood, so does Molly abandon her independence. "By love and
her surrender to him," Wister writes, "their positions had been
exchanged" (350). While the Virginian "was her worshipper
still," he was "her master, too," and before him, Molly "felt pow-
erless" (350). For Wister, Molly's earlier attitudes indicate the
deforming influence of civilization and her change in the
western setting a return to her "natural" gender role. Hopkins
repeats and revises this same sequence of beating and recovery
from a feminist perspective, as a means of further unsettling
the binary opposition of male and female.

As does Molly, Winona has "to be the man through all this
mess," her adoption of that role aided by the change in clothing
that disguises her sex and enables her to infiltrate the all-male
prison. As Tonkovich observes, Winona's "sartorial transgression" symbolizes the "advent of a new woman citizen," one who
is willing to act "to avenge the wrongs she and others have suffered" and who works to restore a "civility and justice that is
both/neither masculine and/nor feminine" (251). Winona's
heroism combines traditionally feminine characteristics (tender
care) with the more masculine adventurous actions. Molly's
unpacking of boxes in *The Virginian* indicates the wavering of
her resolve to move back east. This action transforms the Virginian's stark sick room into a comforting domestic space and
symbolizes as well Molly's transformation from a "new woman
citizen" into one who is traditionally feminine, submissive, and
domestic. Maxwell's jail cell is a far cry from the house where
Molly oversees the Virginian's recovery. The rape that Maxwell
observes indicates the real danger Winona risks by entering this
all-male space. Unlike Molly, whose possession of the Virginian's gun is only temporary, Winona does not return to a submissive role once the crisis has passed. She is rewarded for her
actions with more responsibilities in the camp. When the men
go off to battle, the women take "refuge on the mountainside,"

although, Hopkins writes, "every woman carried a rifle in her hand and was prepared to use it. Winona was in command of the homeguard" (409). She may stay home when the men go off to battle, but she has earned the duties of command and of protecting that domestic space. No longer a ball in a game of toss and catch, Winona enters history as a player, a leading member of a radical political protest group intent on opposing racial oppression.

Simple Justice

Two key incidents in *The Virginian* bring Molly into conflict with the hero—his part in the lynching of the cattle rustlers, Steve and Ed, and the culminating gunfight with Trampas that takes place on their wedding day. In the first incident, Judge Henry convinces Molly of the necessity of such frontier justice. The hanging, Judge Henry asserts, is "proof that Wyoming is determined to become civilized" (Wister 339). The lynching as punishment for violating property rights is an essential step in bringing law to a lawless land. Caught between the necessity of answering Trampas's call for a showdown and Molly's threat to leave him should he fight, the Virginian chooses "the ancient, eternal way between man and man," answering Trampas's insults with his pistol (361). In the end, though, "she could not let him go," and "it was she who renounced, and he who had his way" (387). By accepting the Virginian's reasons for killing Trampas, "Molly finally accepts the masculine principle *as such* as a valid guide to moral action; her conversion and subjection are complete" (Slotkin, *Gunfighter* 182).

Both *Winona* and *The Virginian* represent conflicts between male and female characters over what principles constitute a valid guide to the morality of violent action. Hopkins ultimately defers to divine and feminine rather than legal or masculine concepts of justice. In contrast to *The Virginian's*

argument for the lynching of Steve and Ed, an appeal to heav-
enly vengeance rather than earthly property rights sanctions
John Brown's execution of proslavery prisoners. Winona unlike
Molly intercedes in "the ancient, eternal way between man and
man" and prevents an act of violence that would taint the sanctity of the abolitionists' spiritual purpose with the savagery of
uncontrolled masculine passion and desire for revenge.
Through an act of compassion (preventing the shooting of
overseer Bill Thomson), Patterson argues, "Winona claims a
moral authority far beyond that of any other character" and
thereby establishes her right to determine which acts of violence do or do not represent just retribution in support of a
"divinely sanctioned" collective cause (451–55). Winona's
"mother instinct" tempers vengeance with mercy, and her
demonstrable sanctity and compassion establish her right to
judge in God's stead. Feminine values—"the heart to forgive"—take precedence over the masculine principle as the
ultimate guide to moral action (*Winona* 422).

In the Western, landscape descriptions often signal the
morality of violent acts. "Invariably," Mitchell writes, the setting "is a landscape endowed with the power to transform
casual violence into something at once more venerable and
evocative" (103). Near the end of an extended battle between
the abolitionists and the Rangers Judah—whose rage "carried
in it all the pent-up suffering of two years of bodily torture and
a century of lacerated manhood"—meets Thomson high on a
bluff above the Possawatamie River (*Winona* 414). The landscape descriptions here, a "dramatic scene" of "gigantic rocks,"
steep cliffs, and the "dazzling splendor" of the morning sun,
shape the reader's interpretation of this scene (413–14). The
dramatic Western setting cleanses Judah's desire for personal
vengeance and transforms what might seem like casual violence into an allegorical representation of the vengeance of all
those who have suffered from the oppression of slavery. The

showdown, however, does not conclude in quite the way we expect. Judah, of his own choice, gives Thomson a slight opportunity to live—to jump over the bluff into the river rather than being shot at point blank range. At Judah's count of three, Thomson springs backward off the ledge, and "there came a crashing of underbrush, a sound of rolling rocks and gravel, a plash of water—silence" (416).

The abolitionists greet the news of Judah's seeming execution of Thomson with "a cheer that echoed and re-echoed among the hills," their approval like the earlier landscape descriptions providing a textual clue as to how we are to interpret this act "of simple justice" (418). In response to Judah's deferral to the judgment of the group, "I leave it to you if I'm not right in ridding the world of such a beast as Thomson," we have a series of comments: "I'd kill a snake wherever I f'und him," "This is a holy war," "We've put to flight the armies of the Philistines" (418–19). The defeat of a common enemy (Thomson, who functions here as object of exchange) seems to establish even more firmly the bond between Judah and the abolitionists, but Hopkins indicates ambivalence about such homosocial bonding even in the service of progressive political goals. The repetition of justifications (echoing cheers, approving comments from Brown, Parson Steward, and others) for Judah's action seems overdetermined, and those voices cannot overcome—may even add to—the disquiet the narrative elsewhere reveals concerning Judah's ability to encompass aspects of manhood both savage and civilized. When Parson Steward observes, "That boy's as ferocious as a tiger," Maybee responds, "Well, he's a good boy, is Jude" (424). Assessments of Judah's character remain split—as if the two parts ferocity and goodness cannot be reconciled at the same time by the same observer. Both parts are necessary in a whole man, according to the novel's construction of manhood, but how to reconcile the two?

Having used the landscape as well as a chorus of approving male voices to signal our interpretation of Judah's act, Hopkins immediately begins to question that reading—an indication of her eventual rejection of Western tropes (manly honor, transformative landscape) to signify justifiable violence. Although in Judah's mind his forcing Thomson off the cliff was an act of simple justice, Hopkins acknowledges that, "judged by the ordinary eye," such an act indicates "Judah's nature was horrible" (417). Having followed Judah from youth to young manhood, we know that his essential nature is more noble than horrible, that his desire for revenge is "the natural outcome or growth of the 'system' as practiced upon the black race" (417–18). But how can the black man—made savage by civilization (the "system")—restore that nobility when he must engage in savage acts of violence to win his right to exist as a free man? The answer to this question is complicated by Hopkins's ambiguity about the source of Judah's savagery. For on the same page that she asserts the deformative influence of culture, she also describes Judah's face as shining with the "glitter of the untameable torrid ferocity of his tribe [that was] not pleasing to see" (417). Does his character result from natural ferocity? or is it the cultural product of slavery? To both these questions, Hopkins seems to answer yes.

No such ambiguity appears concerning Maxwell. Only one statement serves to sanction Maxwell's violence, Maybee's observation that "you've got as big a score to settle as anyone of us" (411). The scene of battle represents Maxwell's final transformation. In order to be effective in his support of a just cause, he must awaken the savagery in his blood. He struggles hand-to-hand with Gideon Holmes, one of the ruffians who initially captured him: "At last he had caught the full spirit of the fiercest; the blood mounted to his brain, and with ungovernable rage, thinking only of the sufferings he had endured in the dreadful time of imprisonment, he continued his rain of

blows" (412). Whereas Hopkins feels she must remind the
reader of Judah's link to the greater cause, she describes
Maxwell's actions only in terms of personal vengeance. "Whiteness," Patterson observes, allows Maxwell "the privilege of less
self-restraint" (451). Like the Virginian, Maxwell can act violently without seriously threatening his essentially civil nature.
If he momentarily surrenders to ungovernable rage, he indicates the return of civilized self-control by his actions when he
learns that prisoners are "to be tried by court-martial and shot,
according to the rough justice of the times" (*Winona* 423). As
Parson Steward reveals, "The most of them have been begged
off by young Maxwell. He's the most softest hearted young
feller I ever met for such a good shot" (423). One character in
one sentence of dialogue sums up Maxwell's ability to encompass aspects of manliness both savage (a good shot) and civilized (a soft heart).

Hopkins reintroduces the question of Judah's ability to hold
in balance the savage and civilized aspects of his character by
repeating the showdown scene. Once again Judah faces his tor-
mentor, who has survived his fall. Attracted by the sounds of
battle, Winona stumbles across the mortally wounded
Thomson and looks upon him with "the mother instinct that
dwells in all good women" and that blesses her with "the heart
to forgive" (422). When Judah, his heart still bent on revenge
rather than forgiveness, tries to finish the job by shooting the
defenseless man, Winona steps between the two: "You shall not!
You make yourself as vile as the vilest of them—our enemies.
Let the man die in peace" (422). After Winona's intervention
(seconded by Maxwell who later enters the scene), even Judah
felt "the sheer human repulsion from such butchery master
him" (423). The second showdown between Judah and Thomson replicates the triangular configuration of homosocial
desire we have seen elsewhere, with Winona seemingly in the
position of the woman who facilitates a relationship between

men. Winona functions, however, more as agent than object of exchange, for her actions here alter and shape the relationship between Thomson and Judah.

In order for Judah to encompass both civilization and savagery within his own character, he needs assistance from others. Judah's desire for vengeance, Patterson argues, "connotes 'primitive' selfishness—and he must subsequently be 'managed'" to prevent his regression to savagery (449). As does Micheaux in *The Conquest*, Hopkins realizes that the black man must primarily prove not his ability to act violently (which the dominant culture already assumes) but his achievement of civilized restraint. If we see Maxwell placed in situations that ultimately elicit the "ungovernable rage" held in check by his civilized demeanor, we see Judah placed rather in situations where he must do the opposite—control himself in the face of a rage that threatens himself and others.

Earlier in the book, Winona disguised as Allen Pinks leads the abolitionists to Maxwell's cell. When Bill Thomson arrives to thwart the escape, Judah, who has been lurking in the shadows of the prison, enters the scene "like a wild beast preparing to pounce upon his prey" and captures Thomson, crying out, "It is between you and me, now. Our roles are reversed. It is you who must die" (393). Judah is denied revenge, however, as Brown intervenes—fearing that a pistol shot will reveal the escape attempt to the rest of the enemy camp. Judah "was silent for a moment, but stood as if gathering strength to resist temptation" (394). Although Brown (out of practical rather than moral concerns) must manage Judah here, the choice ultimately belongs to Judah, who demonstrates his ability to gather his strength of will and master his own desire for vengeance. We might read both this scene and the repeated showdown in two ways. Judah's actions provide evidence that the "untameable torrid ferocity of his tribe," his innate racial savagery, places him in greater danger than the white men in the novel of regressing to a bestial state. We might note, however, Mitchell's observation that "restraint can only be demonstrated through narratives of excess, since restraint takes shape as a given capacity only by contrast with surrounding conditions" (167). The cause of Judah's passion, "two years of bodily torture and a century of lacerated manhood," far exceeds that of any of the white characters, and so Judah's desire for vengeance is greater. We might argue that as his passions are so much greater than the white man's, inflamed by the experience of slavery, so must his ability to restrain these passions be greater as well. We could read these scenes as evidence not of Judah's innate primitiveness but of his superior capacity for restraint.

In attributing to Judah the "untameable torrid ferocity of his tribe," Hopkins's word choice is ambiguous. Does "tribe" refer to Judah's racial heritage or to his Indian upbringing? Or does "tribe" refer to the male sex? Judah's "untameable torrid ferocity" echoes the earlier descriptions of the transformation of the Missouri Rangers into beasts during the lynching of Maxwell. In that earlier scene we see "the brute latent in every human being coming out from his lair to blot out the man" (*Winona* 368). As men are portrayed in the book, all members of the male tribe (whatever their race) are equally in danger of losing the civilized self to torrid ferocity. Placed in the context of the novel as a whole, the greatest threat to Judah is not that he will devolve into primitive black savagery but that he will allow his "natur'" to be warped by the white civilization that surrounds him. As Winona states, "You make yourself as vile as the vilest of them—our enemies" (422). Winona's intervention indeed prevents Judah from regressing to savagery, but in keeping with the novel's inversion of the savage/civilized trope, the savage being Judah avoids becoming is not the primitive black but the supposedly civilized white.

With Winona's assistance Judah controls the savage passion that unmans Micheaux's hero at the end of *The Conquest.*

Winona's emergence as an active heroine is a precondition for this restoration of civilized manhood. Her ability to encompass in her own character both masculine and feminine characteristics (as symbolized by her infiltration of the jail) enables her to mediate the two halves of Judah's character. She understands both Judah's desire for revenge and the need for compassion. She has the will to oppose Judah, and also the power to force his masculine desire for revenge to submit to her feminine principles. In spite of his desire for vengeance Judah submits to Winona's management and, by so doing, completes the sequence of beating and recovery. He achieves a restoration of his humanity, a healing of the heart that could not have been accomplished by killing the defenseless Thomson. He is rewarded by Thomson's deathbed confession, which reveals the truth about Winona, White Eagle, and the Carlingford estate.

If Hopkins's portrayal of Judah seems both to refute and to invoke the racial stereotype of black savagery, we should note that Judah is not the only character who needs help in maintaining control over desire for vengeance. Violence committed in battle is one thing, the novel argues, but the execution of unarmed men (an act dangerously close to the lynch mob violence earlier condemned) must be more closely monitored. Brown himself is managed—prevented from enacting a too bloodthirsty revenge. Like Winona, Maxwell acts to intervene and to prevent butchery (the killing of all the prisoners) in the name of justice—an indication that his ungovernable rage is back under control, certainly, but also an implication that most men, in general, need management, even the abolitionists whose fury supports a just cause. Even though the cause is just, Hopkins tempers this scene of extralegal violence with a demonstration of "feminine" mercy, Maxwell's "soft-hearted" intervention. Like Winona's, Maxwell's frontier transformation results not in adherence to a rigidly defined gender role but in his ability to combine masculine and feminine values and behaviors.

As in Micheaux's *The Conquest* and Harper's *Iola Leroy*, romance and marriage play an important, if understated, part in *Winona*. In all three books the lead character is faced with a choice of partners, one black, one white. Winona, in contrast to Iola Leroy and Oscar Devereaux, chooses the white Maxwell over Judah, her adopted brother who becomes her African American suitor. While Hopkins's intent is to present a cross-racial romance as a means of countering a racist discourse that insists on separating black and white, she pays the cost of denying a sexual identity to her primary black male character, whose bitter response, "The white man gets it all—all," is not without justification (378). Unlike most domestic fiction (including Hopkins's own *Contending Forces*), *Winona* does not conclude with a marriage—a point of contrast with *The Virginian* as well. As the final chapter of *The Virginian* indicates, a Western that ends in marriage signals a return to sharply defined gender roles, the submission of the female character to the patriarchal authority of the male hero. We are told that Winona and Maxwell "would marry sooner or later," but the marriage if it takes place at all is not textually represented (435). Judah, the rejected suitor, nonetheless reconciles with both his rival and his beloved and joins the two in escaping America to England, where he succeeds in "service of the Queen," is knighted, and eventually is "married into one of the best families of the realm" (435). Through Judah and Winona, Hopkins represents a political joining of black men and women in a common cause that bypasses the usual symbolic function of marriage in the domestic novel and that does not endanger the newly independent heroine by placing her in a potentially submissive social role.

Although Hopkins does not completely alter conceptions of masculinity (she retains the turn of the century's dominant concept of masculinity as a combination of civilization and savagery), she does rethink relationships between men and women. Manhood in *Winona* does not depend upon the corresponding submissiveness of women. While acknowledging female difference Hopkins imagines the woman's role as that of equal partner who brings her own particular strengths and values to the collective fight for social justice. More so than Love or Micheaux, Hopkins also forecasts the philosophies and concerns of later twentieth-century African American writers, who will likewise emphasize protest over assimilation and accommodation as a response to racial oppression. The male heroes of Richard Wright, Chester Himes, William Gardner Smith, and John A. Williams will have more in common with the struggles of Hopkins's Judah than with the experiences of Oscar Devereaux or Nat Love. Both Hopkins's joining of the Western to the black tradition of literary protest writing and her final shifting of the novel's geography from the United States to an overseas setting foreshadow similar efforts by writers such as Himes and Williams to reconfigure frontier motifs and landscapes in new twentieth-century contexts.

Chapter 4

"Half a Man at Best"

The Ritual Hunt and Manhood Denied

During the early part of the twentieth century, we see a shift in the history of African American migration, from the rural-to-rural (and east-to-west) movement of the Exodusters to the rural-to-urban (and most often south-to-north) movement of the Great Migration. During the first quarter of the twentieth century, such urban centers as Chicago, Detroit, and Cleveland experienced large influxes of African Americans. From 1910 to 1930 New York alone saw its black population increase by 250 percent to 327,763 people (Wintz 14–20). This change in geography is paralleled by a philosophical shift: "In the very process of being transplanted, the Negro is becoming transformed" (6) writes Alain Locke in his introduction to *The New Negro* (1925), an important and influential anthology of the work of black writers and artists. We see during this period a shift away from the integrationist ("Old Negro") model associated with Booker T. Washington to that of the "New Negro" of the Harlem Renaissance, from a focus on assimilation to an emphasis on exploring and celebrating a distinctive African American racial and cultural identity. The work of Harlem Renaissance writers is marked by a "deep feeling of race" (Locke 11), a "wider race consciousness" (14), and a self-conscious effort to build on that sense of racial identity as a means of becoming "a collaborator and participant in American civilization" (15).

We see developing in the period preceding the Renaissance a new militancy among African Americans, sparked both by increasing racial violence against blacks and by the experiences of African Americans who served in World War I. Black troops in France experienced a freedom from racism that contrasted sharply with the way they were treated in their own country. These troops returned to America to find a country embroiled in anti-black violence. The summer of 1919 produced race riots in which white mobs attacked blacks in twenty northern and southern cities. In the face of rising anti-black violence African Americans turned away from the philosophies of Washington and turned more toward political activism and protest as a means of achieving the goal of social equality.

Unlike earlier narratives such as Love's *Life and Adventures* that explore the possibility of erasing restrictive racial markings, writers of the Harlem Renaissance and World War II period foreground the question of what it means to be black— the exploration of black identity and the construction of black subjectivity. Whereas Love and Micheaux construct narratives of journeying west to a frontier environment, we see in the 1920s black writers born in the West, products of earlier migrations, reverse that journey. Langston Hughes (Kansas), Arna Bontemps (California), Taylor Gordon (Montana), and Wallace Thurman (Utah), important figures in the Renaissance, all traveled from western states to the exciting Black Mecca of Harlem.[1] For Arna Bontemps, the African Americans who lived in the East and the South "possessed what he had lost growing up in the West—a culture linked to primitivism, an enduring tie to an African past, an undeniable sense of self" (Flamming 96).[2] Taylor Gordon's autobiography *Born to Be* (1929) sketches out a similar journey—from the familiar western environment of Montana to the strange land of the eastern United States, from what Gordon renders as a "natural," racially unmarked identity to a race-based sense of self that he regards with more ambivalence than does Bontemps.[3]

The beginning of World War II marks another shift in African American migration patterns (once more westward, to California, Washington, and Oregon), sparked in part by job opportunities in the wartime industries in the coastal states. Richard Wright, author of *Uncle Tom's Children* (1938), *Native Son* (1940), and *Black Boy* (1945), and Chester Himes, author of *If He Hollers Let Him Go* (1945) and *Lonely Crusade* (1947), respond to these geographical and political changes by writing works of social protest that also figure the shifting patterns of African American migration. The dominant movement in Wright's stories is northward, from the rural South to the urban North. Chester Himes, through the California settings of his early novels, represents the World War II–era African American westward migration.[4] I will argue that we find in some of Wright's short stories set in the American South motifs associated with frontier mythology (such as the ritual of the hunt). Those motifs are placed, however, in the context of Jim Crow–era Mississippi, a closed frontier where Wright's characters find little in terms of opportunity and where their participation in the archetypal ritual of the hunt is more likely to be as the hunted than as the hunter. Himes's novel *If He Hollers Let Him Go* shifts the ground from Mississippi to a new frontier in World War II–era California—where protagonist Bob Jones experiences the ambiguity of western experience for African Americans, a mixture of opportunity both offered and denied.

For many African Americans, entry into the West is by way of the American South, and black experience in any region of the United States is marked by southern political and social institutions—slavery, segregation, Jim Crow laws. Similarly,

African American writers approach frontier motifs through an African American literary tradition that is rooted in the experiences of blacks in the southern United States, through the slave narrative, for example, the genre from which Micheaux, Love, and Hopkins all draw. Although the slave narrative will remain important to twentieth-century black writers, we will also see the influence of Richard Wright's body of work on the way black writers think about and represent the effect of racial oppression on the development of individual psychology. I discuss Wright's work here in part because of that influence, which will be clearly seen in the novels of Himes, William Gardner Smith, and John A. Williams. Wright's representation of the construction of black manhood under conditions of racial oppression and his articulation of the ritual hunt from the perspective of black and white racial relations provide an important precursor for these later black writers who will both build on Wright's critique of racism and attempt to move beyond Wright by reimagining frontier mythology in new political and geographical contexts.

The Ritual of the Hunt in the American South

Roosevelt adapts the universal ritual of the hunt within the specific context of the American West by substituting for the archetypal categories of hunter and beast the racially opposed positions of the frontiersman (or Indian hunter) and the American Indian. As articulated in the geographical, social, and political context of the American South the ritual of the hunt is marked by another set of racial relations, which are revealed vividly in the short stories by William Faulkner and Richard Wright discussed below. The initial story (entitled "Was") collected in Faulkner's *Go Down, Moses* (1942) sets up the themes addressed later in the book by the more famous story "The Bear," especially in its establishment and parody of the ritual hunt. Central among the various chases and hunts that play against each other in "Was" is the comic hunt for Tomey's Turl, a slave who has "escaped" to visit a black woman on another plantation. In the context of the American South, the hunting ritual ultimately assigns to the black individual the position of the object of the hunt—the "slave" who, like Tomey's Turl, is hunted by his white masters. In Richard Wright's short story "Big Boy Leaves Home" (collected in *Uncle Tom's Children* [1938]), the tone is more tragic than comic, and we see the hunt from the perspective of its object, Big Boy, whose innocent skinny-dipping in a white man's pond leads to his being attacked by a man with a rifle, his accidental killing of that man, and his attempt to escape from a lynch mob that hunts down and burns alive his friend Bobo.

Several of the stories collected in Faulkner's *Go Down, Moses* show the white Ike McCaslin's path toward manhood in Mississippi, which involves being carefully groomed for participation in the hunt as the hunter, a position consonant with his privileged status in the dominant culture. Through the ritual of the hunt, the American man enacts the process of interpellation by which he becomes, as Eagleton describes it, "the image of myself I receive from society" (172). For the white hero of the hunting ritual, to succeed in the hunt is metaphorically to take one's predetermined place in the social order as a member of the gender, race, and class of the dominant culture. It is to become a man according to the dominant culture's definitions of manhood. The act of violence central to the hunt functions as a rhetorical figure that conceals this process of interpellation, the work of ideology. Ike McCaslin's killing of a deer in Faulkner's story "The Old People" initiates him into a masculine identity, marks his passage from boy to man at the same time as it establishes a bond between himself and the other men in the story. After the killing of the deer, Sam Fathers completes Ike's initiation by marking his face with the animal's blood.

Then, Faulkner writes, Sam Fathers's "horn rang in the wet gray woods," a call that brings forth the others in the hunting party, "Walter Ewell whose rifle never missed, and Major de Spain and Old General Compson and the boy's cousin, McCaslin Edmonds... sitting on their horses and looking down at them" (Faulkner 158). McCaslin, who is described as more Ike's "brother than his cousin and more his father than either," asks, "Did he do all right, Sam?" and Sam responds, "He done all right," articulating in simple words Ike's completion of the rite of passage and his acceptance by this company of father figures, "the men, the true hunters" (158–59).[5]

As John E. Loftis points out, the hunt is largely a "European and thus white tradition, and its heroic and mythic dimensions hardly seem available to black American writers" (437); Wright uses his knowledge of this tradition to construct in his short story "The Man Who Was Almost a Man" a parody that dramatizes "the disparity between black and white possibilities of growth and development in American society" (437).[6] Wright's parody hinges on the disjunction achieved by placing one of the frontier myth's dominant tropes, the connection between masculine identity and skill at hunting or using firearms, in the context of Jim Crow–era Mississippi. Wright's protagonist Dave Saunders realizes that guns symbolize manhood, and he thinks to himself, "Ahm ol ernough to hava gun. Ahm seventeen. Almos a man. He strode, feeling his long, loose-jointed limbs. Shucks, a man oughta hava little gun aftah he done worked hard all day" (*Eight Men* 11). Dave's father has never owned a gun. Dave's mother agrees to let Dave buy a pistol even though "Lawd knows yuh don need no gun" (17). But, she notes, "Yer pa does" (17). Unlike the apprenticeship with "true hunters" enjoyed by Ike, Dave's gunless father cannot pass down any skills to Dave; he cannot instruct him in the ritual performance of violence.

After purchasing a gun from the store owner, Dave is unwilling to give up his symbol of manhood to his father. He waits till everyone is asleep before returning home, and he is the first to awake: "The first movement he made the following morning was to reach under his pillow for the gun. In the gray light of dawn he held it loosely, feeling a sense of power. Could kill a man with a gun like this. Kill anybody, black or white. And if he were holding his gun in his hand nobody could run over him; they would have to respect him" (18). In Wister's *The Virginian* the narrator was transformed from "Eastern helplessness" into a man who "had come to be trusted," from an individual who needs an escort for something as minor as an afternoon ride into someone able to cross "unmapped spaces with no guidance. The man who could do this was scarce any longer a 'tenderfoot'" (Wister 294). After viewing his image in the mirror Dave believes that a similar transformation has taken place and that others will recognize this change: "they would have to respect him."

We might explain the difference between Dave's and the Tenderfoot's transformations by reference to Lacan's distinction between the realm of the imaginary and the realm of the symbolic. During the mirror stage the relationship between the infant and the other he sees in the mirror is one that Lacan terms imaginary, a state of being that is pre-oedipal and preverbal. During the process of maturation, the infant grows into a child and, with the acquisition of language, becomes part of the symbolic order, Lacan's term for the systems of representation, language, and law that constitute the social world. In the realm of the symbolic, the assumption of an image of identity is verified by the recognition of an other, a member (or members) of the culture which the developing subject joins. "To exist," Homi K. Bhabha observes, "is to be called into being in relation to an otherness, its look or locus" (44). The narrator of

The Virginian assumes an image of identity and proclaims himself "scarce any longer a 'tenderfoot'" (Wister 294). This
assumption of identity might be interpreted as only "imaginary," the narrator's fiction of self, a fantasy. The novel, however, provides textual evidence to indicate that this fiction of
self is accepted not only by the narrator but also by the others
around him. The primary evidence of the Tenderfoot's transformation is the Virginian's growing friendship with him. The
narrator is a man "who had come to be trusted," with that trust
verifying the reality of his new identity (294). Dave's belief that
the gun can "Kill anybody, black or white"—and thus represents an equalizer that closes the economic and social gap
between black and white—will not be recognized in the social
world where his self-making possibilities are restricted by political and cultural limitations. We might argue that Dave's image
of himself with the gun tied "to his naked thigh," his feeling of
"a sense of power," his belief that "they would have to respect
him" (Wright 18) now that he owns a gun, all exist only in what
Lacan terms the imaginary.

The move from the imaginary into the symbolic depends
upon what Bhabha terms "an objectifying confrontation with
otherness" (52) for that confrontation or encounter represents
the other's recognition of the subject's existence, verification of
the subject's claim to selfhood, one's claim as to the value of
one's individuality. If the white subject is "hailed" by society,
"which recognizes me, tells me that I am valued," that same
society recognizes in the minority subject a different value
(Eagleton 172). What David Palumbo-Liu calls the "encodings
of the dominant culture" limit the possibilities for self-making
for the minority subject, marking out certain identifications,
narratives, and subjectivities as appropriate to his or her "place
in the world of others," a place that is limited by social and
political restrictions (78).[7] Dave Saunders's place in the symbolic order of the South is not the same as Ike McCaslin's.

Although Dave may imagine himself in a position consonant with Ike's, any attempt to assert the validity of that assumed identity in the world of others will be met with resistance rather than recognition.

Through his analysis of Wright's work Abdul R. JanMohamed examines specifically the formation of black subjectivity in a sociopolitical context dominated by "the Jim Crow extension of the fundamental structures of slave society" (109). The status of the black individual under Jim Crow replicates the social death that is a constituting element of slavery. *Social death* is defined as "a mode of oppression through which slaves, and by extension those who grew up under the control of Jim Crow society are coerced and controlled" (107). Under such a structure, the black individual is taught to "perceive his liminality" and accept as his own society's "limited view" of him (114). He (read: he or she) "is incorporated" into society "as an internal enemy, as non-being. He can possess none of the legal, moral, or cultural rights that his masters enjoy" (109). To fight against or protest such restrictions would "probably lead to physical death, and resignation would certainly lead to social death" (117). What the individual trapped in such a social context wants, Bhabha observes, is the recognition by an other of the value of his existence (if necessary, to force the other to recognize his being), for such a recognition "introduces the system of differentiation which enables the cultural to be signified as a linguistic, symbolic, historic reality" and which enables the individual assigned the status of nonbeing within that system to "generate meaning," to claim as his own the legal, moral, or cultural rights that his masters enjoy (52).

As a narrative of self-making, the hunting ritual is closed to Dave. His sense of power is undercut by the fact that, even though he owns a gun, he "was not sure he knew how to fire it" (Wright 18). Unlike Ike McCaslin, Dave has not been taught to participate in this ritual, and his attempt to replicate it on his own goes quickly awry. Dave "shut his eyes and tightened his forefinger," his blind shot accidentally striking Jenny, the mule (19). We might note several parallels here with Faulkner's "The Old People." After shooting the deer, Ike is led by Sam Fathers up to the dying animal and, following Sam's instructions, "drew the head back and the throat taut and drew Sam Fathers' knife across the throat and Sam stooped and dipped his hands in the hot smoking blood and wiped them back and forth across the boy's face" (158). Faulkner writes, "So the instant came. He pulled trigger and Sam Fathers marked his face with the hot blood which he had spilled and he ceased to be a child and became a hunter and a man" (171). The blood that marks Dave's initiation is blood accidentally spilled as a result of incompetence, not skill. Dave reacts in horror when he discovers "the hole in Jenny's side, right between the ribs" (Wright 20). In response, he "stopped and grabbed handfuls of damp black earth and tried to plug the bullet hole" but the "blood came anyhow," his initiation by blood providing a mirror image of Ike's own ceremony (20). As Ike is "marked forever" (Faulkner 159) by the consecrated blood from Sam's hands, Dave finds himself "hot and sticky" with Jenny's blood and rubs "dirt into his palms, trying to dry them," to remove the blood that marks him as guilty of destroying a white man's property (Wright 20).

The shooting of the deer in "The Old People" is followed by a scene where "the men, the true hunters" gather around Ike and his kill, consecrating by their presence and approval of his actions his initiation into the fraternity of true hunters. The collective gaze of these representatives of the dominant order encodes the power to name, to attach signified to signifier and endow the bloody marks on Ike's face with cultural meaning. Their look "hails" Ike, and his recognition of himself in that hailing constitutes his entry into masculine subjectivity, his acceptance of that culturally constructed fiction as the image of his own identity. This scene is paralleled—and inverted—in Wright's story as a crowd gathers around the dead mule and Dave tries to explain what happened: "Ah wuznt shootin at the mule, Mistah Hawkins. The gun jumped when Ah pulled the trigger" (23). Hawkins informs Dave that he has to pay for the mule, and one person in the crowd shouts out, "Well, boy, looks like yuh done bought a dead mule! Hahaha!" (24). Buying the gun represents Dave's rejection of his assigned "place in the world of others." This rejection, however, is inverted in the story. His desire to become a man is exploited by the store owner who sells him the gun, and by Hawkins who uses the killing of the mule to tie Dave deeper into his debt. As a signifier, the gun is beyond Dave's control: "The gun jumped when Ah pulled the trigger" (23). The gun, as does the ritual of blood-letting, signifies only within a system of representation that endows it with cultural meaning. The approving fraternity of hunters in Faulkner's story and their silent acceptance of Ike's action is mirrored by the humiliating laughter of the raucous crowd that Dave must face. The dominant order will not allow Dave to make meaning—to attach signified to signifier—for himself, especially if this meaning contradicts the place assigned him in that social structure. Dave's actions are reconstituted by the representatives of the dominant order to signify the limited view of him that he wishes to escape, that of a "boy" who buys a dead mule, who emerges from his initiation not as someone ceasing to be a child and becoming a hunter and man but as the butt of a joke.

Loftis argues that Wright parodies the hunt tradition as a way of demonstrating how black men have been denied the rituals of manhood available to white men. I would argue as well that Wright goes beyond parody, as Dave continues throughout to resist his status, as he continues to try to make meaning for himself, to take control of the signifier. He refuses to recognize himself in the identity constituted for him by the crowd and rejects the limited view of his own value that the dominant culture wants him to accept as his own image of self. If Dave cannot participate in the culturally sanctioned male rite of passage, he invents his own ritual and teaches himself how to shoot while everyone else is sleeping: "He clutched the gun stiff and hard in his fingers. But as soon as he wanted to pull the trigger, he shut his eyes and turned his head. Naw, Ah can't shoot wid mah eys closed n mah head turned. With effort he held his eyes open; then he squeezed. *Blooooom!* He was stiff, not breathing. The gun was still in his hands. Dammit, he'd done it!" (25). He empties the gun of shells and realizes that "If anybody could shoot a gun, he could" (26). He is immediately faced with the reality of his situation—that his newfound identity will not be accepted or allowed in the South. Although he is out of bullets he wishes he had just one more, so he could fire "at Jim Hawkins' big white house . . . . Ahd like t scare ol man Hawkins jusa little. . . . Jusa enough t let im know Dave Saunders is a man" (26). But the white Hawkins will never acknowledge Dave's masculinity, and although such a violent action would indeed register Dave's demand for recognition, to carry out such an act would undoubtedly transform his social death not into rebirth but into physical death. Caught between physical and social nonbeing, Dave's only hope is to escape. The story ends with Dave searching for a frontier, for "somewhere where he could be a man" (26). That place, that frontier, remains unrepresented and unrepresentable in Wright's story.

In "Big Boy Leaves Home," Wright again explores the relationship between guns, the ritual hunt, and masculine subjectivity in the Jim Crow South. The violent act that Dave avoids is central to the story of Big Boy. "Big Boy Leaves Home" involves "four black boys," Big Boy, Bobo, Buck, and Lester, who we first encounter "laughing easily" and trading playful insults with each other as they emerge from "the woods into cleared pasture" (Wright 17). They cross to land owned by the white

Harvey, who has erected a barbed wire fence to mark off his property, the "thick woods" and the creek where the boys want to swim (23). As Bobo states when the boys confront a no trespassing sign, "ol man Harvey don erllow no niggers t swim in this hole" (25). The boys' trespassing is a minor transgression, although symbolically they cross a racial and geographic boundary in order to enjoy one of the privileges reserved for whites. This transgression becomes major when the boys, naked after their swim, look up to see that a "white woman, poised on the edge of the opposite embankment, stood directly in front of them, her hat in her hand and her hair lit by the sun" (29). In his discussion of the story, Michael Atkinson notes that Wright plays here on the classical myth of Actaeon, the hunter who accidentally sees the goddess Diana bathing and who is punished for his transgression by being transformed into a hart and killed by his own hunting dogs. Actaeon is transformed from subject of the hunt to its object, from hunter to hunted, whereas the boys' position in the hunt is and has always been that of the hunted.

Whereas Actaeon's crime "is seeing, objectifying what he should not see," the boys' transgression "is not seeing, but being seen" (Atkinson 134). Their nakedness is no longer innocent but endowed with "fallen" meaning by the woman's gaze, to which they respond by "instinctively covering their groins" with their hands (Wright 29). As a representative of the dominant order, the power to name encoded by her gaze transforms the subjectivity of the boys, as their nakedness signifies a potential for violation, for bestial behavior. The white woman's entry into the scene is marked by voice as well as vision. Her first response to discovering the boys is the exclamation "Oh!" repeated twice. If Big Boy's transgression is not seeing, but being seen, his entry into subjectivity is signaled not by his own speaking but by someone else's. The woman's voice—and the fear of "bestial" black sexuality that it expresses—assigns to Big Boy a meaning that is "already there," a signification consonant with his position within the symbolic order of the Jim Crow South.

Jim Harvey, "ol man" Harvey's son, enters this scene in a position already marked out for him by the dominant order—as the white hunter, the man protecting the white woman from the "bestial" black "men." Although Harvey kills both Buck and Lester, Big Boy is able to grab the gun barrel, and he struggles for control with the white man. Harvey relinquishes his grasp on the rifle only when Bobo jumps on his back and only in order to "batter the naked boy with his fists. Then Big Boy swung, striking the man in the mouth with the barrel" (31–32). We might note a key difference here between white and African American narratives of man-making. Although conflict with an other is essential to transformation in both cases, African American writers are as likely to draw on the tradition of the fugitive slave narrative and the symbolic conflict between master and slave as on the scenes of battle between whites and American Indians that are central to *The Deerslayer* and *The Winning of the West*. In a famous scene Douglass describes his battle with his white overseer, Mr. Covey, as "the turning-point" in his transformation from slave to man, a moment that "rekindled the few expiring embers of freedom, and revived within me a sense of my own manhood" (*Narrative* 298). "I now resolved," writes Douglass, that, "however long I might remain a slave in form, the day had passed forever when I could be a slave in fact" (299).

In Wright's articulation of the hunt, as in the "battle" between Douglass and Covey, the difference between master and slave is suspended, and the *potential inversion* of the two categories is played out in the struggle for the gun. By taking the rifle from the white man, Big Boy reverses the polarity between subject and object and takes up the position reserved for the white hero—that of the hunter. As in "The Man Who Was

Almost A Man," however, the gun here is a signifier not entirely under the protagonist's control. Wright describes the fight:

> "Give me that gun, boy!"
> Big Boy leveled the rifle and backed away.
> The white man advanced. . . .
> The man stopped, blinked, spat blood. His eyes were bewildered. His face whitened. Suddenly, he lunged for the rifle, his hands outstretched.
> CRACK!
> He fell forward on his face. (32)

Wright describes Harvey's actions during the fight—he breathes hard, he speaks, he blinks, he spits blood, he lunges for the rifle. Big Boy, as a knowing and active subject in the narrative, disappears from the scene of violence. He does not speak during the scene, and he does not look until the fight is over. Harvey lunges, the rifle cracks, Harvey falls, the woman screams, and only then are Big Boy's actions described, as he "and Bobo turned in surprise to look at the woman" (32). Big Boy crosses the boundary between hunter and hunted when he finds himself in possession of the hunter's weapon. This reversal is both accidental—his shooting is seemingly as blind as Dave Saunders's killing of the mule—and temporary.

Big Boy momentarily takes up the position of the hunter, only to have that inversion overturned by an even more brutal assertion of the distinction between hunter and beast, or as those distinctions are articulated in the Jim Crow South, between white and black. Forced to make it through the night waiting for the opportunity to escape north in the morning, Big Boy hides inside a kiln, where he is to meet Bobo. From inside the pit of the kiln, "In spite of his fear, Big Boy looked. The road, and half of the hillside across the road, were covered with men. A few were at the top of the hill, stenciled against the sky. He could see dark forms moving along the slope" (54). Big Boy "saw men moving over the hill. Among them was a long dark spot. Tha mus be Bobo; tha must be Bobo theys carrin" (55). Like Dave Saunders, Big Boy has not been educated or groomed as subject of the hunt. The representatives of the dominant order do not culturally sanction his participation in the hunt as "the men, the true hunters" do for Ike McCaslin. Rather, those representatives join together to form the lynch mob that again transforms Big Boy into an object. Big Boy's accidental shooting in self-defense is likewise transformed. The crime attached to Big Boy and Bobo is not so much murder as rape. As one townsperson states, "Ef they git erway notta woman in this town would be safe" (53). The identity forced upon Big Boy "justifies" the increasing brutality of the mob at the same time as it further effaces Big Boy's subjectivity, as Big Boy becomes a black man, but only as black manhood is defined by the lynch mob.

The violence of the mob expends itself on Bobo, the "beast" of the hunt who is burned beyond recognition while Big Boy watches helplessly. His death completes the hunting ritual for the lynch mob and effectively, if temporarily, ends the hunt for Big Boy. The next morning Big Boy emerges from the kiln overwhelmed by numbness, a state of nonconsciousness interrupted only by physical sensations such as "needle-like pains" and "a dry throat [that] would not make a sound" (59). Voiceless and unable to run Big Boy is hidden away in the back of a truck for the drive north. After finally drinking water, "Hard cold lumps of brick rolled into his hot stomach. A dull pain made him bend over" (61). The witnessed death of Bobo empties Big Boy of consciousness, of feelings, fears, memories, aspirations, leaving him only with an interior life that is physical, consisting of dull pain. If, as Bryant argues, Wright often places his characters "into an intolerable position that forces them to do something violent, final, self-destructive" ("Violence" 18), the violent, final action seemingly belongs not to Big Boy but to the white participants in the hunt—a gesture that is not so much self-destructive as an act that affirms their subjectivity in a racist social order. As the hunting ritual is a white narrative, Wright plays that narrative out to its logical conclusion, refusing, ultimately, to write Big Boy into the narrative as the subject of the hunt.

Wright's stories vividly demonstrate the way the dominant white culture denies the position of the hunter, and the valued subjectivity and humanity that position symbolizes, to the African American man. Wright's representation of the construction of black manhood under conditions of oppression as well as his articulation of the ritual hunt from the perspective of black and white racial relations will influence writers such as Himes, William Gardner Smith, and John A. Williams. These writers not only build on Wright's observations, but also in a sense continue the stories of Dave Saunders and Big Boy by exploring the "new frontiers," the hoped-for places of escape and freedom that Dave and Big Boy strike out for at the end of their narratives.

If He Hollers Let Him Go

By 1850 nearly one thousand African Americans lived in California, with the population centering primarily in two cities, Sacramento and San Francisco. Gold rush fever caused that number to double by 1852 (Quintard Taylor 83–84). In his autobiography, *Shadow and Light* (1902), Mifflin Wistar Gibbs describes his own participation in this modest black migration to gold-rush California. Born free in Philadelphia and trained in carpentry, his desire to "go do some great thing" as a young adult becomes an injunction to go west in search of "hidden opportunities in a new country" (37). Armed with "pluck, tenacity and perseverance," he expects fortune to smile upon him (37). Gibbs arrives in California in 1850, "a moneyless man" set on pursuing opportunity (41). His initial efforts at carpentry are undercut by white fellow employees who strike when working at the same building with him. He moves from carpentry to boot blacking, eventually saving enough money to join a clothing firm and within a year become a partner in the business. Although he concedes that from one point of view the opportunities were good for African Americans in California, he also notes that "from every other point of view they were ostracized, assaulted without redress, disfranchised and denied their oath in a court of justice" (46). Gibbs himself worked to protest a poll tax, refusing to pay for the right to vote when he was legally barred from exercising that right. The protest he organized did not overturn the law, but afterward, "No further attempts to enforce it upon colored men were made" (50).

The largest wave of black migration to the West Coast occurred in the context of World War II, when the African American population grew by 33 percent from 1940 to 1950. This migration drew people from across the country as well as from other western states, from Arkansas, Louisiana, Texas, and Oklahoma particularly. Oklahoma during the 1940s, for example, lost 14 percent of its black population (23,000 people) while California's black population increased by 272 percent (338,000 people). Most African Americans settled in metropolitan areas, Seattle-Tacoma, Portland, the San Francisco Bay Area, Los Angeles, San Diego, with the black population of San Francisco growing by 798 percent and that of Los Angeles by 168 percent (Quintard Taylor 251). Earlier westward migrations, particularly the Exodusters movement, were pushed by a desire to escape white violence and oppression in the South. A dominant factor in this later migration was a labor shortage that "forced the shipbuilders to turn eastward to tap the national labor pool" and that led to President Franklin Roosevelt's anti–racial discrimination Executive Order 8802 (Quintard Taylor 256). Nearly a century after Gibbs's experiences in California, African Americans in the 1940s likewise found that, although opportunities were good from some points of view, other restrictions remained, including limited chances for advancement, exclusion from certain types of jobs, racism within labor unions, and segregated housing.

Chester Himes's novel *If He Hollers Let Him Go* (1945) responds to this second significant African American westward migration. The "leaving home" of Wright's Big Boy parallels the more general early twentieth-century Great Migration of blacks from rural areas to northern urban centers. *If He Hollers* describes a movement from one urban area to another, from a northern city to a western one. The protagonist, Bob Jones, has moved to Los Angeles from Cleveland, Ohio, and found work in the shipbuilding industry at the fictional Atlas shipyard, where he has moved up to the position of "leaderman" of a black work crew: "All I had when I came to the Coast was my height and weight and the fact that I believed that being born in America gave everybody a certain importance. . . . In the three years in L.A. I'd worked up to a good job in a shipyard, bought a new Buick car, and cornered off the finest coloured chick west of Chicago" (153). Like Gibbs, Jones has arrived in California a moneyless man, possessed only of a belief in the American dream that pluck and tenacity will bring opportunity and success. And like Gibbs, Jones discovers that opportunities for African Americans in California are tempered by racial restrictions.

Bob Jones's sense of self-worth, of subjectivity and identity, is articulated through the concept of manhood. He observes: "I'd settle for a leaderman job at Atlas Shipyard—if I could be a man, defined by Webster as a male human being. That's all I'd ever wanted—just to be accepted as a man—without ambition, without distinction, either of race, creed, or colour; just a simple Joe walking down an American street, going my simple way, without any other identifying characteristics but weight, height, and gender" (153). In the novel, manhood is represented through such familiar concepts as property ownership, success at work, a (proposed) marriage. Like the ownership of his car, being "a key man in a shipyard" makes Bob feel as "important as anybody" (10). Because of his blackness, however, and because of what blackness means in the dominant culture, Bob's assertions of subjectivity are continually challenged, his sense of manhood undercut by racial restrictions: "as long as I was black I'd never be anything but half a man at best" (163).

His relationship with his fiancee, Alice, a middle-class light-skinned African American woman, offers the possibility of escape from these restrictions within a protected domestic space: "No matter what the white folks did to me, or made me do just in order to live, Alice and I could have a life of our own, inside of all the pressure, away from it, separate from it, that no white person could ever touch" (169). Near the end of the novel, this realization leads to a sense "of hope, like the beginning of a new life" (170). Bob's image of himself as father and benevolent patriarch makes him feel "very male and important" (171). Earlier Bob considers the life led by Alice and her family (one of accommodation and assimilation) and thinks, "when I could accept being black, when I could see no other out, such a life looked great" (153). For Bob to live as Alice wishes means his accepting rather than protesting the limitations placed on black subjectivity, means agreeing to remain "half a man." The question of whether Bob and Alice could ever be able to maintain a protected space "inside of all the pressure" is left unanswered, as a series of circumstances prevent Bob from acting out this patriarchal role.

In his home state of Ohio, Jones is frustrated by racist hiring practices: "I knew if I kept on getting refused while white boys were hired from the line behind me I'd hang somebody as sure as hell" (3). Like many of Wright's characters, Jones finds himself in a position of asserting his freedom in the only way available, through a violent gesture that seems preferable to denial of self even if it leads to his own death. If Bob leaves Ohio, which "wasn't the land of the free," to escape from racial restrictions, he also tries to escape from his own inevitable response to those restrictions, hoping to find in the West a means of asserting self that does not end in his own destruction (3). The tension of *If He Hollers* derives from the fact that Jones is constantly on the edge of committing a violent act that protests "social death," an assertion of being that will lead not to rebirth but to physical death.

If Bob Jones seems obsessed with a narrowly defined masculine ideal based on violence and conflict, we should note that what Himes demonstrates in *If He Hollers* is the way black men are consistently pushed into identifying with just such a narrow construction of manhood. We see Bob throughout the novel experimenting with different masculine roles, all of which he is excluded from or prevented from filling. By showing how Jones is prodded toward violence, the narrative questions whether violence is an assertion of freedom and subjectivity or an action that reveals how deeply Jones's responses are determined by white racism. Himes plays on the ritual hunt's strategy of inversion as a means of illustrating the construction and negation of Jones's subjectivity. The first-person narrative further obscures the hunting ritual's blurring of the distinctions between subject and object of the hunt as, from Jones's point of view, he seems to be the author of his own actions. However, if Bob plays the hunter, he does so, Himes implies, because he has been positioned there as part of a white ritual of mastery in which the equality between hunter and hunted exists only so that those distinctions may "be asserted more brutally than ever" (Sundquist 142). As in Wright's "Big Boy Leaves Home" Jones's accomplishment in the story is not to succeed in the hunt but simply to survive it, to negate his positioning as prey. Educated and self-conscious, Jones is also able at various points to analyze these actions, and to realize that the moments of self-assertion when he enacts the role of the hunter are possibly his moments of greatest self-delusion.

If Bob initially finds frontier opportunity in California, unlike Micheaux, Love, and Hopkins, Himes does not represent the West in terms of a natural landscape. Rather, frontier freedom is represented by the activities of industry, "the hustle and bustle of moving busy workers, trucks, plate lifts, yard cranes, electric mules, the blue flashes of arc welders, brighter than the noonday sun. And the noise, always loud, unabating, ear-splitting. I loved it like my first love" (Himes 159). The natural world appears only in glimpses, "the hot sunshine," or "the blue-grey stretch of the harbour" where the shipyard is located (159). More important than an Edenic natural beauty is the "motor smell, pungent, tantalizing [that] poured in through the open windows over me, making me want to just squat on the highway and drive a thousand miles" (162). Bob observes that his car, a 1942 Buick Roadmaster, "was proof of something to me, a symbol" (31). The car represents Bob's change in status, his new sense of social, economic, and physical mobility. In spite of restrictions against African Americans, the car, like Dave Saunders's gun, is a kind of equalizer. As in "The Man Who Was Almost a Man," the meaning Bob makes about himself and his ability to own such an object will be consistently challenged by representatives of the dominant order.

The limitations of this "new frontier" quickly become apparent as the novel follows five days in the life of Bob Jones. Each day begins with a vivid dream sequence that illustrates how deeply the racism he experiences in waking life shapes his unconscious as well. Despite such symbols of success as his car, his engagement, his job, Jones wakes every morning feeling scared (2). Observing the wartime removal of Japanese immigrants and Japanese Americans from the coast unsettles him, as does the "crazy, wild-eyed, unleashed hatred that the first Jap bomb on Pearl Harbour let loose in a flood. All that tight, crazy feeling of race, as thick in the street as gas fumes" (4). The beginning of World War II is a double-edged sword, creating opportunities for black workers and at the same time intensifying racial hatred. As Bob observes, the incarceration of people of Japanese descent "was taking a man up by the roots and locking him up without a chance. Without a trial. Without a charge" (3). In a context dominated by the crazy feeling of race, "I was the same colour as the Japanese and I couldn't tell the difference. 'A yeller-bellied Jap' coulda meant me too" (4).

Even on the open road, Bob finds movement restricted in the jostling rush hour traffic on his drive to the shipyard: "If I'd been a white boy I might have enjoyed the scramble in the early morning sun, the tight competition . . . But to me it was racial" (14). A couple crossing the street against the light "looked up and saw we were coloured [and] they just took their time, giving us a look of cold hatred" (13). Bob resists the urge to "grind 'em into the street," although he sits "looking at the white couple until they had crossed the sidewalk, giving them stare for stare, hate for hate" (13). At the entrance to Shell Refinery, "white workers crossing the street looked at the big new car full of black faces and gave off cold hostility. I gave them look for look" (13). In *Being and Nothingness* Jean-Paul Sartre writes that, in looking, "I am fixing the people I *see* into objects. . . . In looking at them I measure my power" (356). Each day for Bob is an existential battle in which he must assert his subjectivity against gazes that seek to fix him into an object. Writing from the perspective of film theory, Rey Chow notes that the gaze of the camera in classic cinema is often associated with the "masculine" viewpoint of the film and the movie's spectator, "while images on the screen, in the state of being looked at and thus eroticized, are 'feminine'" (16). Bob's subjectivity—and his masculinity—is constantly challenged by an objectifying white gaze that positions him in a state of being looked at, that symbolically "feminizes" him. Bob rejects this positioning by returning the white gaze, stare for stare, hate for hate, and look for look, although the effect of meeting these existential challenges to his identity is a sense of exhaustion, sickness, fear.

At the shipyard, Bob has traveled as far west as possible, to the edge of the shore. If the drive to work symbolizes not tight competition but racial restriction, the interior of the ship further emphasizes the claustrophobia of these restrictions. The decks are littered with tools and equipment, forcing Bob "to pick every step to find a foot-size clearance of deck space, and at the same time to keep looking up so I wouldn't tear off an ear or knock out an eye against some overhanging shape. Every two or three steps I'd bump into another worker" (16). Himes describes "cramped quarters aft, a labyrinth of narrow, hard-angled companionways, jammed with staging, lines, shapes, and workers who had be contortionists first of all," and an atmosphere "thick with welding fumes, acid smell, body odour, and cigarette smoke" (20). The cramped ship condenses American racial relationships as white and black workers play out these tensions within the confined space of the setting. The constricted space also represents the restrictions of race. As Bob notes later in the novel, "But the things had gotten me. Now I felt depressed, walled in, black again" (120). In this social setting, the black self is as walled in as the black body inside the cramped ship.

Like "Big Boy Leaves Home," *If He Hollers* is a lynch drama played out according to the rules of the ritual hunt. As in "Big Boy," central to that drama is a white woman, in this case Madge Perkins, "a peroxide blonde with a large-featured, overly made-up face" (19). An early encounter with Madge results in Bob's losing his leaderman position and his draft exemption. At the end of the novel, he accidentally walks into a room aboard the ship where Madge is sleeping. She locks the door and yells rape. As a result of the accusation, Bob is beaten by a mob of white workers, escapes, is chased through Los Angeles, arrested, and forced to choose between joining the armed forces or going to prison. He both stalks and is stalked by Madge, as the two characters throughout the narrative oscillate between the positions of hunter and hunted, sexual predator and sexual prey.[8]

This ritual of the hunt is often articulated in visual terms or via visual metaphors. The demarcation of the boundaries between self and other connoted by seeing is readily adaptable to figurations of the hunting ritual and to the measuring of power such rituals encode. In the scene from Cooper's *The Deerslayer* in which the captured Natty Bumppo is assaulted by one of his captors, for example, the Panther—whose eyes, Cooper writes, "gleamed on the captive"—with a yell tosses a tomahawk at Natty, but "the loud tones of the speaker had drawn the eye of Deerslayer toward him," and Natty catches the tomahawk in the air (473). Cooper represents the conflict between the Panther and Natty Bumppo as an exchange of glances. Deerslayer's eye is more "sartain" than the Panther's, and he reduces his opponent to an object with a violent act that carries out the threat of his "kindled eye." Natty's toss follows the line of his gaze and strikes his opponent "directly between the eyes," a blow that disables the Panther's ability to look back not only by killing him but also by striking directly at his ferocious "glare," effectively blinding the gaze that initiated the conflict (473).

Himes uses a similar technique in his representation of the game played by Bob and Madge. Meeting accidentally in the tight quarters of the ship's interior, "We stood there for an instant, our eyes locked, before either of us moved" (19). If the "locked" eyes refer back to earlier matching of gazes between Bob and a series of white opponents, Madge moves the challenge to a different level by acting out the part of the hunted, the prey of the "bestial" black man by "deliberately put[ting] on a frightened, wide-eyed look and back[ing] away from me as if she was scared stiff, as if she was a naked virgin and I was King Kong" (19). Bob observes later in the novel, "I'm just like some sort of machine being run by white people pushing buttons. Every white person who comes along pushes some button or other on me and I react accordingly" (166). Madge is particularly adept at pushing his buttons, controlling him "like a puppet on a string" (168). In this initial meeting, her reaction sends a "blinding fury through my brain," a response that provides Madge with a "sexual thrill" (19). Bob's blind fury gives way to an equally unseeing and unconscious response: "Lust shook me like an electric shock" (19). When one of his crew needs a "tacker," Bob discovers that only Madge is available, and "I knew the instant I recognized her that she was going to perform then—*we both would perform*" (27, emphasis mine). She goads him, saying "I ain't gonna work with no nigger," eliciting Bob's response, "Screw you then, you cracker bitch," a statement that causes him to lose his leaderman position (27).

If Wright plays the hunting ritual out to its logical conclusion by refusing to write Big Boy into the narrative as the subject of the hunt, Himes similarly describes Bob's limited ability to author his own story. Bob must contend with external racism that has become internalized, "with the white folks sitting on my brain, controlling my every thought, action, and emotion, making life one crisis after another, day and night, asleep and awake, conscious and unconscious" (Himes 150). Even sexual desire is not necessarily his own but something that acts upon him "like an electric shock." Prohibitions against sexual relations both create and inhibit sexual desire. Madge's ability to put into play that dialectic of prohibition and desire places her in position as master of this particular game, as the hunter and sexual predator who stalks Bob, even during the times when he believes he is tracking her. Meaning is made offstage or unconsciously as Bob performs a script already written, controlled from within by the "white folks sitting on my brain" and controlled from outside by the individual white characters he encounters. Attempts to disengage from the script—to make meaning for himself—are corrected (often by chance or by accident) to return him to the story line to perform the action that will lead to accusations of rape and the justification for mob violence. Madge's acting, her performance of fear in his presence, attempts to draw him into the drama; in the end, when he refuses to play out his predetermined role in the lynch drama, Madge names him rapist anyway.

He redirects his fury away from Madge and toward Johnny Stoddard, a white man who blindsides him during a dice game, knocking him unconscious. Bob returns to consciousness "scared of what I might do" (34). Armed with a borrowed knife, Bob hunts Stoddard through the shipyard: "I was going to kill him if they hung me for it, I thought pleasantly. A white man, a supreme being. Just the thought of it did something for me; just contemplating it. . . . I felt just like I thought a white boy oughta feel; I had never felt so strong in all my life" (38). As Bob performs the role of the hunter, he leaves behind the "sick, scared, gone feeling" (36) that had dominated his senses since the encounter with Madge. Instead, he feels strong, like "a white boy oughta feel." Bob confronts Stoddard, shows him the knife, but decides not to attack: "As long as I knew I was going to kill him, nothing could bother me. . . . I had a peckerwood's life in the palm of my hand and that made all the difference" (45). After work, reinforced with his .38 Special, Bob stalks "his white boy" through the urban wilderness of Los Angeles, tracking him to his home. Again, Bob decides to defer killing him, preferring to "save him up for killing like the white folks had been saving me up for all these years" (44).

Through his stalking of Stoddard, Bob prepares himself for "a more dangerous game"—Madge—for it is she and not Stoddard "standing there between me and my manhood" (123). His

obsession grows until Madge is "all I could see," her existence
controlling his gaze and disrupting his ability to assert his subjectivity: "I was going to have to have her. . . . I was going to have
to so I could keep looking white folks in the face" (123). He
tracks her through the crowded ship, coming up to her as
Madge "looked me square in the eyes" (123). As they exchange
glances, waiting for Bob to take the next (verbal) step in the
game, "I lost my nerve. I couldn't say a word. . . . She was pure
white Texas. And I was black. And a white man was standing
there. I never knew before how good a job the white folks had
done on me" (124). Unlike the earlier workplace confrontation
with "his white boy," this scene ends not with Bob putting away
his knife of his own volition—delaying the conclusion of the
hunt to prolong his own pleasure in the act of hunting—but in
his sense of impotence and objectification, of being "absolutely
subhuman," leaving the field of battle knowing "she was
watching me," unable to return her gaze, the object rather than
the subject of the look (124–25).

Bob realizes that the "whole idea of going to bed with her to
get even with Kelly and Mac and the other peckerwoods out at
the yard seemed silly" (140). "I'd always figured myself too
smart," he observes, "to let the white folks catch me out there on
their own hunting-grounds." Despite feeling "relieved and kind
of half-way clever, as if I'd gotten out of a trap the white folks
had set for me," he still finds himself drawn to search for Madge
(140). The central battle takes place in her apartment: "We tus-
sled silently back and forth across the bed until we were both
panting for breath" (145). If the battle across the bed represents
the possibility of inverting the positions of subject and object
of the hunt, Madge reasserts those distinctions by opening her
robe to reveal her nude body and stating: "This'll get you
lynched in Texas" (147). As viewing the nude goddess in the
Actaeon myth transforms the hunter into the hunted, so does
Madge's strategic positioning of herself as the object of Bob's

gaze result ironically not in his sense of his own subjectivity but in his objectification. Bob collapses, sitting on the bed, defeated "just because she was white" (147). Madge teases him back into the fight, and "we locked together in a test of strength in the middle of the floor" until Madge yells out, "All right, rape me then, nigger!" (147). Madge's power in the hunt is the power to name: "the word scared me, took everything out of me, my desire, my determination, my whole build-up" (148). As in "Big Boy Leaves Home" the woman's voice assigns to Bob a meaning that is "already there," that evokes, he notes later, the "whole structure of American thought" (187).

Sexual desire is part of the trap, fooling Bob into thinking that he is the hunter, the sexual predator, when he is in fact the hunted animal. In his hunting of both Madge and "his white boy," his own thwarted assertions of identity are funneled into prewritten roles, into the two identities ascribed to the "bestial" black man—rapist and murderer. What seems to be the exercise of his own desire and will, his individual protest, is revealed to be part of the elaborate way his actions and psyche are formed and shaped by whites. Although Bob leaves Madge's apartment thinking "the white folks had won again," he has in fact escaped another trap—of committing a sexual act that would place him more fully under Madge's power and control by providing a basis for her threatened accusations of rape (148).

When he comes across his gun in his glove compartment, "I jerked my hand back as if I'd touched death, felt the shock run clear down into my soul. To realize that I'd been so close to murder" (162). The gun, he understands, represents another trap narrowly avoided: "It gave me a funny feeling of having been drawn outside of myself, of having been goaded beyond my own control" (163). As in Wright's story, "Almost a Man," the gun is revealed to be a signifier not entirely under the protagonist's control. Although Bob plans to use the gun to make meaning for himself, to assert his subjectivity through violence, he also realizes that such a momentary inversion of the hunter and the hunted would only result in asserting those distinctions more brutally than ever. Johnny Stoddard, like Madge herself, is only a signifier, a piece in a larger game. The real hunter in this game is the whole structure of American thought that Bob is oppressed by and opposes, which is always both offstage and everywhere at once, sitting on his brain, working through individual white characters, existing within the official and unofficial system of legal and social restrictions placed on African Americans. None of the individuals who physically embody "the whole structure of American thought" emerges to symbolize that system in the way Covey does in Douglass's *Narrative* so Bob is continually frustrated in his efforts to force recognition of his being through an encounter with a symbolic other—one who represents the laws, values, privileges, of the dominant culture. That white other in Himes's story remains elusive, both everywhere and intangible.

Bob escapes one trap only to fall into another. At work the next day, he accidentally stumbles onto Madge napping inside a cabin and finds himself locked inside the room with her: "Looking at each other; our eyes locked together as in a death embrace; black and white in both our minds; not hating each other; just feeling extreme outrage. I felt buck-naked and pow-erless, stripped of manhood and black against the whole white world" (181). In a reversal of the earlier scene, Bob—not Madge—is revealed (metaphorically) "buck-naked." In the encounter at Madge's apartment Bob avoided the fate of Actaeon—metamorphosis into an animal—by retreating. In this final encounter, retreat is not possible, and Bob's sense of nakedness symbolizes the power of the white gaze to see and name, to transform Bob into the hunted animal. Bob thinks later, "I could see myself trying to prove my innocence and nobody believing it. A white woman yelling, 'Rape,' and a Negro

caught locked in the room. . . . American tradition had convicted me a hundred years before" (187). The door bursts
inward, and Bob sees "a hundred million white faces" coming
after him, protecting the innocent white woman from the "bestial" black man (181). As do Micheaux's Devereaux and Hopkins's Judah, Himes's Bob Jones battles throughout the book
not only with individual white characters but also with the
imagery of black savagery. Although Jones is repeatedly coerced
by others who try to make him lose control, he ultimately
proves his ability to restrain himself. Such proof of civilized
behavior, however, has little effect on the way the dominant culture interprets his actions. "Yours was a crime of uncontrolled
lust—the act of an animal," he is told later by the company
president (202). Despite his assertions of subjectivity, Madge's
false accusations (despite the fact, Bob later realizes, that no one
in authority actually believes her) succeed in transforming him
into a beast, an animal. The uncontrolled act of violence he has
narrowly avoided committing throughout the narrative is
attributed to him anyway.

At the end, Bob is led off to join the armed forces with two
young Mexican American men. One of the two comments,
"Looks like this man has had a war. How you doing, man?"
(203). Bob responds, "'I'm still here,' I lisped painfully" (203). As
in Wright's two short stories, Himes's novel ends with Bob
leaving home, his interior life nearly as hollowed out as Big
Boy's, his body in pain, but nonetheless a survivor. Ordered
into the armed forces, Bob's next migration is not his own—
but he is headed toward a frontier that will be important for
later writers, overseas, outside the national boundaries of the
United States, perhaps to Europe or Africa. For Himes and
Wright, the position of the African American man in the frontier myth is that of the beast hunted by the white hero of the
myth. His primary accomplishment is to survive the hunt and
to resist being objectified by the narratives and discourses he

finds himself caught in—to establish a sense of subjectivity in spite of repeated attempts to negate such self-making. Unlike in the frontier scenarios of Turner and Roosevelt, neither Big Boy nor Bob Jones makes a first contact with an other not encountered before. Each story ends with the protagonist setting forth for a new land, to the north for Big Boy, to an overseas military frontier for Bob Jones.

Chapter 5

"How Does It Feel to Be a White Man?"

New Frontiers in The Stone Face

William Gardner Smith is the author of four novels, *The Last of the Conquerors* (1948), *Anger at Innocence* (1950), *South Street* (1954), and *The Stone Face* (1963).[1] Jerry H. Bryant in "Individuality and Fraternity," an excellent overview of Smith's achievements as a novelist, writes that *The Last of the Conquerors* "seemed to have launched its twenty-year-old author on a comfortably successful literary career in America," making the bestseller list and eliciting "warmly favorable" reviews, including a *Saturday Review of Literature* article in 1949 that "talked of Smith as one of the bright new novelists in America" (1). Joseph Friedman's 1963 *New York Times* review of *The Stone Face* notes that the book is "a solid achievement. Among the most worthy younger writers, Negro or white, count this one" (53). However, despite being well reviewed, Smith published no further novels.

Bryant's article notes that Smith "has suffered a gradually dwindling reputation" ("Individuality" 1). Bryant argues that Smith's four novels register changes taking place in African American literature as a whole from World War II through the

Vietnam War. Whereas his first two novels are "part of the literature of black social protest begun by Richard Wright," in the
space between writing *Anger at Innocence* and *South Street*
"Smith undergoes an important change of attitude" (2). For the
earlier novels, Smith envisions a white audience. He intends
these novels as "a means for transforming white American racial
attitudes. Smith has said that in these novels he still had some
hope that he could 'communicate' with white people, could
make them understand the general significance of his own
acute discomfort in America" (2). In the process of writing
South Street, however, he abandons his attempt to change the
minds of a white audience "and has written a novel for blacks"
(3). This change in imagined audience is "not a change involving his idea of the function of his art, which he sees as a semi-
political instrument for improving his people's condition. It is a
change in his view of American society" (3). According to
Bryant, Smith "discards the assumption that his satisfaction as a
black man depends upon his 'communication' with whites" and
focuses instead on transforming the views of black society (3).

Smith's *The Stone Face* represents as well an effort in the
1960s to reformulate the frontier myth in a context informed by
both black activism in America and nationalist independence
movements in Africa. The significant action takes place not in
the western United States but in Europe, primarily in Paris
during the Algerian war for independence. If the frontier offers
"a gate of escape from the bondage of the past" as Turner argues
(59), the protagonist, Simeon Brown, leaves America for
Europe in order to escape the past of white racism. In Europe
he experiences a "first contact" with whiteness, in the form of
an interracial romance. Whereas, in the traditional version of
the frontier myth, the hero becomes Americanized by his experience, Smith's African American hero endeavors to lose his
Americanness, reversing the traditional pattern although still

retaining the idea of the frontier as place of transformation and rebirth.

Smith's novel reconfigures two essential components of the traditional frontier narrative of pioneers in the American West—a newly encountered geography, and a meeting point between two or more cultures. This new landscape—Paris in the 1960s—is social as well as geographic, for Simeon's sense of frontier freedom depends on the absence of the racial restrictions associated with American society. Europe is a frontier in another (and for the African American novelist more important) sense of the word. Europe functions as the border between America and Africa. The question of racial identity that is central to the work of Wright and Himes is placed in a new context, a colonial situation in flux. Within this context Smith substitutes the conflict between the French and the Algerians for the traditional frontier encounter between European colonists and American Indians. The primary encounter with otherness, the most important first contact, is not with a white woman but with another man, one engaged in fighting white oppression in his own country. Simeon's contact with the Algerians results in a transformation of his psyche and ends in his return to America with a new willingness to engage history not escape it, and to fight against oppression.

The Stone Face *and the Frontier Denied*

> *It was the massive head of a man sketched so harshly that it looked as though it had been carved out of stone; the jaw was clamped tight, the mouth was a compressed bitter line, the skin was deathly pale, the eyes were flat, fanatic, sadistic and cold. It was an inhuman face, the face of* un-man, *the face of discord, the face of destruction.* —SMITH, *The Stone Face*

Arriving in Paris, Simeon observes, "America was behind him, his past was behind him," a past that is associated with racial violence and with what Simeon refers to as the stone face (3). Simeon is an artist, both a painter and a writer, and supports himself in Paris through hack work for an American men's magazine called *He-Man,* while he tries to use his painting to work through his fear of the stone face: "For years that face had been at the center of all his dreams. Sometimes the face simply floated in the air. Sometimes it perched itself on the bodies of people Simeon knew. . . . Sometimes it shone burning in the sky, a horrifying sun" (18). What remains elusive in Himes's *If He Hollers*—"the whole structure of American thought" (187), the dominant values and beliefs about race that have been internalized by black and white characters alike— appears in Smith's novel in personified form, in the figure of the stone face.

In the novel the stone face exists not only as part of Simeon's very unconscious, "at the center of all his dreams," but also embodied in the form of individual characters. Simeon first experiences this stone face when a white teenager named Chris, with "a solid reputation for hating Negroes," attacks him with a knife and blinds him in one eye (26). The attack begins with Chris hailing Simeon, "Hey, *nigger!*" (26). Simeon wants to respond defiantly, to reject the name attached to him by the other's address, but his muscles freeze, and he notices that his tongue is paralyzed. The other boys with Chris surround Simeon, and "Chris' face came into frightening sharpness. He had an inhumanly cold face with dull, sadistic eyes." Smith writes that "Simeon was less frightened by the danger than by the coldness of the eyes" (27). Chris's gaze as well as his act of naming inscribe an identity for Simeon—"nigger." While Simeon's paralyzed tongue prevents him from rejecting the name by verbally representing himself otherwise, he does not acknowledge that act of naming (by refusing to speak and thus answer

Chris's address). By so doing he refuses to acknowledge any "truth" in Chris's appraisal. Chris's gaze and hail symbolize the authority possessed by representatives of the dominant culture to assign an identity to the minority individual—an authority reinforced by potential violence. Simeon speaks only after Chris places a knife to his throat, threatening him: "*Answer* me, nigger, or I'll *blind* you" (28). When Simeon again lapses into silence Chris carries through with his threat. Chris's phallic knife and his act of penetrating and blinding Simeon symbolizes the dominant culture's denial of his emerging masculine identity.

As Simeon is mutilated physically so is his sense of self damaged by his experiences, and Simeon's one blind eye symbolizes his limited possibilities in a racist society. If the presence of the stone face intercedes between Simeon and all his dreams, he also responds to the knife attack by forging a new identity, one that establishes his American self, as "the place where he had once had an eye" becomes central to his self-conception, to his "I" (29). The teenaged Simeon begins wearing a black patch over the empty socket to make himself look mysterious and romantic, an image he views in a mirror with satisfaction. Simeon tells the other boys in the neighborhood that his eye "is a gift to the gods. I gave them the eye; they give me other things" (29). In exchange for the eye, Simeon claims, he has received "Strength, courage, bravery," a bravery he proves by shoving the blade of a borrowed penknife through the palm of his hand. Smith writes, "Simeon smiled. He was a man (30). The self damaged in Chris's knife attack repeats that very act of violence in the form of a self-inflicted wound, an action meant to assert a masculine identity to the world and to himself. At the core of this new identity, however, is a self-hatred that is only partially concealed by the fantasy of manhood generated by Simeon's identification with his romanticized image in the mirror. Simeon must leave America not only to rid himself of the stone face but also to rid himself of the identity forged in reaction to that face.

In America, Simeon has a double identity. On one hand the black patch represents his sense of identity as "the Man of Mystery" (29). Opposed to that assertion of self is the identity constituted by Chris's address—"nigger"—and by the dominant culture attitudes that Chris exemplifies. Simeon's fiction of self will not be accepted as fact in the world of others, and his attempts to represent himself as he wishes to be seen in that world will be met with resistance and violence. As does Micheaux's pioneer hero in the first part of *The Conquest*, Simeon finds success in the white world, becoming the only black reporter on a white newspaper in Philadelphia—achieving the status that is one of the traditional indicators of masculine identity, success in the workplace. Simeon's success does not, however, provide him with protection or bring him the praise of a white community. While he is visiting friends in a primarily white area of the city he is spotted by the police, arrested, stripped, and beaten. Mike, one of the policemen, tells Simeon, "I'm gonna personally keep my eye on you. Anytime you act up, I'll bring you in for treatment again" (42). As Mike beats him with a hose, Simeon notes the sadistic eyes and realizes, "*It's the same face,*" the stone face of white racism (42). Simeon has stepped outside his "place," his new job bringing him into a geography reserved for whites, a transgression that is punished by violence. The policeman says to Simeon, "I'm your guardian angel; we're married from now on, you and me" (42). The fictional identity Simeon creates in the mirror ("He was a man") is contested by the brutally masculine Mike, whose insistence that Simeon is "married" to him feminizes Simeon, denies him his masculine identity. As with Judah in Hopkins's *Winona*, the damage caused by this beating extends beyond the physical to the psychological—and likewise results in an all-consuming, potentially self-destructive desire for revenge. Before any healing of his damaged psyche can take place, before Simeon can have any hope of completing the sequence of beating and recovery that is familiar to us from Hopkins's *Winona* and Wister's *The Virginian,* he must leave America.

The force of white violence does not end with the encounter with the policeman, and after a series of racial attacks, Simeon buys a gun for protection. Only the fact that his gun jams saves him from committing murder and leads him to examine his situation in America:

> In bed that night he forced himself to be calm. But the face—of Mike, of Chris, of the sailor—would not leave his mind. . . . Murder in a bar, then the electric chair, what a ridiculous way to end life! To die for a cause, that would be one thing. But in a barroom brawl!
>
> He told himself slowly and lucidly: *I'm going to kill a man someday.* In a moment of anger, humiliation, an instant of illusion, of hallucination. No! Not that waste, not kill himself through his own irrational act! (55)

Simeon finds himself in the position of having to choose between living a life of submission that forces him to repress and deny his own desires for self-making or committing a violent gesture that may protest repressive conditions but that will also lead to the electric chair. He fears the possibility that "an instant of illusion" will cause him to act irrationally, with a determined response to white racism and not an act of free choice, an act as self-destructive as stabbing himself with a penknife.

The self he forms in relation to the stone face is one that mirrors the irrationality of white violence. To escape that self he would go away, "leave America. Go where? Anywhere. Europe, for example. France" (55). When Simeon leaves America, Smith to a certain degree also leaves behind the conventions of the protest novel. The violent gesture his hero is on the verge of committing in America is avoided. Wright and Himes protest the limited choices of identity available to African Americans by representing the damaging effect those limitations have on the black psyche. Smith seeks to move beyond representing those limitations. There is a hope here of another kind of violence that is regenerative rather than self-destructive and that leads not to the electric chair but to transformation and rebirth.

Frontier France

The narrative of *The Stone Face* traces the movement of Simeon's desire to be a man, to force acknowledgment—in the realm of the symbolic—of the identity Simeon constructs for himself in the mirror. This desire initiates the novel's shifts in geography, with those shifts corresponding to Simeon's identity transformations. Smith reconfigures the frontier myth's East/West, Wilderness/Metropolis dichotomy in terms of national boundaries, with America representing the civilized East and France imagined as the wilderness West. Smith's Paris, the streets, rooms, and cafes where Simeon lives, are places imagined to be outside the deforming influence of civilization/America. *The Stone Face* progresses through a series of rebirths, a series of changes in subjectivity for Simeon, with the argument of the novel presenting those changes as a steady evolution in Simeon's character, a structural pattern that is visible in narratives of the frontier myth as early as John Filson's 1784 *The Discovery, Settlement and Present State of Kentucke*. As Slotkin notes in *Regeneration through Violence,* Filson presents Daniel Boone's adventures as "a series of initiations, a series of progressive immersions that take him deeper into the wilderness," with each immersion awakening "Boone's sense of identity" and deepening his understanding of the wilderness (278). For Simeon, each immersion in the wilderness of Paris moves him further away from the civilized world of American racism and further away from the consciousness he has formed in reaction to that racism. There are several stages in Simeon's awakening: the new man he becomes within a few days of his journey into Paris; the sense of freedom he attains in an interracial relationship; his "baptism" during a raid on the Algerian quarters where he is visiting; his decision to reject his membership in a private club that will not allow his Algerian friends to join him there for dinner; his final rebirth after he defends a woman and child being attacked by a policeman. Each journey is a movement deeper into a new sense of identity. Each immersion takes him further from seeing the world through white eyes, further from accepting the value judgments of white people, and deeper into the world of the novel's other, the Algerians.

If the frontier offers an "escape from the bondage of the past" (Turner 59), Simeon finds in Paris a place to escape the stone face and to escape the self (de)formed in America. After a few days in France Simeon notes an immediate change: he "felt he had gone through his initiation now, this was *his* city. The old tension like poison had already begun to seep out of him, and he could feel himself growing strong and whole. He would become a new man. He wondered what that man would be" (11). Simeon's rebirth and emergence as a new man in Paris is accompanied by his enjoying new privileges and protections. When white Americans enter a bar and complain loudly about the presence of blacks, the bartender responds, "There are certain things you have to leave behind when you come to France. At least when you come to my club" (37).

At the same time Simeon's assertions that he is a new man are contradicted by some of his actions. If white Americans have a hard time leaving certain things behind when they come to France, Simeon also brings certain things with him. Sometimes he "dreamed that he was back in Philadelphia, unable to escape" (34–35). When he and his friend Babe go to meet two

Swedish girls for an evening out, Simeon "felt a vague unease, a readiness for battle as they left the taxi and walked to the cafe where the girls waited for them" (35). Upon his arrival in Paris Simeon feels that everyone is staring at him (6). A woman laughs when he trips over a table leg, and "the old insidious thought came to him, the conditioned reflex. *Racism*" (6). The same woman who laughed at him, however, moments later embraces and kisses "A tall African, black as anthracite" (6). The crowd at the cafe pays no attention. If for Simeon France is a place where the representatives of the dominant culture do not seek to return him to an inferior place, he still must contend with that part of his unconscious that causes him to interpret the actions of others according to his conditioned reflex. If the stone face belongs in America, Simeon's painting of that face that he keeps inside his Paris apartment reminds us of how much his psyche remains shaped by his American experience: "As he stared at the portrait—the face of Chris, of Mike, of the sailor, he felt his old inescapable torment of emotions—horror, disgust, fear, hatred, and a desire to kill" (7).

Eventually, Simeon's experiences in Paris allow him to get rid of some of his reflexes conditioned by racism, to release some of the "old tension" (11). His newfound freedom in Paris is represented most clearly by an interracial romance with a Polish woman, Maria, who like Simeon is partially blind. Maria tells him, "your eye . . . my eyes . . . our eyes bring us together, perhaps" (76). Maria is also a fugitive, leaving behind her past in Poland and leaving behind as best she can her memories of being held prisoner in a German Occupation labor camp during World War II (75). If the interracial romance with Maria represents a type of freedom for Simeon, one outside the boundaries of white racism, she also allegorically represents one of the choices he must make. She, like Simeon, has sought to escape the past and to escape her own impulses to irrational violence: "For years, after the war, I dreamed of nothing except that camp, that line-up, the faces of my parents and the face of that commander. For years I dreamed how I could torture and kill that man" (78–79). Haunted by her own version of the stone face, she seeks in Paris an escape into the present moment where "I don't want to think about. . . . I want to pretend it never happened" (79).

Places of lovemaking and conversation, the various rooms and coffeehouses of Paris function as wilderness spaces outside the "civilized" world of racial prejudice where we can identify a first contact between Simeon and a representative of another culture, someone who is white but different from the white people he encountered in America. Maria's feminine presence aids Simeon's psychological recovery from the damage caused in America—at least partially. The sequence of beating recovery familiar to the genre of the Western is not played out in quite the same way as in the novels discussed earlier. Maria has also been damaged, and she represents a method of healing that the novel eventually rejects. Healing in *The Stone Face* depends not on a feminine presence that aids in the recovery of manly restraint but on a symbolic confrontation with another man—one whose embodiment of the stone face justifies the release of violent passions that Simeon otherwise struggles to contain. Restraint in the novel functions as self-defense, as a means of avoiding a violent act that would lead to violent retribution, not as proof to white society of the black man's ability to achieve civilized manliness. Rather, the novel demonstrates Simeon's path toward a violent act that is not self-destructive, because that violence occurs in the context of a just and collective cause. This justification for extralegal violence parallels the argument made in *Winona* on behalf of John Brown's abolitionists, although Smith does not connect the Algerians' cause to the divine justice emphasized by Hopkins.

Simeon leaves America to escape a hideous "marriage" to the stone face. When Maria comments that Simeon's painting "looks like somebody I knew before," he rolls it up and "toss[es] it into the closet" (72). In place of the marriage to the stone face he plans to marry Maria, but he must adapt to her one condition, that "he must be content to live and love in peace. . . . cut off from the troubles of the world" (129). Simeon responds, "Perhaps the Negro who might want to marry you might not be able to flee. Not forever. Because of something inside" (130). The stone face remains that "something inside," momentarily closeted and deferred but still a part of his consciousness, that his relationship with Maria cannot erase. The various interiors in the novel, the places where Simeon and Maria develop their relationship, are also womblike spaces that eventually become confining to the hero's growth. In the end, the transformation of Smith's hero depends on his rejection of this feminine space and the breaking of his bond with Maria.

Crossing the Border into Indian Country

The Conquest presents Micheaux's alter ego, his narrator Devereaux, as an example for African Americans who will not accept white models of success, encouraging readers to identify with his own imitation of the ideal of white success. In *The Stone Face* Smith also wishes to transform the consciousness of his African American audience, but not through representing an image based on white values. Smith is interested in inventing a black hero who will serve as a model of a new identity. In order to create such a hero, he must rid himself of the gaze of the white other that causes Devereaux, for example, to keep his "place as regards custom" (Micheaux 155). Both Micheaux and Smith refer explicitly to *Exodus* 2:22—"I have been a stranger in a strange land," which Smith quotes as an epigraph to the novel. Devereaux's journey to South Dakota, Micheaux writes, makes him "a stranger in a strange land, inhabited wholly by people not my own race" (77). For Smith the strange land is Paris in

1961 during Algeria's war for independence from France, which establishes one of the significant borders Smith's hero must cross.[2] In contrast to Micheaux's *The Conquest* Smith introduces the possibility of identification with a group of people "not of my own race" who are not white, an identification not with the dominant culture and its values but with a group in opposition to those values.

While the new man that Simeon becomes in Paris is based in part on his interracial romance, the most important relationship in *The Stone Face* is between Simeon and Ahmed, a young Algerian man living temporarily in France as a student, who, in the argument of the novel, represents the appropriate identification for African American men, a "brother," a member of a group whose oppression and whose violent and collective revolt against that oppression (the Algerian war for independence from France) serves as a model for remaking African American manhood in America. As Simeon's initiation in Paris leads to his emergence as a new man, he also is initiated into the Algerian situation through his encounters with Algerians living in Paris, culminating in a night of peaceful protest that ends in violent attacks on the Algerian protestors. At one point Ahmed tells Simeon, "I told you, we're twins," and Smith sets up Ahmed as Simeon's double as he draws parallels between the Algerian situation and the situation of African Americans in the United States (189).

Earlier in the book, Simeon is hailed by a friend of Ahmed's, Hossein, who asks him: "How does it feel to be a white man?" (55). Smith writes that "Simeon knew somehow that the words were for him," and he answers the address by turning to see "four Algerians sitting at a table" (55). Hossein asserts that for Simeon, France is "the land of the free," but for the Algerian Arabs, "We're the niggers here" (56–57). Later in the book, Simeon observes Ahmed and Hossein: "Simeon looked at the two men. Their skins were white, all right: they looked like

Southern Slavs. The way Hossein jokingly called him 'white man' was ridiculous, he thought—as though he, Hossein, were not white! One of the Brazilians had explained to Simeon that in South America when an Indian or Negro became rich or became a general, he was officially considered white" (92–93). The divisions between the Algerians and the French replicate the frontier myth's Indian/white man border with Simeon moving back and forth across those lines, at times identifying with the oppression of the Algerians and at other times enjoying the freedoms they are denied. Through his relationship with the Algerians, Simeon realizes that his own sense of freedom in Paris places him in a position of privilege that he finds disturbingly close to the position in society held by white people in the United States. The novel's narrative follows Simeon's steady movement from one side of the border to the other, as he moves from a position of being officially considered white to one of identification with and acceptance by the Algerians. For the Algerians Paris is no wilderness space outside the deforming influence of civilization, and this understanding forces Simeon to rethink the novel's initial drawing of the Metropolis/Wilderness border. His relationship with the Algerians shifts that boundary—as Simeon begins to think of Paris as civilization and of the Algerian section as the novel's version of Indian Country.

Simeon enters the Algerian/French conflict initially as an ally of the French—he calls the police in to arrest an Algerian man who is beating a woman. In the section of the novel entitled "The White Man," Simeon begins to resist his "white identity." His encounters with the Algerians lead to, as Hossein puts it, the "Education of the white man," an education that results in Simeon "passing" as Algerian (92). The police raid the Algerian apartment building where Simeon is visiting with his newfound friends. A policeman with a submachine gun looks at Simeon, stating, "You're not an Arab," and demands to see his passport (94). When the raid is over Simeon states, "I feel . . . baptized" (95). Hossein, impressed with Simeon's composure, comments, "You're not so bad for a white man" (96).

While Smith sets his novel in the context of the colonial relationship between the French and the Algerians, his construction of his fictional Algerian characters is far less complex than the psychoanalytical portrait of colonial and postcolonial subjectivity we find in the work of theorists such as Frantz Fanon and Homi K. Bhabha. Postcolonial theories of subjectivity may be useful in examining Smith's novel, but primarily as a means of looking at Smith's characterization of Simeon and his shifting identifications and migrations rather than at his creation of Algerian revolutionaries. Bhabha writes that Fanon's designation "Black skin, white masks" as a metaphor for colonial identity is a "doubling, dissembling image of being in at least two places at once" (Bhabha 44). While Simeon is racially marked by his black skin, he wears in France a symbolic white mask that enables his enjoyment of rights and privileges denied him in America. In France, his passport validates his wearing of that mask, allows him to pass as officially white, validates his imitation of white freedoms and his membership in exclusive clubs, and marks him as distinctly different from the Algerians.[3]

Simeon's black skin and his passport reveal that he is "not an Arab," but his "baptism" into a new identity in this scene initiates a new type of passing as he begins to play the role of the Algerian revolutionary and begins to wear an Algerian mask to accompany his white mask. Simeon's "double passing"—his attempts to continue to enjoy the new freedoms of Paris at the same time as he tries to establish a solidarity between himself and the Algerians—will place his sense of identity in conflict. In *The Stone Face,* the occasional slippage between Simeon's masks registers the novel's most disturbing moments, when Simeon is "difficult to place," "unhomely," to use Bhabha's phrase (62), as when the French policemen are puzzled by

Simeon's presence in the Algerian quarters.[4] Simeon's passport validates his "passing" at the same time as it marks him as not French. He is "not an Arab" and at the same time "not bad for a white man," two negative designations that simultaneously place and displace him. If Simeon is both and neither the "us" of the Algerians and/nor the "us" of the French, where and what in fact is he?

Simeon's relationship with the Algerians is tested—as is his own attempt to occupy without contradiction two places at once—when he takes Ahmed and his friends to a club in Paris: "Simeon liked being a member simply to show that he *could* be one for once in his life; it was the kind of exclusive club that never would have admitted him in the United States" (106–7). In France, Simeon has the ability to pass as white, to be a member of white society. To enjoy the privileges of that community, however, he must also (as do Devereaux and Love) accept its values and judgments. Ahmed's presence in the club causes Simeon to realize his position of privilege and reveals the accuracy of Hossein's description of him as a white man. He is shocked by the reaction in the club and for a moment can not decide how to act: "But he was afraid of something. Of losing something. Acceptance, perhaps. The word made him wince. Of feeling humiliation again. For one horrible instant he found himself *withdrawing* from the Algerians—the pariahs, the untouchables! He, for the frightening second, had rejected *identification* with them! . . . How could this be? Simeon thought. Escape—that was what he had wanted. Sitting here with the Algerians he was a nigger again to the eyes that stared. A nigger to the outside eyes—that was what his emotions had fled" (108). Simeon's subjectivity is split as he looks from two places at once. He identifies with the eyes of the dominant culture as he sees and judges the Algerians ("untouchables!") from the point of view of a member. At the same time, he shares with the Algerians the experience of being transformed into an object, a "nigger to the outside eyes." Observing the gazes of the people in the club, Simeon recognizes for the first time how his own look coincides with the gaze of the dominant culture as he sees his friends as well as himself with "outside eyes." For a frightening second Simeon experiences a crisis of identity, an "unhomely moment" when his split subjectivity makes it difficult for him even to locate himself, a moment when he is out of place in his own psyche. In the end Simeon seeks to "hold the respect and good will" of the Algerian men rather than members of the dominant culture. Smith writes, "The bad moment had passed. He had crossed the bridge, and felt at one with the Algerians. He felt strangely *free*—the wheel had turned full circle" (109).

Simeon resolves his crisis of identity by fixedly identifying with (and romanticizing) the Algerians, by assuming the mask of the revolutionary as an authentic image of identity. In my discussion of Turner, "The Significance of the Frontier in American History," I argue that the American Indian man functions to facilitate the colonist's transformation. As is Turner's colonist, Smith's protagonist is aided in his transformation by the figure of another man encountered in the wilderness—his Algerian friend Ahmed who serves as the ideal image of masculinity and mastery. At one point in the novel, Ahmed leaves France briefly in order to join the battle in his home country. Upon his return, "Simeon was shocked at the change in Ahmed's physical appearance, or rather a contrast between Ahmed's appearance and his own. Ahmed's bearing was more erect and proud. . . . His eyes had lost all their boyish shyness and shone with serene determination" (187). Simeon's transformation depends on his assuming the image that he himself has in a sense produced—the projection of his own desires to be whole onto the figure of Ahmed. The image of Ahmed causes Simeon to note the contrast between himself and what he desires to become. Simeon's twin has become a mirror that reflects back to Simeon his own lack. He knows now that he is not the man he could be. He wants to become that man, to replace, perhaps, his own damaged gaze with eyes that shine "with serene determination." Simeon's renewal of his acquaintance with Ahmed "had somehow given him strength" (190). In a scene early in the novel the teenaged Simeon, his eye damaged by a knife attack, observes his image in the mirror with "satisfaction" (30). Through his journey to France, Simeon replaces that admired mirror image with another—the "erect and proud" Ahmed freshly returned from the battlefield.

Making a Slave a Man

> It is precisely from this edge of meaning and being, from this shifting boundary of otherness within identity, that Fanon asks, "What does a black man want?"
>
> —BHABHA, The Location of Culture

> Suddenly Simeon saw something more brutal than anything he had ever seen before in his life. A few dozen yards away from him a policeman was swinging his club over a woman who was holding a baby. . . . Then suddenly he saw the policeman's face.
>
> He saw it clearly as though it were only inches from him—that face he knew so well, the face in America he had tried to escape—it was Chris, Mike, their face. The policeman's face was distorted and twisted with the joy of destruction, his eyes narrowed, red dots of excitement on his deathly pale skin.
>
> The face exploded in front of Simeon. . . . [He] stumbled forward, almost fainting from the pain in the socket, weaved between the parked cars, and swung his fist into the hated face, with all his strength.   —SMITH, The Stone Face

The final section of *The Stone Face* involves several key events, culminating in an Algerian protest against a government curfew. The police crack down on the protesters. Smith writes, "The corpses of more than two hundred Algerians, Ahmed's among them, were to be fished out of the Seine the next day and for days afterward" (202). During the curfew protest, Simeon wanders through the Algerian section of Paris, observing police brutality firsthand but only discovering the next day that his friend Ahmed has been killed by the police, and finally observing a scene of such brutality that he chooses to act in solidarity with the Algerians by attacking a policeman. Simeon's decision to act violently against police oppression represents his final rejection of the freedom he has enjoyed in Paris and his engaged commitment to a type of freedom that can be achieved only by struggling collectively on behalf of all who are oppressed. In *The Stone Face,* an act of regenerative violence not only solidifies Simeon's bond and identification with a group of Algerian revolutionaries but also leads to his final transformation. Unlike Love's violence in his *Life and Adventures,* Simeon acts against—not in conjunction with—the dominant culture.

Simeon's violent act also connects *The Stone Face* specifically to the African American slave narrative tradition, especially to Douglass's *Narrative* of 1845. Central to Douglass's figuration of his own transformation from nonbeing to subject is a violent encounter with his white overseer. Through this violent assertion of self, Douglass argues, "a slave was made a man" (294). George P. Cunningham argues that within the discourse of slavery, the individual designated as slave is assigned a position in the symbolic order consonant with nonbeing, nonsubjectivity, non-man. In counterpoint to the slave's negation of identity is the master, who embodies "the figure of the father" and "reserves to himself the masculine authority to generate meaning," to name, and to control a "literal and symbolic inheritance" (113–14). There are several points of comparison here with events from *The Stone Face*. We might argue that the figure of the father appears in the novel in the form of the stone face itself and in the form of the various individual embodiments of that face—Chris, Mike, and so on. These characters have the masculine authority to generate meaning, to assign to Simeon a name—"nigger." They also have the authority to enforce the boundaries set by a racist discourse of segregation, boundaries both geographical and symbolic. They police the dividing line between their identity as men and Simeon's enforced identity as non-man.

Cunningham argues that even though in the struggle between master and slave "the basic contest is between two men, a third party—a woman—is essential to Douglass's figuration of his desire" (119). The first pivotal moment in the *Narrative* occurs when Douglass as a young child observes his master, Aaron Anthony, whip his Aunt Hester. Such scenes of a woman or child being whipped by a master are standard in slave narratives, and Cunningham argues Douglass uses this standard scene to set up his famous battle with the overseer Covey. By drawing parallels between the two scenes Douglass recalls those moments in other male slave narratives where "the slave's fight for self is conflated with the fight for a woman or child" (Cunningham 121). This conflation enables Douglass to enter into the triangular relationship in the preexisting position of the father, filling the father's role as the patriarchal protector of the woman or child, thereby marking his "entry into a gendered and symbolic order" as man rather than as non-man (Cunningham 119).

Simeon's is also the story of "entry into a gendered and symbolic order" that uses triangular configurations to channel and articulate desire. Smith figures Simeon's transformations in Paris through the triangular relationship between Simeon, Ahmed, and Maria. The novel's climactic scene also figures and focuses Simeon's final transformation via another triangular relationship—one that replicates the standard slave narrative scene of a woman or child being beaten by the master. The violent attacks Simeon experiences in America place him in a position consonant with the woman or child in the slave narrative. In one case he is penetrated by Chris's knife/penis; in the other case, like Aunt Hester in Douglass's narrative, he is stripped and beaten, a symbolic rape that ends with a forced "marriage" between Simeon and Mike, whose "whispered joy" as he beats Simeon with a hose signifies Mike's erotic investment in this scene (Smith 42). In both these scenes, a single male acts violently against Simeon within the view of a group of white, male, participant-observers. The desire focused through these attacks is not Simeon's but that of the other participants in the triangle. Simeon's position is that of the "object of desire," "the woman," whose difference not only reinforces for the others their own sense of masculinity (they occupy the male, not the female, positions in the triangle) but also solidifies a bond between the members of the group. The feminized Simeon serves as an object of exchange that enables groups of white men to act out symbolically the establishing of the bonds between men that are necessary for the continuation of racist hegemony.

Simeon's story culminates in a scene that repeats and reverses these earlier triangular configurations. During the Algerian protests, Simeon observes a woman and child being beaten by a policeman. Before he takes the place of the father/master in this triangle, that of the patriarchal protector of the woman and child, Simeon identifies with the woman—he felt "those blows against his own body" (203). This identification with the feminine and with a feminized position changes when he sees the policeman's face, "that face he knew so well, the face in America he had tried to escape." The woman disappears from his consciousness as his gaze becomes locked on the enemy. Simeon swings "his fist into that hated face, with all his strength" (203). As Douglass does in his *Narrative,* Simeon uses a violent confrontation to invert the symbolic master/slave, white/black relationship. What the black man wants, according to Bhabha, is "the objectifying confrontation with otherness" that negates his "primordial identity" and enables the individual "assigned the status of other" within that system to "generate meaning" (Bhabha 52). What Simeon ultimately wants is not escape (as Maria does) but this objectifying confrontation with otherness, a demand for consideration that is played out as desire to become a man, to gain for himself the rights and privileges that belong to the "father" but are denied to black men. The French policeman provides—or seems to provide— just such an objectifying confrontation.

After Ahmed's return from Algeria, Simeon sends a letter to Maria breaking off their relationship and instead sees "Ahmed almost every day" (Smith 191). Ahmed and Maria represent two differing and opposed notions of freedom, and Simeon cannot remain married to both characters. To escape, as Maria suggests they do, is to remain in the imaginary, for Simeon. After an eye operation that restores her sight, Maria escapes further into fantasy as she leaves Paris behind to become a movie star. Maria's desire to escape, although it parallels Simeon's desires throughout most of the novel, is a desire that the novel genders as feminine. To escape is to remain in the imaginary, to reject the risk of engagement with representatives of the symbolic order ("the world of others") and remain a non-man. As *The Stone Face* comes to a close, Maria, preparing for a film career, thinks to herself, "Acting would mean a metamorphosis, it would wipe out the past, destroy memories. There would be no little Jewish girl named Maria who had been profaned by a monster in a concentration camp" (184). While Maria's acting is dismissed as a mere role, Simeon's "act" is also acting, a metamorphosis facilitated by playing a role, as he imitates the revolutionary violence of his admired Algerian friends. Before the night of protests, Simeon observes that the expatriates in Paris, himself included, "lived in a fantasy.... They were not involved in current realities in France just as they were not involved in what was happening in their native countries" (175). Simeon's defense of the woman and child indicates that he no longer lives in such a fantasy, that he has become engaged in current realities. The relationship between Simeon and the French policeman is not exactly the same, however, as that between master and slave or as that between the French and the Algerians, a difference in position that Simeon's asserted solidarity with the Algerians elides.

Bryant argues that Simeon's relationship with Ahmed and the Algerians brings him to a realization and discovery of a collective manhood, an "African tribal feeling" ("Individuality" 3). Simeon awakes from unconsciousness to find himself contained in another womblike space, the inside of a police van, his immersion into the world of the other figured here as quite literal, as he is buried beneath "a pile of bodies, some squirming and some inert" (Smith 204). Simeon is reborn from this pile—"he pushed his arms forward to try to open a path to air," a final emergence that initiates him into a new identity: "Most of the Algerians paid no particular attention to Simeon, but two or three glanced at him and smiled faintly, without surprise, '*Salud, frère,*' a man said. *Frère:* brother. Simeon smiled. '*Salud, mon frère*'" (204–5). Unlike such narratives of assimilation as *The Conquest* and *The Life and Adventures of Nat Love,* which detail their heroes' attempts to become part of "[white] men's relations with other [white] men" (Sedgwick 2), *The Stone Face* imagines the possibility of a new set of homosocial bonds between men of different oppressed groups—and imagines a black father whose look and address replaces the gaze and voice of the master, the white father who refuses to recognize the African American individual's value as a human being. By so doing, the novel posits the creation of a black patriarchy as a means of opposing white patriarchal and colonial society.[5] Smith does not, as Morrison does in *Paradise,* consider the possible negative consequences of such a social structure.

Although Smith's "African tribal feeling" posits an alternative to the structures of white patriarchy, he fails to imagine a method of protest and political activism that would include women as active, knowing subjects as well. His novel at moments entertains the possibility of disrupting such binary oppositions as male/female and black/white through the relationship between Simeon and Maria, but Smith seems unable to reconcile feminine aspects of identity with the masculine ideal. Maria, in a sense, functions like Molly in Wister's *The Virginian.* As Molly tries to prevent the Virginian's showdown with Trampas, so Maria tries to convince Simeon to escape confrontation for a life of domestic happiness. As indicated by his defense of the woman and child, Simeon believes, like Cooper's Natty Bumppo, that "Men are'n't apt to see females in danger, and not come to their assistance" (95). Simeon's action is linked not only to a manly defense of a woman in danger but also to the greater cause of the collective fight against oppression, to the higher principles of political and social justice that are secondary to manly honor as justifications for violence in *The Virginian* and *The Deerslayer.* In the end, however, women in *The Stone Face* function as objects of exchange between men—for Simeon's relationship with the Algerians is facilitated by his acting to protect the woman and child, who having served their purpose disappear from the narrative, leaving only Simeon and the other men, his brothers. The critique of such homosocial bonding, even in support of a progressive cause, that we see in Hopkins's *Winona* and Morrison's *Paradise* is absent from *The Stone Face.*

Simeon's assertions of "at oneness" with the Algerians actually are often accompanied by scenes that call into question that unity. In the discussion of Turner's summary of frontier transformation I note that, in the process of becoming "a new product that is American," something essential (a particular quality of masculinity) is transferred to the colonist from the American Indian. Having passed along that quality, the American Indian simply disappears from Turner's account of American history. For Turner, the essential element of the American Indian (his primitive masculinity) remains, incorporated into—and thereby enabling the evolution of—the white American man. We might note a similar transference between Simeon and his double, Ahmed, who likewise disappears from the narrative, his offstage death occurring nearly simultaneously with Simeon's own violent entry into the symbolic. Ahmed's essential masculinity remains, incorporated into and thereby enabling Simeon's evolution. If Smith draws on frontier mythology in constructing his story, he also repeats a problematic element of both Turner's and Roosevelt's versions of the myth. The hero's emergence as a new man seems to turn on the death and/or disappearance of the savage other.

At the end of the novel, Simeon's asserted masculine identity is acknowledged by the address of the Algerians, but he is only "passing," as is indicated by his ability to act out a choice denied to the Algerians—he leaves the compound where they are imprisoned. The French administrators do not recognize Simeon's brotherhood: "That's right, you can go. You're not Algerian" (209). Simeon "was astonished to have gotten off so easily, and felt guilty as the guard led him across the stadium floor before the eyes of the Algerians" (209). As a guest in France, Simeon enjoys some of the privileges of the master/father, one of those privileges being his ability to act violently without fear of reprisal. Whereas Simeon's violent act resolves the dilemma of his double identity by eliding the difference between him and the Algerians, the French administrator reintroduces the questions that Simeon believes his actions have answered. I noted earlier Bryant's observation that

Smith rejects in his later novels "the literature of black social protest begun by Richard Wright" ("Individuality" 2). This rejection is in a sense symbolized by the opposition between two types of violence that Smith sets up in *The Stone Face*—the "irrational" violence based on "an instant of illusion" (55) that Simeon is in danger of committing in America; and the violent act he does commit in France, an act based not on illusion but on the fact that "the reality had penetrated" (213). In a sense, Smith begs the question here. Simeon's position in France ("neither" and "both") allows him to act without retaliation from French officials—a position unattainable for Wright's characters in books such as *Uncle Tom's Children* and *Native Son*.

Simeon's journey to the frontier is followed by his return to civilization, to engage with rather than escape from the social situation in America and to find the sense of freedom and identity he asserts he has found in France but perhaps has not. At the end of *The Stone Face* Smith writes: "Where would he go? He asked himself the question though he knew the inevitable answer. . . . Back to the States—not because he liked it, not because his antipathy to that country and its people had changed, not because he felt any less anger or bitterness or frustration at the mere thought of living there again, but because . . . America's Algerians were back there, fighting a battle harder than that of any guerrillas in any burnt mountains. Fighting the stone face" (210). Simeon's journey to Europe echoes a similar overseas trip described in the "Twenty-one Months in Great Britain" chapter of Douglass's second autobiography, *My Bondage and My Freedom* (1855). A change in geography for Douglass as well as for Simeon results in a shift in the way others treat him. Douglass notes that when he boards ship in America his movements are carefully restricted, but "In two days after leaving Boston, one part of the ship was about as free to me as another" (223). In England, Douglass writes, "I seem to have undergone a transformation. I live a new life" (225). "In the southern part of the United States," Douglass writes, "I was a slave, thought of and spoken of as property," and in the North, "a fugitive slave, liable to be hunted at any moment" (226). In England, though, "I breathe, and lo! the chattel becomes a man" (226). "I employ a cab," Douglass writes, and "I am seated beside white people—I reach the hotel—I enter the same door—I am shown into the same parlor—I dine at the same table—and no one is offended" (226).

Douglass closes his chapter with a return to a ship heading for America and a return to racial restrictions. His first-class cabin is given to someone else; he is moved to a cramped berth in the stern of the ship and "denied the right to enter the [shipboard] saloon, lest my dark presence should be deemed an offense to some of my democratic fellow-passengers" (239). Although Douglass returns to a world of racial restrictions, his status in American society has been fundamentally changed by his trip. Friends in England (against his stated wishes) have collected money and bought his freedom during his stay. If, in his own mind, Douglass left America a free man, his sense of his own humanity was not legally recognized. Under the system of slavery, he remained designated as property. His trip to England results in a change in that status, a legal transformation from property into humanity. Simeon's transformation in *The Stone Face* is more akin to the one in Douglass's *Narrative* of 1845, symbolic rather than legal, one that takes place within his own mind, perhaps at an unconscious level. Simeon's experience opens up for him a new understanding of oppression, one that allows him to move physically and psychologically beyond national boundaries. His willingness to be critical of his own sense of frontier freedom may also indicate a fundamental change in his character, a remaking of his sense of self at an unconscious level. If Bob Jones in *If He Hollers* remains frustrated by his inability to confront the other, the "whole structure of American thought," perhaps Simeon Brown discovers a potential solution to that dilemma—by confronting the white father, the symbolic figure of the white master, in the place where he does the most damage, inside Simeon's own mind.

CHAPTER 6

The Frontier Myth and Metaphors of Vision in *The Man Who Cried I Am*

John A. Williams's *The Man Who Cried I Am* (1967) is the story of the radicalization of Max Reddick. The novel follows Max's early struggles to become a writer, his success as a novelist and the first African American correspondent for a major American newsmagazine, and his eventual exposure of a government plan (named the King Alfred Plan) targeting people of African descent. King Alfred is the American contribution to a group called Alliance Blanc, a coalition of European nations joined with the United States and created in response to growing African independence movements. Alliance Blanc, Williams writes, rose out of white fears that "all of Africa might one day unite" (*Man* 364). If "there were a United States of Africa, a cohesiveness among the peoples . . . should not Europeans anticipate the possibility of trouble?" (364).[1] In anticipation of such trouble, the King Alfred Plan proposes the elimination of the black race. Although doing so causes his own violent death, Max leaks the existence of the King Alfred Plan to Minister Q (a fictionalized version of Malcolm X). Max Reddick hopes to revolutionize other African Americans by demonstrating that

"all the new moves" made by the American government—the
New Frontier, the Great Society—"to gain democracy for them
were fraudulent" (368). Knowledge of the existence of the King
Alfred Plan would make African Americans realize that the one
alternative left "would be not only to seek that democracy with-
held from them as quickly and violently as possible, but to fight
for their very survival" (368).

The structure of *The Man Who Cried I Am* is complex, shifting back and forth from past to present as Williams narrates the
story of Max Reddick's life. In the present the story takes place
in a twenty-four-hour period in 1965, as Max, dying of rectal
cancer, has traveled to Europe to visit a friend, fellow writer
Harry Ames, one last time. The narrative begins in Amsterdam,
where we learn in a flashback that Ames has died in Paris, under
mysterious circumstances. In the present the novel moves geo-
graphically from Amsterdam to Leiden, where Max travels by
car to meet Ames's mistress who, at Ames's instructions, passes
on to Max a briefcase containing the King Alfred manuscript.
During these twenty-four hours, we are taken through Max's
consciousness as he meditates on the last thirty years of his life.
We are shown his early struggles and subsequent successes, his
time spent with an all-black army division in World War II, his
trips to Europe and Africa, his many sexual relationships and
his two main romances—the first with Lillian Patch, a middle-
class black woman, that ends with her tragic death; the second
an interracial marriage to Margrit Westoever, a white Dutch
woman, that eventually disintegrates under the pressure of
white racism in America.

He also forms relationships with fictionalized versions of
important historical figures of the era, including fellow novelists Harry Ames (Richard Wright) and Marion Dawes (James
Baldwin), civil rights leaders and black activists Paul Durrell
(Martin Luther King) and Minister Q (Malcolm X), and an
unnamed president of the United States modeled after John F.

Kennedy.[2] Max himself is based primarily on novelist Chester Himes, although Williams draws on his own experiences as a journalist and fiction writer in constructing his protagonist. In Max's travels he participates in such historical moments as World War II and as a reporter observes such historical occurrences as lynchings in the southern United States, the boycotts and marches of the civil rights era, as well as the growing independence movement in Africa during the 1950s and 1960s. Literary history and political history intersect throughout the novel. CIA agents follow the movements of Harry and Max. Expatriate writers Alphonse Edwards and Roger Wilkinson are revealed to be secret CIA operatives. As public events invade and disrupt personal relationships in the novel, so racial politics permeates the literary world, as revealed most clearly by the retraction of a literary fellowship won by Harry Ames, an event in the novel based on an incident in Williams's own life.[3]

As Smith does in *The Stone Face,* Williams writes in a context informed by both black activism in the United States and independence movements in Africa. The optimism for the future that we see at the end of *The Stone Face* is tempered by the historical events that preceded the writing of Williams's novel—escalating racial tension and violence, including the murders of three civil rights demonstrators in Mississippi in 1964; riots in Los Angeles resulting in thirty deaths, more murders of civil rights activists, and the assassination of Malcolm X in 1965; extensive rioting in Cleveland, Atlanta, and other cities in 1966. As Smith does early in *The Stone Face,* Williams documents the struggles of his hero to attain a masculine identity in a racist society. Although Max's attempts to gain entry into the white publishing world are consistently rebuffed early in his life, the Supreme Court's 1954 desegregation decision opens slightly the previously closed world of American publishing, and Max Reddick finds himself in "one of the citadels of white power" as "a pioneer, a 'first Negro first,'" when he lands a job as the first

African American correspondent for *Pace* magazine (240–41). This job creates other opportunities for Max—journeys to Europe and Africa, two geographical spaces that the novel represents as potential African American frontiers. In Europe Max finds, as Simeon did in *The Stone Face,* a sense of freedom denied him in America—symbolized in both books by an interracial romance. The primary first contact in *The Stone Face* is between two men, Simeon and Ahmed, representatives of two cultures and geographies, African American and Algerian Arab, America and Africa. Although Max also has contact with individual Africans, his primary encounter is with the otherness of African culture, or more precisely with African history. The change in consciousness brought about by this first contact with Africa and African history enables Max to begin to uncover the hidden history of the present—the existence of the Alliance Blanc and the King Alfred Plan.

Both *The Stone Face* and *The Man Who Cried I Am* are existential parables, with the main plot involving the individual's commitment to a particular act, a choice freely and rationally made. Both writers emphasize clarity of vision, for it is only when their characters can "see precisely" that they can make a free choice. In neither book is freedom from racism a goal in and of itself. Such freedom is important only when it allows the character to achieve his manhood and then confront the very racism he initially escapes. John M. Reilly argues:

> This bleak and remarkable novel shows us that, to escape becoming victims of history, we must neither leave history unquestioned nor relate it as inevitable. Politics may be oppressive, but in the act of narration politics becomes subject to will and knowledge and inventive craft. Strictly speaking, of course, history is not a text, neither a master text such as the King Alfred Plan nor even a masterfully conceived novel such as

The Man Who Cried I Am. Still history becomes accessible only through texts; it is the absent cause of fictions. . . . To know history, then, we must act as we read and write, with the same creative force and imagination that produce narrative. (40)

Max's final choice in the novel is an act of narration, through which he hopes to intervene in the political history of the moment by revealing the conspiracy of Alliance Blanc. As Max thinks at one point, "What wouldn't they do, the white folks, to keep you from having a history, the better, after all, to protect theirs" (223). Muller argues that more insidious than the genocidal King Alfred Plan is the history "manipulated and written by Western powers," for this writing of history represents a form of "cultural genocide" that deprives oppressed people of their own history "and consequently of their identity" (82). Smith personifies racial violence through the image of the stone face; Williams figures racial violence in a more discursive form—in the violence of history itself, especially as that history is made accessible through texts that represent a white point of view.

Shooting Straight, Seeing Precisely

Yes, but you are not seeing precisely. I am an abomination. Ugly, black, cutting back on my thoughts so I wouldn't embarrass people, being superbly brilliant for the right people. I was born seeing precisely, Mr. Reddick. There were times when I chose to. Death, for example. . . . By my acts I decided how I would die. But those acts had more in them. This world is an illusion, Mr. Reddick, but it can be real. I went prowling on the jungle side of the road where few people ever go. —Williams, *The Man Who Cried I Am*

I am an invisible man. No, I am not a spook like those who haunted Edgar Allan Poe; nor am I one of your Holly-wood-movie ectoplasms. I am a man of substance, of flesh and bone, fiber and liquids—and I might even be said to possess a mind. I am invisible, understand, simply because people refuse to see me.

That invisibility to which I refer occurs because of a pecu-liar disposition of the eyes of those with whom I come in contact. A matter of the construction of their inner eyes, those eyes with which they look through their physical eyes upon reality.   —ELLISON, *Invisible Man*

In the first meeting of Max Reddick and Harry Ames at a party shortly after the publication of Max's first book, Ames good-naturedly engages Max in a shooting contest: "Max rec-ognized the challenge. The people would be sympathetic if he missed. Even Ames. The comparison would be obvious. It might even carry to the writing of novels" (*Man* 40–41). As Wil-liams signifies on the frontier myth in general, he also com-ments specifically on the hunter archetype. Max is masterful with the rifle, his skill and wilderness awareness placing him in a long line of frontier heroes in American literature, from Natty Bumppo to Ike McCaslin. Max's wilderness skills, revealed not only in the shooting competition with Harry Ames but also in several hunting scenes dispersed throughout the novel, set up a sharp contrast between Max and Wright's short story charac-ters such as Big Boy and Dave Saunders. Whereas the violence of those characters was often accidental and unskilled, Max's violence is carefully controlled, calculated, and skillfully ac-complished, whether shooting at a tin can, leading a party of soldiers during World War II in Italy, or hunting deer.

Shortly after his return from World War II, Max joins Harry Ames for a hunting trip. In the middle of a conversation, "they turned to watch the buck break out of the brush" (92). Williams writes, "adrenaline pumping suddenly through their bodies, their rifles swinging up, they sighted." As in the earlier scene in which Harry and Max matched skills with the rifle, Max again prevails: "Harry Ames, too long away from a rifle and the woods, hesitated for just the small part of a second as he started to lead the deer in his sights" (92). Harry observes out of the corner of his eye "Max leading the dear at the height of its second bound, heard his rifle crack sharply . . . and saw life go out of the buck," as Max's keen sight and quick reflexes enable him to shoot the deer straight through the heart (93).

Important to *The Man Who Cried I Am* (as it is to *The Stone Face* and to *If He Hollers*) is a figuration of and play on metaphors of vision, especially as a means of representing assertions of subjectivity and as a means of articulating power relationships between individual characters. In this hunting scene Max becomes a "deerslayer" because of his ability, like Natty Bumppo's, to sight and dispatch his prey quickly. The moment of violence in Cooper's *The Deerslayer* when Natty Bumppo first kills a man leads to a moment of transformation and rebirth for the hero in which he receives a new name and identity. Violent skill is intimately related to vision, to Natty Bumppo's "sartain eye" (he becomes Hawkeye after all, not Lightningfinger). The gun is an extension of the "eye," a symbolic representation of the subject's power.

In *The Man Who Cried I Am* Williams plays on the connection between "I" and "eye," representing Max's hunting ability not so much as a display of heroic skills as a symbolic assertion of self in a racist society that denies his subjectivity. Williams articulates in visual metaphors the sense of new power and sense of self that Max enjoys upon the publication of his second novel. Max thinks to himself, "There was nothing quite like success, American Negro writer Harry Ames, nothing quite like it. It means that you stare at the cops just as long as they stare at you and a host of other things, right, Harry?" (89). Earlier in the book, as Max interviews convicted murderer Moses Boatwright in his prison cell, he experiences a "stab of fear" as the prison door locks behind him, "just as he did whenever he saw a policeman and the cop put that extra something into his casual stare. Perhaps it was that the look carried a threat, a menace" (54). The casual stare of the police officer objectifies Max Reddick, marking him as the racial object of the policeman's subjective gaze: "Black boy, I could have you whenever I wanted to, it said, that look" (54). The figure of the policeman represents the cultural and political authority of the dominant culture, and his "casual stare" encodes the power to enforce through acts of violence the limitations placed on black subjectivity.

For Max, the casual stare of the police officer renders him in a sense invisible. It turns him into an object, a black boy. His success in the field of the verbal (as a novelist) allows him to assert himself in the field of the visual, to return the gaze of the police officer and oppose the racial identity constructed for him by that gaze. To *look* is not only to see but to force the other into seeing as well, into acknowledging the gaze of another subject; to look is to become visible. The importance of Max's "sartain eye" goes beyond the physical act of sighting a rifle, as "seeing precisely" in the novel has more to do with uncovering hidden truths than with violent skill. As Bryant notes, the acts of "discovery" and "revelation" are repeated motifs in the novel ("Williams" 93). Max's ability to "see precisely" enables visual acts of discovery that in turn lead to verbal acts of revelation and narration. The various hunts in *The Man Who Cried I Am*—for jobs, for success, for the truth—ultimately find their object in the text of the King Alfred Plan. The woodland hunts in *The Man Who Cried I Am* prefigure and symbolize the novel's primary hunt, which takes place in a more tangled wilderness, the history of racial politics.

Through Williams's use of the term *black boy* here and his references to Richard Wright throughout the book, he plays on the coming to consciousness that Wright narrates in *Black Boy* (1940) and other works. As JanMohamed notes regarding Wright's autobiography, the Jim Crow culture of the South "not only expects [Wright] to follow the rules but to internalize them until he becomes totally resigned to the prevailing distribution of power" (117). This process of internalizing the dominant culture's limited view of the minority individual's subjectivity appears most explicitly in *The Man Who Cried I Am* through the voice of Saminone (or Sam I None), a character who exists only within Max's consciousness. In one of the scenes of internal dialogue between Max and Saminone, Max asserts, "I am. I am a man." Saminone replies, "Know what youse is? Wanna know? Youse a stone blackass nigger" (187). Earlier in the novel Williams writes that Harry Ames "no longer believed, as they had taught him and his father and his father's father, that he was a nigger" (138). In America, despite Harry's beliefs, voices both black and white, internal and external, continue to tell him that he is "a nigger"; to escape those voices, he leaves for Europe. In one of the many parallels between Max and Harry, Max also must face the voices that tell him he is "a nigger," including the voice that lives inside his own consciousness.

Williams also demonstrates the deforming effect of the dominant culture on the formation of African American subjectivity through the figure of murderer Moses Boatwright, who "was a cannibal even though a graduate of Harvard" (52). As a reporter for the *Harlem Democrat,* Max interviews Boatwright, who has been convicted of killing—and then eating "the heart and the balls" of—a white man, a crime for which he is eventually executed. Ames suggests that he turn the material into a novel, one that would provide the "other side of the coin to my last book" (61). Unlike Bigger Thomas in Wright's *Native Son,* Boatwright represents a black man from a middle-class background, educated and bright, but with "New pressures. New disappointments, frustrations. Hope, but after all, no hope. Right, Max?" (61).[4] Boatwright recognizes the deforming effects of white racism, and he chooses to reveal that recognition by internalizing and manifesting through his actions the image that white racism has created of the black man, as a monster, subhuman, perverse. Moses Boatwright wishes to "see precisely." Like Boatwright, Max's existential act will be to choose his own death. However, as a model for Max's own actions, Boatwright is a cautionary one. His actions are irrational. They are directed against individuals at random and do nothing to change the structure of racism that creates individuals such as Bigger Thomas and Boatwright himself. Through his actions, he creates a text to be read, directed at the white audience that victimized him. Boatwright's acts may have revealed the world as an illusion, but his death and his actions do little to change white perceptions of the truth. Only Max and Harry see and read Boatwright's actions correctly. Boatwright signifies resistance through acts of physical violence, whereas Max—like Harry Ames and Richard Wright himself—will resist through a different discursive strategy, through the writing of fiction, through the act of narration.

It is Harry who articulates for Max the existence of the closed frontier for black men, and who advises Max on how the discovery of that denied opportunity influences—or should influence—the black writer's acts of revelation: "In our society which is white . . . there has got to be something inherently horrible about having the sicknesses and weaknesses of that society described by a person who is a victim of them; for if he, the victim, is capable of describing what they have believed nonexistent, then they, the members of the majority, must choose between living the truth, which can be pretty grim, and the lie, which isn't much better. But at least they will then have the choice" (49). Max Reddick and Harry Ames represent two methods of resisting through writing the black boy identity that preexists them. Harry tells Max that "Your job is to tell those people to stop lying, not only to us, but to themselves" (50). By describing the sicknesses and weaknesses of that society from the perspective of a person who has been victimized by those weaknesses, Harry wishes to place whites in a position of making a choice, of living an illusion or living the truth. What Harry wants to make visible is the process of objectification that creates black boys. If the narrator of Ellison's *Invisible Man* recognizes that there is a flaw in the inner vision of white people, Harry Ames argues that the black writer's job is to correct that flaw. Williams argues for a different kind of visibility, one that is not based on describing objectification but based on looking back—on returning and thereby resisting the objectifying gaze.

A Frontier Denied

While Max notes after World War II that "being a man was still tied to being at war" (*Man* 78), that sense of manhood is called into question when he returns from the war—as is highlighted by his tragic relationship with Lillian Patch, in 1946. Early in the novel, Max is described as a "bit petit bourgeois" (120). With his middle-class background, "Reddick never knew, except in passing through them and reporting on them, the horror of the ghettoes Ames had known. Nor had Reddick, except for his time in the Army, really known the oozing horror of being a Negro in the South" (120). Before Max is able to uncover the large-scale political conspiracy of Alliance Blanc, he must discover the closed frontier that American society represents for the black individual. Through his 1946 relationship with Lillian Patch, Max attempts to act out a masculine identity that Williams argues is denied the black man, that of patriarch, the man who finds his sense of self in the workplace by providing for his family. He cannot find a job, however, and his inability to play out his chosen role leads to increasing anger and frustration: "Max Reddick was evil. He wanted to punch out every white face he saw. Evil was beyond anger" (106).

Personal relationships, Max learns, provide no escape from racism, as racial politics invade and disrupt private life. Max's attempt at constructing a masculine identity for himself through his relationship with Lillian only reveals more precisely how that subject position is denied, a fact underscored by Lillian's death as the result of an illegal abortion she undergoes when it becomes clear that Max will not find a job. As Max observes, Lillian's values are those of a dominant white culture that gave her "the photograph, the image of the American Family Group, but when she looked very, very closely, she wasn't in it" (116). Lillian wants to make her life like the image in the photograph, to claim for herself the very values inculcated as the norm by white culture at the same time that white society denies black Americans access to that ideal. Her inability to achieve that ideal forces her to choose abortion rather than to raise a child in impoverished circumstances, a decision that results in her death. At the same time as Williams protests the racist conditions that cause Lillian's death, the relationship between Max and Lillian is represented ambivalently in the novel, as a trap. Max abandons novel-writing in order to seek more stable and traditionally-middle class employment. Harry views her critically, noting that "Max is still hurting for that girl and a good job. Marriage. By now he may know what kind of marriage it would be. Nothing wrong with the girl, except that she can't do Max no good. All she sees is a house with a white picket fence, a refrigerator and a washing machine" (106). Fictional literary critic Bernard Zutkin observes that the "reality of his girl's death might be good for him," might make him a better writer by ripping "the last ragged curtain of illusion from Reddick" (120). Lillian's death becomes a means to an end for the male protagonist, a ripping away of an illusion that prevents Max from "seeing precisely."

After Lillian's death, Max thinks to himself: "I'll never forgive them. Never. And they don't even know what they did! *They don't even know!* He felt a rage growing within him, small at first, like the cyclone on the horizon, and then it came spinning up, blacker and redder, faster and faster" (116). Desire in the novel—especially as that desire is manifested in the form of rage—is channeled and focused through triangular configurations, as it is in both *The Stone Face* and Douglass's *Narrative.* Symbolic battles between master and slave hinge on a female figure whose presence enables the male protagonist to enter into the triangular relationship in the preexisting position of the father, filling the father's role as the patriarchal protector of the woman and/or child. Missing from the triangle of desire at this early point in *The Man Who Cried I Am* is an embodiment of the white father/master. As in *If He Hollers* the father/master exists as an omnipresent figure who circulates everywhere but only in the inaccessible and disembodied form of the "them" that Max will never forgive. Max's desire, his undirected anger, remains unfocused, "spinning up, blacker and redder, faster and faster" (116).

Despite his growing rage, Max realizes that such a violent reaction would make him just another victim of white racism, another Moses Boatwright whose protest ends not with freedom but with death. Max directs his violence inward, where it reemerges in the form of rectal cancer: "He was sure of one thing: that he was; that he existed. The pain in his ass told him so" (18). Like the racial attack that leaves Simeon blind in one eye, Max's cancer is a mutilation of his body that signifies the limitations placed on his subjectivity. Like Simeon's eye patch, Max Reddick's eventual success as a writer masks his hurt and rage. Despite Max's mask of success, his cancer—the pain, the physical odor of sickness and decay that accompanies him— returns as a consistent reminder. The physical injuries endured by the black male protagonists of *The Stone Face* and Hopkins's

Winona symbolize the psychic damage caused by living in a racist society. Whereas Smith and Hopkins represent the possibility of recuperation from these injuries, Max's cancer is terminal.

New Frontiers

The years following Lillian's death are marked by Max's increased alcoholism and eventually by the continuation of his career as a novelist. Early in the 1950s, he finds a job with the *Century,* a liberal Jewish newspaper, a job that contributes to his education by sending him to the southern United States where he witnesses and reports on lynchings and racial unrest. In the wake of the Supreme Court's 1954 integration decision, Max begins working at *Pace* and becomes "the first Negro hired by a major news magazine" (249), and this position leads to other opportunities. The president of the United States, upon the recommendation of literary critic Bernard Zutkin, offers Max a job as an advisor and speechwriter. Zutkin believes that hiring a black man "to help the President speak" represents a history-making moment (290). Through the president, "Max's words would at least now have voice" (291). Max is less certain. He remembers that he had not liked Washington on his last trip there, as Jim Crow had been virulent in the nation's capital at the time (296). He does hope that the administration of the unnamed (but clearly modeled after Kennedy) president will indeed provide a "new frontier" for racial relations, and he optimistically observes upon his arrival that "because of the President," this "Washington was new indeed" (297). The continuity between the old Washington and the new is soon revealed when the Civil War Centennial Commission announces it will "maintain segregated facilities for the observances of the celebrations" (299). Max writes a speech on the subject of the centennial, certain that "the President would take some action" in the face of segregation in his own city (299).

Max, in spite of himself, enters Washington with the hope that this president will be different, but he learns that "Washington's determined look . . . [was] misleading," that the hand "was quicker than the eye," and although the eye "was drawn to the radiant faces which beamed back so much good will," one had to watch "the hands that were busily engaged in the shell game" (307). The president tells Max "to behave as though civil rights is our most urgent problem," to write "what you think about it," but his administration is continually preoccupied with other issues such as Yury Gagarin's first human space flight or the failed invasion of Cuba (303). In the wake of the Freedom Rides South and rioting in Montgomery, Alabama, Max finds himself "awaiting the summons [from the President] that never came" (307). After discovering the president's efforts to keep a young black student, William MacKendrick, from entering the University of Mississippi, a disillusioned Max resigns. Whereas Zutkin hoped that the president would provide Max with a voice, Max observes at the end of his four-month tenure that "I helped to write not one speech" (315).

Max discovers in Europe a new physical terrain where he enjoys freedom from the racial restrictions imposed by America, a place where African Americans could "be just people, which would be all right for a change" (228). Europe, for Max, also provides the possibility of a first encounter with whiteness. There he would find "White people, sure, but maybe a different kind of white people" (156). Max's European freedom is symbolized most explicitly by his relationship with and eventual marriage to a white Dutch woman, Margrit Westoever. Williams like Smith in *The Stone Face* initially rearticulates the frontier myth's Metropolis/Wilderness opposition in terms of America/Europe. As a frontier, however, Max discovers that Europe is already compromised, already embroiled and implicated in the history of racial politics. The novel's first setting is Amsterdam, where Max sits waiting for Margrit "three hundred forty-five years after" the first Dutch slave ship sailed from that city into Jamestown (4). While Max's eventual marriage to Margrit represents a reconciliation in the present between the descendants of those early Dutch and African actors on the historical stage, this personal relationship will eventually prove unable to bear the burden of resisting the racial politics set in motion centuries before.

Max meets Margrit in 1958, many years after Lillian's death, and at the same time that he has been assigned to *Pace*'s newly opened African desk. When we first see him, he is in a cafe in Amsterdam, waiting to meet Margrit, whom he has not seen in a number of months. In the last pages of the novel, after Max has been murdered, we see Margrit in the same cafe, waiting for his return. In between, the story of their courtship, marriage, and eventual estrangement provides an important counterpoint to the other events in the novel. Marriage is an act both personal and political, one that challenges and disrupts the boundaries set by racist discourse. Through his relationship with Margrit, Max enters into a different kind of relationship with white people or at least recognizes the possibility of such relations.

He hopes that Africa might provide a hospitable and enabling space for their relationship.[5] On a plane from Africa to Amsterdam, after deciding that he will ask Margrit to marry him, Max imagines life with her in Africa: "He could see her already, topping the foaming, hissing surf at Tarkwa Bay, vanishing for an instant beneath the monstrous blue waves and then emerging with a steady pink stroke, coming on toward the ivory-colored beach" (339). Max "thought of them together, skin against skin, mind to mind, of her whispered words of barely muted awe (for there *was* all of history and distance, the displacement of old values that been overcome)" (339). As the name Margrit Westoever implies, the hoped for relationship is "ever west," on a frontier that is always tenuous and disappearing.[6] Even in the midst of Max's Edenic vision of life in Africa with Margrit, he thinks to himself, "Later, of course, there would be America" (339).

In New York, after they are married, Margrit "kissed him suddenly on a corner where many people were milling around a newsstand for their papers. He (she felt it keenly, like a rebuke) submitted, but they walked on in silence until he said, 'Maggie, for Christ's sake, I don't like to be kissed on the street'" (350–51). In St. Thomas, on vacation, Max surprises her by kissing her in public. That night, however, in a bar, Max "tipped the table getting up quickly, breaking the top of his glass and wheeling on a group of American sailors with it in a single, frightening motion" (352). Later, in a Puerto Rican bar, Margrit notices Max observing a drunk American, "and she just started to understand that Max was watching the American, waiting for him to make a move" (352–53). Margrit realizes that she is in the middle of a battle between Max and these white men, and she recognizes as well, at least subconsciously, that she is involved in a battle over the kind of man Max is going to become, whether he will be the man she married in Europe, a man with a loving gaze, or a man whose eyes "she did not know" (353). In this instance, Margrit successfully intercedes, convincing Max through a silent but "agonizingly long instant when their eyes met" to leave the room and the potential fight behind (353). Williams writes that Margrit "knew if they did not make love that night, the morning would be unpleasant. . . . for she wanted him to know in the fullest way that white could love black and did, and they both sensed that the drunk American downstairs had to be erased with love" (353). Still, the drunk American, or the racism he represents, cannot be permanently erased, as racial politics will continue to invade their relationship. As do Winona's actions in Hopkins's novel, Margrit's intervention in a conflict between the black hero and the white villain prevents excessive male violence. *The Man Who Cried I Am,* however, ultimately rejects feminine values— the heart to forgive as represented by Winona, the power of love as represented by Margrit.

Through marriage to a white woman, Max believes, he will lose his "black anonymity" and end the "*boyhood* that came with being Negro" (339). The "old myths goaded by hatreds would make him highly visible," would put his manhood "on the line as never before, for now it would always be challenged," and "he would become *recreated* as a Negro in the process" (339). In the battle scenes that follow their marriage, Max's desire—the rage that earlier was undirected or internalized—is focused through a series of triangular configurations involving himself, Margrit, and white American men such as sailors in nightclubs or drunks in bars. Max's visibility depends on Margrit's presence, for her whiteness forces the white other to see and consider Max's challenge. As Williams's language here explicitly refers to Ellison's invisibility trope, it also plays on Douglass's scene of re-creation—his movement from slave-hood to manhood via his battle with Mr. Covey. Although Williams places Max repeatedly in situations reminiscent of Douglass's scene of transfiguration, the proliferation of these battles indicates that they ultimately do not satisfy his desire for a confrontation with otherness—that on some level Max real-izes that these individuals are merely markers in a larger game and that the player who pushes the pieces in the game remains out of reach.

These various battles also indicate the difficulty of locating an African American frontier, a geography free from American racial attitudes and oppression. America, Max discovers, seems to be everywhere on the globe. The scenario of transfiguration articulated by Douglass fails to provide Max with a means to symbolize a sense of manhood achieved. The hunting ritual of the frontier myth likewise remains closed. For Roosevelt, defeating the savage other in battle enables the civilized white man to acquire the other's primitive masculinity and thus facilitates his own evolution into a new man. During the hunt, the hunter becomes like the beast but only in order to prove his superior status by emerging the victor in the battle. As in Himes's *If He Hollers* those moments when Max believes he acts as the hunter—as in the Puerto Rican bar when he essentially reduces Margrit to functioning as bait to entice the drunk American into making a move—are perhaps his moments of greatest self-delusion. While Max seems to be the author of his own actions, he is himself baited by these white figures to act out the role already assigned to him, that of the violent black man whose irrational, animalistic acts prove him to be not the civilized hunter but the savage beast. Margrit intervenes to save him, and to demonstrate that he can play an alternative role, that of a man who loves rather than a man who hates. Max, however, remains pessimistic about the possibility of escaping to a space where such a role can be enacted. Ultimately, *The Man Who Cried I Am* (as does *The Stone Face*) presents the argument that—even if possible—to make such an escape would be to remain in the imaginary and to reject the risk of engagement with representatives of the symbolic order. It would be to accept one's "place in the world of others" along with the limitations inherent in that place.

Masculine identity in *The Man Who Cried I Am* is represented as a series of choices made by Max Reddick. In his relationship with Margrit, he bases his sense of self on his ability to love someone else. To a certain extent his marriage to Margrit represents his attempt to live out the patriarchal ideal he was denied in his relationship with Lillian Patch. There are moments in the novel, however, when the relationship between Max and Margrit represents the possibility of something new. In the face of increasing white violence against blacks in the 1960s, Max turns away from that possibility to a more traditional masculine identity—as indicated in the novel by his obsession with phallic signifiers. Max marks his first wedding anniversary by buying a new rifle to add to his growing collection (354). Mark A. Reid argues that while Max Reddick fights against white patriarchy he is "unable to consider the desires and needs of the two women he loves," is unable to recognize his complicity in the very patriarchy he opposes (58). As a consequence, Reid argues, "Lillian's death and Margrit's return to Holland move Max to a . . . form of resistance that prevents gender equity and transracial intimacy" (58). What is lost in this move is the possibility of imagining masculinity—and of imagining resistance to the narrative of white patriarchal history—otherwise.

Homosexuality as an alternative masculine identity surfaces primarily in the form of homophobia, especially in Williams's unflattering portrayal of the Marion Dawes (James Baldwin) character. In the opposition between the novel's two white literary critics, the Jewish Bernard Zutkin and the homosexual Granville Bryant, Williams sets up for Max an opportunity to establish a cross-racial identification between African Americans and another oppressed group. Through his relationship with Zutkin, Max establishes an alliance (very often an uneasy one) between the histories of black and Jewish oppression. On the other hand Max's relationship with Bryant serves to deepen his suspicions of the critic's motives. Bryant is represented as the "Great White Father" who engineers literary success for those black writers (such as Dawes) who have sex with him, and Max keeps his distance, "for one was either in the Bryant camp or the Zutkin camp and he preferred the latter" (*Man* 39). In a dreamlike scene that occurs while Max is recovering from surgery, Bryant appears by Max's hospital bed, telling him the story of how homosexuals arrived on earth via a craft from another planet and began "mix[ing] with the populace" (189). Although they have been "hated, legislated against, harassed, made vulnerable," Bryant prophesies, they have "the power within their grasp" to take over and "improve the earth" (189–90). Homosexuals "too are outcasts" who have "a natural empathy for your people," Bryant asserts, an argument that Max rejects (190).

Williams nonetheless expresses a dissatisfaction with the masculine identity the novel ultimately privileges, a dissatisfaction most clearly exemplified by the relationship between Harry Ames and Max Reddick. Unlike Dave Saunders in Wright's "The Man Who Was Almost a Man," Max's "fathers" (ranging from Harry Ames to Minister Q to the white president) are not unskilled, are not marginal or nearly absent figures. Harry in particular serves as a model and teacher for Max, a figure who enables and assists Max's development as a writer and who also serves as Max's chief rival. At the end of the letter he sends to Max accompanying and explaining the King Alfred manuscript, Harry tells Max, "I suppose you're next in line to be father" (370). In Harry—in his competitiveness, his suspicion, his jealousy, his increasing isolation—Max sees the damage done by the masculine ideal, to Harry, to his relationships with his wife and with his friends. Both Harry and Max dislike but are nonetheless unable to change the competitiveness of their relationship, and both realize that competition results from a white power structure that continually compares black writers to each other and that practices a philosophy of "divide and conquer or, divide and pay less money for talent because everyone's scufflin' to get there" (104). While Max's observation of Harry does not prevent him from becoming very much like Harry, Max's understanding does enable him to interpret (and avoid repeating, himself) the complicated motives behind Harry's final act, passing on the briefcase containing the King Alfred Plan to Max.

The Only Frontier Left on the Globe

> *Africa. The continent had been like something you knew you had to buy or see or go to, but always forgot. . . . The Africans had kings and princes and great armies and wealth and culture. . . . The books in the Schomburg Collection up on 135th Street near Lenox also said as much. The Collection was some place. Every Negro feeling the toe of the world halfway up his ass could duck in there and read about how great Africa was and how great black people in general were, but few had done it. The white man's hate-self-serum had created a hard stale rind of disbelief.*
>
> —WILLIAMS, *The Man Who Cried I Am*

For the majority of the novel, Max's adventures seem to demonstrate the truth of Baker's observation that "all frontiers established by the white psyche have been closed to the black man" (*Long Black Song* 2). It is through his representation of Africa, a "bright new world," that Williams most clearly and explicitly reimagines the frontier from an African American perspective (*Man* 137). Africa is a frontier in the novel not only because it is unexplored territory for Max but also because of the contemporary changes taking place there. Harry Ames tells Max: "Can you imagine that? A free Africa. Big, rich, three hundred million people, untold wealth. Can't you see what will have to happen to the white man's politics? Africa, Max, I tell you, that's the only frontier left on the globe" (97). As African nations come into freedom and independence, they emerge on the world scene in the form of a first encounter. For the first time, diplomats from independent nations move back and forth from Africa to Europe and America. In Harlem, disbelief regarding African history gives way to "Black Fever," as Max observes "more and more Negroes in African dress—kentes, agbadas, shamas—these days without laughter" (262). The attraction to African dress represents a resistance to the "white man's hate-self-serum," an attempt to create a positive African identity in opposition to the negative images of Africa propagated by white culture, a negativity (the "hard stale rind of disbelief") internalized by the black psyche (97). In the mirror of Africa, African Americans begin to see a new model of blackness and of self-respect.

As in *The Stone Face,* Europe functions as a frontier between America and Africa, a space that enables the protagonist's first contact with the continent. Max "had come to [Africa] via Europe, passing from one ancient ruin to the next in growing, ill-concealed irritation, yet drawn inexplicably to the best of the white man in the past" (273). Williams writes: "Not until [Max] had climbed the hill to another ruin, the pyramids at Gizeh, *did he lose Europe* and begin to feel both the size and the un-plumbed history of Africa stretching out over the white sands behind the free tombs, stretching outward southward to Nubia, Cush, the Sudan" (274, emphasis mine). Williams writes that "Africa stunned Max," ridding him of the irritating influence of Europe (273). The expanse of land stretching before him is not virgin land or a tabula rasa but a text already written—if unread—by European civilization. As Minister Q states in a speech that Max covers for *Pace,* "We have a history, but no white man is going to reveal it" (251). Only by ridding himself of white images of Africa can Max come to see for himself that hidden history—and, as the head of *Pace's* West Africa desk, narrate that discovery. If the frontier represents for Turner "a gate of escape from the bondage of the past" (59), for Williams the African frontier represents both an escape and a return, a discovery of something new that is also a discovery of something old. The African frontier enables Max to escape not from history itself but from history as written from the point of view of white civilization.

Like California in Himes's *If He Hollers,* Africa represents for Max an opportunity to succeed in the workplace, to advance in his career from reporter to administrator, as the head of *Pace*'s West Africa desk. African independence "came as an unexpected boon" not only for Max but for African Americans working in U.S. agencies, "releasing them from the narrow alleys and dead ends of their careers back home into the Foreign Service. Just like many whites in the Service, they'd never had it so good, with cooks, houseboys, gardeners and drivers" (328–29). Williams notes the irony of the new status achieved by African Americans upon leaving the United States to live in other countries. Max himself hires a driver who calls him "Sir" and a houseboy who refers to him as "Mastuh." As Max observes, "'Mastuh,' then, was anyone who paid your salary whether black, white or red striped" (328). In Africa, Max falls on the side of the haves rather than the have-nots.

In *The Stone Face,* the ironic result of enjoying one's freedom is a loss of racial identity, a symbolic transformation into a white man. Simeon Brown ultimately resists that loss through identification with the Algerians. Max's response is more complex, as his journey to Africa results in his awareness of both his difference from and his similarity to the African people he meets. Williams casts a more critical eye on the projection of desire onto and identification with the image of the other than we have seen in frontier narratives from Turner to Smith. Through the African setting, Williams both reconfigures frontier mythology and critiques some of its more problematic elements. Although he retains the idea of a journey into the wilderness and an encounter with otherness as a means of self-transformation, he dismisses the civilized/savage dichotomy of Turner's thesis. Max discovers in the otherness of Africa not savagery but civilization, and one that is evolving and changing at that. Max discovers that postcolonial African identities are far from monolithic, that these identities emerge in part from desires created by the history of colonialism and in part by the past and present mixing of European and African cultures. Max notices "wig-wearing Bakongo girls" who had what "looked like a healthy hunk of African hair" but was really "a gob of synthetics" (331). Max observes Africans in the wake of colonialism engaged in creating for themselves an "authentic" African identity—one achieved, ironically, through artificial means. Whereas American blacks, according to Max, "had gone through that phase of disengagement with the white man's culture," Africans "were just getting the full effects of the European presence" (331–32). As a frontier space in the novel, Africa is not the furthest point of colonial incursion ("the meeting point between savagery and civilization") but the point of cultural contact where the complex processes of decolonization are taking place.

In Nigeria, Max observes a "new generation of Nigerians moving from farm, rain forest or desert to the hot pavement and reeking sewers of Lagos," where their contact with "the outside world" results in a complex mixing of various tribal and regional identities with American and European influences. Max sees in that mixture a potential revolution, as the "not having" of the Africans "would be underlined by contact from outside." This new generation of Nigerians "would be eventually a part of the inevitable revolt which all have-nots must begin" (325). One of Williams's accomplishments in this novel is to rearticulate the American concept of the frontier in a postcolonial context. By so doing, he anticipates the contemporary revision of the frontier we see in the critical work of Annette Kolodny, Arnold Krupat, and others, in which "the frontier is understood as simply that shifting space in which two *cultures* encounter one another" (Krupat 4–5). Max's journey to the

African frontier results in his discovery of just such an encounter between two cultures, two civilizations. The African other does not simply disappear. Contact initiates a dynamic process of change for both cultures, and a transformed Africa, Max believes, will eventually become a revolutionary Africa.

Simeon Brown in *The Stone Face* strongly identifies with Algerian culture, and his relationship with Ahmed and other Algerians elides the cultural and racial differences between African Americans and Algerian Arabs. Max Reddick's reaction to Africa is more ambivalent. For a long time, he is uncertain whether he likes or dislikes it. Recalling his journey, Max "suddenly knew why it had taken him so long to make up his mind: he had been setting aside the fact that most of the Africans he had met did not like black Americans" (*Man* 276). The Africans, Max notes, "who with their independent status preferred white diplomats, were not terribly happy about the Negroes" (331). Williams's African characters emerge as complex and imperfect individuals, and Williams carefully establishes that the Africa that appears in the novel is filtered through Max Reddick's impressions of a culture—and cultures, for Max's travels reveal the diversity of the African people—that are alien to him. His experiences in Africa highlight the fact that he is African American, that "nothing was farther from the truth" than the "black-being-compatible trap" (334). Having made this realization does not keep Max from the knowledge that "he was going back," that Africa nonetheless offers him something he can not find in America or Europe— history from a black perspective, a potential counter discourse to a Western history written by white powers (276). As is Himes's California in *If He Hollers,* both Europe and Africa in *The Man Who Cried I Am* are ambivalent frontiers. Both spaces are entangled in the same web of racial politics and the same history of racial oppression as America. For Williams, no place exists outside history, but through his journey to Africa Max does discover the possibility of coming to a new understanding of (not an escape from) the past. One cannot escape history as such, but one can rethink, contest, and revise it.

A Rebel against History

The most important African character in *The Man Who Cried I Am* is the Nigerian Jaja Enzkwu, first minister to the premier in his own country. Enzkwu is not an idealized African other, who introduces the protagonist to a more authentic identity. Max's first meeting with Enzkwu turns him violently against him, as he is embarrassed by Jaja's obvious attempt to pick up Max's date for the evening, a white French reporter named Janine (219). As Max observes, for Enzkwu, "every white woman who was courteous to him was really offering to share her bed with him," and with that knowledge behind him, Enzkwu's "suggestive conversation" proceeded with "no guidelines" or "courtesy" accorded to the object of his attempted seduction (220). Whatever his character flaws, however, Jaja discovers the existence of Alliance Blanc and the King Alfred manuscript. While Jaja begins investigating in order to protect his country, this desire soon gives way to self-interest, as he realizes that he could use King Alfred to prove that African leaders "had failed to protect their people from the new colonialism" (367). Having proved this point, he plans to gather all African nations under his own rule. With the information that the Americans were behind King Alfred, "Jaja started to deal," agreeing to hand over the papers "if the Americans gave him Nigeria" (368). While the Americans agreed with the deal, they "ran out of patience" and, thinking that they could "find the material without him," killed Jaja—but not before he passed on a key to a safe deposit box to Harry Ames (369).

As the events of Max's past unfold in the novel he has been in a cottage in Leiden, reading through the briefcase of notes about the King Alfred Plan passed on to him by Harry Ames. In a letter accompanying the material Harry explains his reasons for sending the briefcase to Max: "But there was America itself. You and *Pace*. You must have access to outlets where this material would do the most good. The choice is yours and yours alone" (370). Max has two choices to make here; first, whether or not to make King Alfred public; second, a decision as to where to address this information, to a black audience or to *Pace*'s white audience. Even Max's choice of a black audience is potentially conflicted, as there are two possible conduits for the information—Paul Durrell (the fictional representation of Martin Luther King) or Minister Q (Malcolm X). Well before he comes into possession of the King Alfred manuscript, Max's encounters with Durrell reveal that he might be the wrong outlet. In part, Max is suspicious of Durrell because he represents for whites "the old and comforting image of the Negro preacher as a leader" (246).

His primary reservations about Durrell, however, derive from his observation that he behaves like "a man who might have a lot to sweat about" (314). Max fears that the white power structure has saved "Durrell from his mistakes," specifically from an accusation of grand larceny (258). If he were indeed guilty, he had "indebted himself to white America," and one day "the leadermakers would call in the chips" (258). As Max is looking through the King Alfred material, the words of Minister Q run through his mind, "I call now for black manhood. Dignity. Pride. Don't turn the other cheek any more" (388). At the end of the novel, Max answers Minister Q's call for black manhood: "I know the truth and can do something about it" (388). If Paul Durrell indeed had indebted himself, the King Alfred manuscript might be the chip the leader makers would call in. Max has no fear that Minister Q is compromised—or that he will not know what to do with the information.

Harry Ames has advised Max that his job is to tell white America the truth about the effect of racial politics on African Americans. Max, at the end of the novel, comes to a different conclusion. Max "knew the Alliance and King Alfred were not stopped by the faintest consideration that they would be discovered. Max knew that people who believed as he now believed had to adopt that view, too, and at once, for the secret to converting *their* change to *your* change was *letting them know that you knew*. And he now knew to what extent they would go to keep black men niggers" (386). Max's purpose is not to change white minds, not to give whites a choice. Letting white Americans know what they have done to black Americans has little effect. As King Alfred demonstrates, they already know that. The key for Max is to let them know that you know, and by so doing, to show that "you" are a knowing and considering subject as well. Whereas in *The Stone Face* Simeon Brown's culminating action is a violent attack on a police officer, here Max's final actions are revelatory rather than violent, although the choice he makes sets into motion violent events including his own death: "But now the truth literally had been placed in Max's lap. That truth told him that change could no longer be imperceptible, without cataclysm" (386).

The briefcase containing the King Alfred Plan—and thus literally full of meaning—functions as well as an effectively complex signifier of the relationship between Harry and Max. Central to Harry's identity has been his subject position in a racist society—as an initiator of a counter discourse that contests the truth propagated by the dominant culture. As that briefcase passes from one to the other it represents Harry's acknowledgment that Max is taking his place as the black "father," his adversarial subject position. The passing on of the suitcase (the possession of which condemns Max to death) represents as well a final move in the gamesmanship between Harry and Max,

Harry's revenge against Max for sleeping with his wife. While Harry's letter tells Max he is "next in line to be father," Max realizes the pettiness of his motives. "You were the father," Max thinks. "I'll never take your place as you knew very well when you wrote that last line" (379). Max notes that both Harry and Jaja were "made giddy by the presence of that massive, killing evil, had dared to toy with it" (376–77). Whereas greed caused Jaja Enzkwu's mistakes, Harry Ames suffered from "the unopening mind that opened in one, small, killing direction," one that saw in the existence of King Alfred a means of personal revenge (377). While the other men involved in passing along the information contained in the briefcase did so for personal gain as well, Max makes his decision "with the same cold objectivity that made the Alliance so formidable" (385). Max realizes that "he didn't hate the way Harry had, not that killing hatred that turned in upon yourself and those close to you" (385). Max passes on the information orally to Minister Q, and then, instead of imitating Harry and sending the briefcase to someone else, he burns the papers, realizing strategically, "No papers and therefore no end" (394). The Alliance Blanc "would always know that someone else knew. That fact would gnaw at white men in power for as long as they held it" (394). After burning the manuscript he takes the empty briefcase with him: "Let the emptiness, when they discovered it, speak for itself" (394).

At the end of the novel, Muller argues, Max emerges as "a rebel fighting history itself" (82). Max's intervention in the making of history takes place on two levels. First, he speaks the hidden truth of the King Alfred conspiracy and thus produces an alternative view of history that contests official history. Second, through the empty briefcase he resists the efforts of official history to achieve closure. If Max Reddick's final transformation involves becoming an agent in—rather than being subjected to—history, we might note Bhabha's observation that "Our task remains, however, to show how historical agency

is transformed through the signifying process; how the historical event is represented in a discourse that is *somehow beyond
control.* This is in keeping with Hannah Arendt's suggestion
that the author of social action may be the initiator of its
unique meaning, but as agent he or she cannot control its outcome" (12–13). In his discussion of the poem "Strangers on a
Hostile Landscape" written by Meiling Jin (a British poet born
in Guyana of Chinese parents who emigrated to England in her
childhood), Bhabha argues that the invisible eye/I that represents the migrant woman protagonist of the poem produces a
subject that "cannot be apprehended without the absence or
invisibility that constitutes it . . . so that the subject speaks, and
is seen, from where it is *not*" (47). This invisibility presents "an
anxious absence," a "disembodied evil eye" that "wreaks its
revenge by circulating, *without being seen*" (Bhabha 47, 55).

Max's death at the hands of undercover CIA operatives
Roger Wilkinson and Alphonse Edwards—he cannot be
coerced by bribe or torture into revealing what has happened to
the manuscript—leaves just such an absence. At the end,
Alphonse Edwards considers the absence of papers, thinking
that he will have to trace Max's steps to locate them, and realizes, "Goddamn it . . . it might not even end there" (402). Max
enters into history by disappearing, by introducing into signification the briefcase, literally emptied of its meaning, and
transformed by that emptying into "an anxious absence," a signifier circulating within the discourse of the dominant culture
that wreaks its revenge by disrupting the other's ability to make
and control history. His strategic emptying of the briefcase
makes it impossible for the white makers of history to achieve
closure. That empty signifier, as Alphonse Edwards realizes, will
circulate as an always unanswered question in the dominant
discourse.

In Toni Morrison's *Paradise,* the disappearance of the bodies
of the Convent women serves a similar function. Billie Delia

asks herself not where the women went but when "will they return? When will they reappear, with blazing eyes, war paint and huge hands to rip up and stomp down this prison calling itself a town? A town that had tried to ruin her grandfather, succeeded in swallowing her mother and almost broken her own self" (308). Given that the effort made by the New Fathers throughout the novel to control and limit meaning is part of what stifles the town, the mysterious disappearance of the bodies of Consolata, Mavis, Gigi, Seneca, and Pallas represents the possibility of positive change in Ruby. Although Billie imagines a physical revenge from beyond the grave, the women wreak their greatest vengeance by remaining "an anxious absence," for this absence will always circulate through the "official story" of Ruby and will always disrupt any efforts to sanitize the story of what happened at the Convent.

Through what Max terms a "black act," he reveals the truth concealed by the rhetoric of the New Frontier and the Great Society, that "all the new moves" made by the American government to gain democracy for African Americans "were fraudulent" (399, 368). In *The Stone Face*, Simeon Brown's intervention in the history of the moment is physical and embodied. Max Reddick's intervention is discursive and disembodied, an act of narration that puts into circulation a counter discourse in opposition to the dominant white version of history. At the end, Williams writes, Max "felt exhausted, as if he had been running beneath a gigantic, unblinking eye that had watched his every move and determined just when movement should stop" (376). Much as he earlier returned the "casual stare" of the policeman, Max here looks back at the "gigantic, unblinking eye" of the Alliance Blanc conspiracy, an act that signals his willingness to engage not simply representatives of the dominant culture but the entire discursive structure that supports white racism.

Conclusion

In concluding, I would like to summarize three points about the way African American writers have revised frontier mythology, the first concerning the geography of the frontier, the second concerning the Turnerian definition of the frontier as "the meeting point between savagery and civilization," and the third concerning the way these writers have imagined and constructed masculinity. Love, Micheaux, and Hopkins traditionally locate their frontiers in the geography of the American West—the unsettled western states and territories of the cattle drives for Love, the newly opened for settlement South Dakota for Micheaux, and Kansas before statehood for Hopkins. Himes, Smith, and Williams reimagine frontier mythology in a mid-twentieth-century context. Although Himes uses the western setting of California, he does not emphasize the natural landscape of the West as do the earlier writers. Frontier freedom is represented by the hustle and bustle of industry, by the new opportunities for black workers opened up through wartime mobilization, and by the possibilities of movement represented by the automobile—by the "motor smell, pungent, tantalizing [that] poured in through the open windows over me" (Himes 162).

While most of the writers I have discussed here imagine the frontier as a place that is free from racial oppression, we have also seen the specific meaning of the frontier (whatever the location) change according to the writer's particular historical, philosophical, or political perspective. For Love and Micheaux, migration to the frontier represents assimilation into the dominant culture. Hopkins, from a different political perspective, uses a frontier setting to construct a society (the John Brown encampment) that accommodates both racial and gender difference. Smith and Williams reimagine the frontier in a context of independence movements in Africa. The geography of the frontier is overseas, in Europe or in Africa, and the first contact with an other or others of African descent represents the possibility of reimagining the African American self in terms of a pan-African identity and in terms of political alliance with other oppressed peoples.

The African American writer's adaptation of the frontier myth's basic dichotomy (wilderness/civilization, savage Indian/civilized white) is complicated by the dominant culture's construction of black manhood as similarly savage or primitive. For Nat Love, the violent dispossession of American Indians is a precondition of his employment, and he repeats without criticism the frontier myth's designation of the American Indian as savage other. American Indians exist as foils, as the true savages against whom Love violently establishes his own humanity. Oscar Micheaux likewise accepts the stereotype of American Indians as savages, although he primarily represents the savage/civilized dichotomy in *The Conquest* in terms of civilized and uncivilized African Americans. Although for Micheaux the frontier symbolizes freedom from white racism, it also represents escape from a black community that he represents as having as great a detrimental effect on black achievement as race-based restrictions. Savagery exists in the civilized East, especially in urban black communities. Although Micheaux does not refute the stereotype of black savagery, he uses the frontier myth's savage/civilized dichotomy to distance himself from that racist imagery, recasting the opposition in terms of "civilized" blacks (like himself) and "primitive" blacks (like the Rev. McCraline).

The border between Missouri and Kansas in Hopkins's *Winona* is social as well as geographic, the frontier between two political systems (slave state, free territory). Hopkins follows the strategy initiated in John Marrant's *A Narrative of the Lord's Wonderful Dealings with John Marrant, a Black* by inverting the savage/civilized trope. The greatest savagery resides in civilized Missouri, whereas the greatest civility exists in the wilderness of Kansas, as yet untainted by the slave system on which civilization is built. In Missouri, Hopkins's African American characters endure slave status, their position in the dominant culture that of savages, beasts, chattel. The journey across the border to Kansas represents a shift in existential status from savage beast to civilized humanity. Through adaptations of the ritual hunt Wright and Himes demonstrate the way the dominant culture attempts to keep the black individual in his designated place, as the objectified beast of the hunt. As in *Winona,* the primary struggle in the stories of Wright and Himes is existential. The black man's greatest accomplishment is often to survive the hunt and thereby to establish a sense of subjectivity in spite of repeated attempts to negate such self-making.

The Man Who Cried I Am and *The Stone Face* revise the frontier myth from a postcolonial perspective. The frontier is not the point of furthest colonial incursion ("the meeting point between savagery and civilization") but the place where the complex processes of decolonization are taking place. In Smith's *The Stone Face,* a shift in the geography of the frontier from America to France creates a corresponding change in the savage/civilized opposition. The division between the Algerians and the French in *The Stone Face* replicates the frontier myth's white/American Indian border. Simeon moves back and forth across these lines, identifying with the oppression experienced by the Algerians but also enjoying freedoms denied to them. If the journey to the frontier for Micheaux's Devereaux represents escape from the black community and potential assimilation into the dominant culture, a similar frontier journey for Simeon Brown results in the opposite—identification with a minority culture and a rejection of membership in white society. As does Williams in *The Man Who Cried I Am*, Smith ultimately rejects the inferior/superior implications of the savage/civilized dichotomy in favor of a more contemporary concept of the frontier as a social and geographic landscape where two cultures—Western and African—meet and interact.

We have seen the protagonists and characters in these stories struggle with the image of black manhood as that identity has been constructed by the dominant culture—as primitive, savage, unable to control passion. Writers such as Micheaux and Hopkins have responded to these dominant constructions of black manhood by writing narratives that emphasize restraint. Writers such as Wright, Himes, Smith, and Williams have explored the way the dominant culture closes off other aspects of identity to black men leaving them only with violent or self-destructive behavior as a means of self-assertion. The journey to the frontier represents the possibility of constituting a black manhood denied or misrepresented in "civilized" America. In the process of asserting black manhood, the writers discussed here have often articulated their desires to be accepted as human, as the subjects rather than the objectified others of contemporaneous racist discourse, through dominant concepts of what it means to be a man. They have often repeated problematic elements of the dominant culture's masculine ideal without much critical self-reflection. Thus, an often violent and patriarchal masculine ideal has remained central to the ways these writers have constructed black manhood.

As does Hopkins's *Winona*, Era Bell Thompson's *American Daughter* (1946) provides an interesting contrast to the frontier narratives written by men. Her autobiography is first and foremost a family history, the story of her entire family and their western experiences rather than the story of a lone male (such as John Marrant, Oscar Devereaux, Nat Love, Simeon Brown), leaving family behind to journey to the frontier, a stranger in a strange land. Concerned primarily with the welfare of his sons, her father observes "we'd better take the boys to Dakota. . . . They need to grow and develop, live where there's less prejudice and more opportunity" (Thompson 21). As it does for Devereaux in *The Conquest*, the Dakota frontier represents for Tony Thompson an opportunity that is unavailable in the civilized East, an environment where his sons may grow and develop in accord with the growth and development of the family farm. Thompson writes that her father soon left "for far-off North Dakota to find a new home in the wide open spaces, where there was freedom and equal opportunity for a man with three sons. Three sons and a daughter" (22). The American daughter, Thompson indicates, is peripheral to her father's enterprising vision. As a daughter Thompson does not share with her father and brothers the desire to establish a patrimony, but her position on the periphery as an observer of her father's and brothers' attempts to fulfill this masculine ideal enables her to cast a critical eye at her father's vision.

Although her father experiences many of the same travails as Oscar Devereaux, Thompson emphasizes light humor (often at her father's expense) over Micheaux's very serious representation of a heroic black farmer shaping the wild land into a profitable enterprise. *American Daughter* begins in Iowa where a "touch of gardening," she observes, must have put "farming in Father's blood" (18). If so, "it was later a touch of farming that took it out" (18). Tony Thompson's attempt to remake himself in terms of a Devereaux-like heroic farmer results either in failure or in the occasional qualified success. Throughout the book, Thompson provides several scenes which indicate that her father achieves a masculine identity not in the traditional place of the frontier myth (the wilderness, the outdoors, the fields) but in the domestic space of the kitchen. "In a hot kitchen," she writes, "he was again Tony the cook, quick, sure, skillful" (85). "On the farm," however, "he was lost, confused" (85). When a populist movement, "the Nonpartisan League, a political organization composed entirely of farmers," takes the governorship and legislature of North Dakota in 1916, the new governor calls Tony Thompson to come to the capital and teach the uncouth farmers manners (59). "We never been to one of these here fancy things," a farmer-politician frets. "All them dishes and things—Tony, you been around, we'll set by you an' watch, see how you do" (78). Tony's domestic skills precipitate his entry into the public sphere. During the legislative session, "he was shaking hands, rubbing elbows with the public, and it gave him back some of the confidence he had lost during his brief struggle with the soil" (79). In Thompson's autobiography, her father emerges as someone who flourishes when asked to bring together masculine and feminine spheres. When he tries to remake himself in terms of a narrower, heroic masculine identity, he struggles—and is lessened by the narrowness of the role he tries to act out.

Pearl Cleage's play *Flyin' West* (1995) and Toni Morrison's novel *Paradise* (1998) similarly explore experiences largely ignored by the male writers I have discussed—the stories of black families and black communities settling in the West. Cleage's play uses a turn-of-the-century setting in Nicodemus, Kansas, to tell the story of a group of black women who have fled race rioting and lynching in Memphis to start a new life in the all-black town. The play follows Sophie Washington's efforts to convince the citizens of Nicodemus to pass a rule "saying nobody can sell [their land] to outsiders unless everybody agrees," with the hope that keeping the town an all-black community will assure the continuance of freedom, safety, and opportunity (Cleage 12). Like the men of Haven and Ruby in Morrison's *Paradise*, the characters in *Flyin' West* envision a black utopian society in the West: "We could own this whole prairie. Nothing but colored folks farms and colored folks wheat fields and colored folks cattle everywhere you look" (13). As in Micheaux's *The Conquest*, landownership is crucial to the play's utopian vision, for it is "the land that makes us free women" (65).

In contrast to the utopia envisioned by the men of Haven and Ruby, *Flyin' West*'s version of paradise is distinctively feminist and women-centered. Sophie declares her freedom not only from white people but also from black men: "Two things I'm sure of. I don't want no white folks tellin' me what to do all day, and no man telling me what to do all night" (21). Sophie's efforts to maintain the town's unity are undercut by white investors seeking to gain a foothold in Nicodemus and by Frank Charles, a light-skinned black man embittered by having been cut from his white father's will. Charles, husband to one of the four primary female characters, Minnie Dove Charles (the others are Sophie Washington, Fannie Dove, and Miss Leah), uses physical violence to force Minnie to place his name with hers on the deed. In an effort to gain back the inheritance he has lost, he seeks to sell his wife's share to the white investors. In the Eden of Nicodemus, the snake enters in the form of white investors, but Adam rather than Eve gives in to temptation. Appropriately, retribution for Adam's transgression will involve an apple.

Frank Charles represents the savage other who threatens the "sacred bond between us with all our trust" established by the women in the play (45). Wil Parrish, a male neighbor, offers to "settle" the problem "man to man" (73). As does Hopkins in *Winona*, Cleage revises this conventional trope of the Western by having one of the female characters intervene in Wil's attempt to settle the score according to the dictates of manly honor. In contrast to Winona's actions, Sophie intervenes not to prevent violence but to assert that it is her right and duty to be the agent of that violence: "I appreciate the offer, but the day I need somebody else to defend my land and my family is the day *that* somebody's name will be on the deed. I need you to help me do what needs to be done. Not do it for me" (77). Although Sophie carries a shotgun and knows how to use it, *Flyin' West* inventively revises the Western showdown by choosing a less phallic weapon for taking care of Frank Charles. Through a cleverly deployed apple pie containing poison, the threatening Charles (who indicates that he deserves the retribution he receives by savagely beating his wife) is dispatched, the harmony among the female characters restored, and Nicodemus made safe (at least temporarily) from the white investors.

Central to the construction of masculine identity in the work of many of the male writers discussed here is participation in homosocial bonds with other men. The male writers consistently demonstrate the way black men are excluded from "men's relations with other men," from full participation in the homosocial bonds between white men that constitute the power structure of the dominant culture. We see in later novels an attempt to rearticulate a system of homosocial bonds with black men—between Simeon and his Algerian brothers, for example. In *The Stone Face*, manhood achieved (as it does in *The Life and Adventures of Nat Love*) turns on an act of violence that serves as Simeon's initiation into a homosocial bond with the Algerians. Of the writers discussed in the preceding chapters, only Hopkins and Morrison view such homosocial bonds with decided ambivalence. Although the joining together of black men and white in one group (John Brown's war party) is represented as a progressive development, *Winona* is careful to demonstrate the necessity of active women participants as a means of controlling the excesses of such homosocial bonding.

Like *Flyin' West*, Morrison's *Paradise* examines the tensions between men and women in the black community of Ruby,

Oklahoma. Like Nicodemus in *Flyin' West,* the all-black town represents a potentially utopian refuge, segregated but safe, where the community can grow and develop, protected from white racial violence and free from the limitations of white society. Whereas the utopia of Nicodemus is distinctively feminist, *Paradise* presents a male-dominated social structure. In *Paradise,* Morrison casts a critical eye at the desire to create a black patriarchy (even as a defense against white oppression) in the West. At the end of the novel, Billie Delia observes that the town had become a "backward noplace ruled by men whose power to control was out of control and who had the nerve to say who could live and who not and where; who had seen in lively, free, unarmed females the mutiny of the mares and so got rid of them" (308). Whereas acts of violence in the name of protecting women serve as a means of furthering or establishing homosocial bonds in such works as Roosevelt's *The Winning of the West* and Smith's *The Stone Face,* Morrison reveals that male violence, rather than being protective, is just as likely to be employed against women.

JanMohamed observes that literature or any other work of the imagination can be "productive" for the minority individual "because it is the realm of 'as if,' a space in which one can investigate human potentiality in ways that are immediately unconstrained by the contingencies of actual life," a distinction between possibility and constraint analogous to the Lacanian concepts of the imaginary and the symbolic (118). We might argue that the landscape of the frontier myth allegorically represents the imaginative realm of "as if." For the African American writer, the frontier, whatever the geographic location, is an imaginative space free from racial oppression where the human potentiality otherwise constrained may be investigated. If frontier mythology offers an existing structure for investigating potentiality and possibility, however, that myth also encodes existing constraints. With its central opposition of civilization and savagery, self and other, especially as the dichotomy is articulated along racial lines, the frontier myth both offers the African American writer a set of motifs for exploring self-making possibilities and restricts those possibilities through a dominant discourse that associates the black individual with the racial other and not with the white subject of the myth. Through the story of Dave Saunders, for example, Wright demonstrates the difficulty of transferring an identity discovered in the realm of "as if" into the realm of the world of others, whose attitudes, beliefs, and values constitute the constraints of "actual life."

We might argue that the relationship between the realm of "as if" and the realm of constraint is dynamic and interactive. In *The Stone Face*, the journey to France-represented-as-frontier introduces Simeon to the possibility of forming a self in a context of freedom from racial restriction. If Simeon's transformation is in a sense imaginary, an acting out of the role of revolutionary in a context that enables him to do so without experiencing the same consequences as his Algerian friends, the playing of that part nonetheless convinces him to return to America, to the civilization left behind. The identity formed in the realm of "as if" precedes—and empowers—his new willingness to work to change the constraints and limitations that constitute "actual life" for African Americans in America.

Oscar Micheaux inserts a black presence into the "master narrative" of the frontier myth in part by weaving elements of African American literary tradition into his story—by joining together a Turnerian story of frontier transformation with a narrative of racial uplift inspired by Booker T. Washington. By imagining a black man at the center of a story inspired by frontier mythology, even if he does not imagine a way out of the contradictions inherent therein, Micheaux participates in a process of revising and adapting that mythology to accommodate African American experience. As does Micheaux, the writers studied here expand the possibilities of self-making available in the literary realm of "as if." Women writers such as Hopkins, Morrison, Thompson, and Cleage extend that realm further by representing the frontier from a female perspective, by creating multidimensional and active female characters, by criticizing patriarchal masculine ideals, by representing men who embody masculine identity in ways other than the heroic ideal. Examining the literary "realm of 'as if'" expands our understanding of the complex ways African Americans have experienced, imagined, and represented the American frontier. Studying responses of African American writers to the reality and the mythology of the West likewise increases our knowledge of the multiple purposes to which the concept of the frontier has been employed, and it expands our historical understanding of the way African Americans have participated both in the settling of the American West and in the imaginative representation of westward migration.

NOTES

Introduction

1. After he merges into the "brotherhood" of white cowboys, Love refers only rarely to his racial identity. We see a similar erasure of racial identity in the as-told-to biography, *The Life and Adventures of James P. Beckwourth* (Bonner). Beckwourth's story tells of his various adventures on the western frontier as fur trader, army scout, adopted member of the Crow Indians, and founder of Beckwourth Pass through the Sierra Nevadas. As William Katz observes, however, Beckwourth's biographer "failed to include any mention that he was a black man" (31).

2. In his introduction to Flipper's memoirs, Theodore Harris notes that although no evidence exists to suggest that Flipper's relationship with Dwyer was "anything other than a purely platonic friendship," such a "public interracial social contact" was bound to cause disapproval (Flipper 6). Whether Flipper's allegations of a plot by certain officers to force him from the service were valid or "the product of accumulated pressures, tension, anxieties, and his pervasive sense of loneliness, is unclear" (6). In 1976, the Army Board of Corrections for Military Records declared that, although it did not have the authority to reverse Flipper's court-martial, it did "convert his separation record to a certificate of honorable discharge," and Flipper's remains were moved in 1978 to his birthplace in Thomasville, Georgia, "and buried with full military honors" (15). On February 19, 1999, President Bill Clinton granted a full pardon to Flipper.

3. In terms of the "reality" of this encounter, we might note Jameson's discussion of Althusser's notion of history as an "absent cause": "What Althusser's own insistence on history as an absent cause makes clear, but what is missing from the formula as it is canonically worded, is that he does not at all draw the fashionable conclusion that because history is a text, the 'referent' does not exist. We would therefore propose the following revised formulation: that history is *not* a text, not a narrative, master or otherwise, but that, as an absent cause,

it is inaccessible to us except in textual form, and that our approach to it and to the Real itself necessarily passes through its prior textualization, its narrativization in the political unconscious" (35).

4. For discussions of Adams and Singleton, see Painter, especially pages 82–146. For a personal perspective on the exodus, see Henry Clay Bruce's autobiography *The New Man* (1895), which contains a brief description of his own migration to Leavenworth, Kansas, in 1864.

5. The popular genre known as the Western represents one specific variation of the frontier myth. Lee Clark Mitchell in *Westerns* argues that books such as Wister's *The Virginian* and Zane Grey's *Riders of the Purple Sage* (1912) and movies such as *Stagecoach* (1939), *Shane* (1952), and *High Noon* (1952) have developed a set of expectations and conventions that mark the genre: an attention to grand landscapes, Indian attacks, cowboys, outlaws, gunslingers, cattle roundups, lynchings, showdowns, "the transfiguring potential of western life" (Mitchell 125). Whereas few of these elements appear in Micheaux's *The Conquest* (a frontier narrative more concerned with farming than with ranching or gunslinging), both Hopkins and Love indicate an awareness of the Western's generic conventions, although they approach these conventions from quite different political perspectives. For a discussion of the influence of the dime novel Western on twentieth-century versions of the genre, see Daryl Jones, *The Dime Novel Western*. For a more general discussion of the dime novel phenomenon as a whole, see Michael Denning, *Mechanic Accents,* Henry Nash Smith, *Virgin Land* (especially chapter 9), and Jane Tompkins, *West of Everything*.

Chapter 1

1. George Rogers Taylor writes that Turner's essay "The Significance of the Frontier" gradually provoked "such widespread interest and support that it presently became the most widely known essay in American history and literally revolutionized the teaching of American history in the colleges of the United States" (vii–viii). Slotkin emphasizes the influence of both Turner and Roosevelt on twentieth-century understanding of the idea of the frontier. Although Turner has received greater acknowledgment of that influence, Slotkin argues, "Roosevelt's version of the Myth is closer in style, emphasis,

and content to the productions of industrial popular culture . . . and has had a greater (though unacknowledged) impact on the ideological underpinnings and policy-practice of twentieth-century administrations" (*Gunfighter* 26).

2. The recognition of the self in the mirror signals the "assumption of the armour of an alienating identity" (Lacan 4). For Lacan, the subject is defined by lack and loss. By assuming the identity of "I," the subject enters into language by accepting this linguistic marker as a signifier for the self. Although this assumption of identity is necessary for enabling the subject to negotiate the systems of representation used by human beings to communicate and interact, this move is also alienating. When the subject becomes a subject by entering into language, into a system of discourse that preexists the self, the subject "has no meaning of its 'own,' and is entirely subordinated to the field of social meaning and desire" (Silverman 173).

3. Potkay and Burr chose this undated edition because it is both unique and the most complete of the extant texts: "The title page of this imprint states that it is 'Enlarged by Mr. Marrant, and Printed (with Permission) for his Sole Benefit, WITH NOTES EXPLANATORY'; one R. Hawes of No. 40, Dorset Street, Spitalfields, prints the story 'FOR THE AUTHOR.' By contrast, the title pages of the first six 'editions' printed by London's Gilbert and Plummer indicate that William Aldridge, Marrant's amanuensis/editor, had direct control over Marrant's story because he 'ARRANGED, CORRECTED, AND PUBLISHED' it to be sold to his parishioners at the Jewry Street Chapel where he was a pastor" (72–73). Although Aldridge himself sold these other editions, he did not sell the one published for Marrant, "a clear indication that he did not take responsibility for its contents" (73).

4. Gates is writing before the rediscovery of the fourth edition and bases his interpretation of Marrant's book on the 1788 London edition reprinted in Richard VanDerBeets's *Held Captive by Indians* (1973).

5. Compare this emphasis on warfare to Turner's argument, which focuses more on the geology of individual frontiers: "In these successive frontiers we find *natural boundary lines* which have served to mark and to affect the characteristics of the frontiers" (36, emphasis mine). After a long discussion of various rivers, mountains, and arid areas Turner acknowledges that each of these "natural" frontiers "was won by a series of Indian wars" (37).

6. Cooper makes a similar observation in *The Deerslayer*. Natty Bumppo meditates, "a red-skin is by no means as sartain with powder and ball, as a white man. Their gifts do'n't seem to lie that-a-way. Even Chingachgook, great as he is in other matters, is not downright deadly with the rifle" (122).

7. Bederman argues that Roosevelt "repeatedly contrasts the virile manliness of the Americans to the brutal unmanliness of the Indians. . . . Manliness meant helping the weak; Indians attacked the weak. Therefore, Indians . . . were the opposite of manly" (181). We might argue here that Roosevelt's representation of Native Americans is inherently contradictory; they are both seen as examples of unmanly behavior and at the same time seen as possessing a savage and masculine ability in warfare that the American man desires to appropriate in order to enhance his own manhood.

8. Sutton Griggs's *Imperium In Imperio* (1899) takes the idea of an all-black haven in the West a step further by imagining an African American shadow government located in Waco, Texas, that operates as a separate legislative body and alternative to the federal government. At the end of the novel, Griggs proposes establishing in Texas a black nation within the larger United States as a means of securing individual rights and liberties for African Americans.

Chapter 2

1. For a similar story of an African American farmer in the West, see Robert Ball Anderson's *From Slavery to Affluence* (1967), a memoir of his homesteading endeavors in Nebraska beginning in the late nineteenth century. By the time of his death in 1930 Anderson "was the largest black landowner in the state of Nebraska" (Wax 67).

2. Oscar Micheaux's seven published books are *The Conquest: The Story of a Negro Pioneer* (1913), *The Forged Note* (1915), *The Homesteader* (1917), *The Wind from Nowhere* (1944), *The Case of Mrs. Wingate* (1945), *The Story of Dorothy Stanfield* (1946), and *The Masquerade: An Historical Novel* (1947). Both *The Homesteader* and *The Wind from Nowhere* rework the story he first told in *The Conquest*.

3. For overviews of Micheaux's films see Thomas Cripps, *Slow Fade to Black;* Joseph A. Young, *Black Novelist as White Racist;* J. Ronald Green, "'Twoness' in the Style of Oscar Micheaux." For more infor-

mation on specific films see, for example, Jane Gaines, "Fire and Desire," for a discussion of *Within Our Gates* (1919); or bell hooks's discussion of *Ten Minutes to Live* (1932), in bell hooks, *Black Looks*. For book-length studies, see J. Ronald Green *Straight Lick*, and Pearl Bowser and Louise Spence, *Writing Himself into History*.

4. See Barbara Will, "The Nervous Origins of the American Western," especially 293–96, 304–8.

5. For a discussion of the critical dismissal of Micheaux's creative work based on his ostensible "race hatred," see Gaines, "Fire and Desire."

6. For a discussion of the function of marriage in male slave narratives, see Houston A. Baker Jr., *Blues, Ideology, and Afro-American Literature*, 48–56.

7. For a discussion of what they call the continual development of Micheaux's "biographical legend," see Pearl Bowser and Louise Spence, *Writing Himself into History*.

8. Micheaux's adaptation of his own novel *The Homesteader* (filmed in 1919) was in fact one of the earliest films about black frontier life, but this movie has been lost, as have a number of his other silent films. Preceding *The Homesteader* was the Lincoln Motion Picture Company's *The Realization of a Negro's Ambition* (1916), the story of a black protagonist journeying west to seek fortune in California oil fields. Only a fragment of this film still exists. See Reid, *Redefining Black Film* (7–18).

Chapter 3

1. Richard Yarborough notes in his introduction to the Schomburg Library of Nineteenth-Century Black Women Writers edition (1988) of *Contending Forces* that Hopkins was "the single most productive black woman writer at the turn of the century" (xxviii). Between 1900 and 1905 Hopkins "published four novels (three of them serially), at least seven short stories, one historical booklet, over twenty biographical sketches, and many other essays and feature articles" (xxviii). Her three serial novels, *Hagar's Daughter: A Story of Southern Caste Prejudice* (1901–2), *Winona* (1902), and *Of One Blood, or, the Hidden Self* (1902–3), appeared in the *Colored American Magazine*. The novel *Contending Forces*, published by the Colored Co-operative Publishing Company (which also sponsored *Colored American*

Magazine), is her best-known work and the first to be republished (in 1978, with an afterword by Gwendolyn Brooks). For further discussion of Hopkins's life and work, see Hazel Carby, *Reconstructing Womanhood*, Claudia Tate, *Domestic Allegories of Political Desire*, and John Culler Gruesser, ed., *The Unruly Voice*.

2. Elizabeth Ammons, for example, argues that Hopkins's use of the Western "cannot be reconciled with the slave narrative or the racialized protest novel, the two other genres most important to Hopkins in *Winona*" (215–16).

3. Jones points out that the adventure story in many nineteenth-century dime novel Westerns "derives from a recurrent pattern of capture, flight, and pursuit—a plot pattern whose origins lie in both religious and secular versions of the Indian captivity narrative" (137). This particular plot pattern, not at all unreconcilable with African American forms, provides Hopkins with a point of contact with the fugitive slave narrative in which escape and pursuit are often important components.

4. As Quintard Taylor points out, "it would be naive to assume no racial tension existed" between black and white cowboys (160). He notes that, although excluding blacks from trail herds was rare, "discrimination in work assignments was common" (160).

5. For a discussion of the repetition of this narrative structure, see Robert B. Stepto, *From Behind the Veil*, and Valerie Smith, *Self-Discovery and Authority in Afro-American Narrative*.

6. Louis Althusser argues that subjectivity is constructed through a process that he terms interpellating or "hailing" the subject. Terry Eagleton describes this process: "It is as though society were not just an impersonal structure, but a 'subject' which 'addresses' me personally—which recognizes me, tells me that I am valued, and by that very act of recognition makes me into a free autonomous subject. Enthralled by the image of myself that I receive from society, I subject myself to it. I willingly adopt the subject position that society has told me is mine." (172) We might note the similarity here to Lacan's notion of the mirror stage. The assumption of identity in the mirror stage, however, is imaginary, a fiction of self that has no meaning in the "symbolic," the world of others, of language, law, society. "Interpellation" takes place in the realm of the symbolic, for the assumption of identity here is endowed with meaning by the recognition of another

subject. The process of interpellation is described by Althusser in *Lenin and Philosophy*.

7. For a discussion of the way male writers of slave narratives use property acquisition as a means of symbolizing their own transformation from slave to human, see Baker, *Blues, Ideology, and Afro-American Literature*, especially pages 35–48.

8. James Cutler's *Lynch-Law* records nearly two thousand lynchings of African Americans in the South between 1882 and 1903, an average, as Slotkin notes, "of just under two Blacks lynched in the South each week for 20 years" (*Gunfighter* 183–84). Near the end of this period, "lynching itself became more atrocious," as victims were "routinely subjected to torture, including eye-gouging, castration, flaying alive, and burning to death" (184).

9. Nellie McKay writes that the *Colored American Magazine*, founded in 1900, "was the first significant twentieth-century African American journal owned and published by blacks" (3). Shortly after the founding of the magazine, Pauline Hopkins became a member of the board of directors, a shareholder, and a creditor (3–4). Until she "left (or was forced from) the staff in 1904," Hopkins's writing "made up a substantial portion of the literary and historical materials the magazine promoted," and she apparently served as the "appointed editor of the Women's Department from 1901 to 1903" and as literary editor beginning in 1903 (4–5). The magazine's financial problems in 1904 resulted in Booker T. Washington's surreptitiously gaining control over it, a shift in ownership and philosophy that led to Hopkins's resignation, supposedly because of ill health (7). McKay notes, "critics believe, as Du Bois explicitly stated a few years later, that she was forced out in a clash of political ideologies between herself and the new owners" (7).

10. Ammons notes that Hopkins deliberately constructs this interracial family to stand "as a trope for what could be the human family in North America: multicultural, multiracial, anti-imperialist, unnational, antimaterialistic, environmentally attuned" (214). This "idealized family unit" in *Winona* also "presents major problems" (215). The primary American Indian character (White Eagle) "is not native but nativeness taken over by a white man," while the only real Indian, Nokomis, is silenced, peripheral to the plot, and stereotypically written (215). Both Love and Hopkins use the setting of the

American West to create a place of potential refuge from racial oppression, a frontier space that enables the emergence of a new man and a new woman. However, Tonkovich observes, Hopkins fails to recognize that "expansion into Dakota and Kansas territories presupposed dispossession of Native Americans who inhabited the land" (262). For Love this dispossession is a preexisting condition that establishes the necessity of his employment. American Indians exist as foils—as the true savages against whom Love violently proves his own humanity. Although both writers respond (albeit in different ways) to racism against African Americans, neither writer recognizes or protests the violence and dispossession that serve as a precondition to their protagonists' experiences of freedom.

11. Ammons notes that "the name Hopkins gives Winona in drag, Allen, is the same name she gave herself when she wanted to publish anonymously in the *Colored American Magazine,* Sarah Allen—her mother's name" (217–18). Allen Pinks may also refer to Allen Pinkerton of the famed Pinkerton Detective Agency. In addition to operating the actual agency, Pinkerton and his son also wrote a series of dime novels (including such titles as *The Molly Maguires and the Detectives* and *Strikers, Communists, Tramps and Detectives* [both 1877]), loosely based on the experiences of Pinkerton agents. The Pinkerton detectives, in fact and fiction, were noted for going undercover in order to infiltrate the various organizations under investigation (see Slotkin, *Gunfighter* 139–43). Winona certainly uses a similar technique to break into the prison and aid Maxwell.

Chapter 4

1. Wallace Thurman's *The Blacker the Berry* (1929) follows the path of main character Emma Lou Brown from the Boise, Idaho, of her childhood and adolescence, where she was "the only Negro pupil in the entire school," to Harlem, a movement from west to east that we also see in Taylor Gordon's autobiography *Born to Be* (1929), which begins in the Montana of Gordon's childhood (Thurman 22). See also Langston Hughes, whose life growing up in Kansas is detailed in fiction, in *Not without Laughter* (1930) and in his memoir, *The Big Sea* (1940).

2. Rather than refute the construction of blackness as primitive, Bontemps and other writers chose to celebrate those aspects of black

folk culture that are often condemned as evidence of inferiority. For Bontemps, an authentic black identity could be found in "aspects of Afro-southern folk culture" (Flamming 88). Whereas Bontemps himself traveled from west to east in order "to discover his own identity as a black American," his novel *God Sends Sunday* sketches out a journey in the opposite direction (Flamming 85). Flamming notes, however, that "*God Sends Sunday* is not about the black West . . . but about the black South," with the main character, Little Augie, represented as an example of authentic Afro-southern culture (95). We might note a few connections, however, to black western writing. As in Love's *Life and Adventures* horsemanship plays an important role in *God Sends Sunday*. Augie's ability as a jockey is significant to his life "primarily because of the curious transformation it promptly wrought in his character. With horses he gained a power and authority which, due to his inferior size and strength, he had never experienced with people" (Bontemps 20). His ability gains him a measure of freedom, even in the South. However, when his luck runs out "and bad days [come] upon Little Augie," he begins a long journey to California (103). His initial sight of the semirural Mudtown reminds him "of savage wildness," but this impression of what seems a traditionally represented western landscape becomes with the light of day the realization that "Mudtown was like a tiny section of the deep south literally transplanted" (117–19). He is already an elderly man when he arrives in California, and Augie's journey west does not lead to transformation. He soon discovers that his southern bad luck has followed him west.

3. For a discussion of Gordon's *Born to Be* see Michael K. Johnson, "Migration, Masculinity, and Race in Taylor Gordon's *Born to Be*."

4. For discussions of Himes's two California novels, see Robert E. Skinner, "Streets of Fear"; Stephen F. Milliken, *Chester Himes*, especially pages 70–100; and David Wyatt, *Five Fires*.

5. As the later stories in *Go Down, Moses* indicate, the South is a closed frontier and the mythic hunt degraded by the development of civilization. If "The Old People" illustrates Ike's interpellation, the later stories represent his rejection of that identity, symbolized by his refusal to accept the inheritance of the family's land. If the frontier represents, as it does for Turner, an "escape from the bondage of the past" (59), Ike's moments of wilderness experience have their counterpoint in moments when he acquires knowledge about the history of slavery, and of the effect of this history on the present which Ike

cannot escape. The movement of *Go Down, Moses* represents increasing entanglement with rather than escape from the past. The transformation that Turner celebrates of "unowned" land into property farmed by white settlers Faulkner sees as the key to the present fallen state of the world. As Annette Bernert notes, "the primal injustice" in the book is "the ownership of land," for from that ownership is derived "the greater horror of the ownership of people, which can lead to the final secret of the commissary ledgers, old Carothers's begetting, without acknowledging, a son upon his mulatto daughter," a "double crime" against both land and people, resulting in a cursed South, "a legacy of guilt and shame" that Ike has inherited from his grandfather (181–82).

6. Despite the difference in publication dates in book form, Faulkner's "The Old People" and Wright's "The Man Who Was Almost a Man" (collected in *Eight Men* [1961]) are roughly contemporaneous. Loftis notes that Faulkner's "The Old People" appeared in *Harper's Magazine* nine months after Wright's original version of "The Man Who Was Almost a Man" was published in the January 1940 edition of *Harper's Bazaar* (437). This version of the story, "Almos' a Man," while detailing the same events as "The Man Who Was Almost a Man," entailed one key change in the character of the protagonist. In the change from Dan of "Almos' a Man" to Dave of "The Man Who Was Almost a Man," Wright made his protagonist "into a more juvenile character" who (unlike Dan) is unmarried, childless, and still living with his mother and father (Bradley xii). The purpose of this change, Bradley argues, is to make the protagonist's escape at the end of the story unambiguous, as critics could otherwise argue that the hero "acted irresponsibly in abandoning a wife and child—in fact turned away from manhood" (xii). The plot of the 1961 story remains basically the same as that of the 1940 story, and as a character Dave has more in common with Ike McCaslin of "The Old People" than Dan does.

7. Drawing from the work of Frantz Fanon, Jean-Paul Sartre, and Jacques Lacan, Palumbo-Liu argues that the minority individual's "meaning" or "place" in the world preexists the individual. This meaning is limited by social and political restrictions and enforced by "the look of the dominant Other," which inscribes those limitations in the minority subject's self-conception. Palumbo-Liu describes this

inscription in terms drawn from Sartre's philosophy: "In Sartre, the Other's objectification determines one's ontological status. In his well-known analogy of the keyhole, Sartre sets up the following scenario: one is absorbed in looking through a keyhole at another, when one suddenly senses that one is being looked at—one's gaze upon another is the object of an Other's gaze. This forces upon one a recognition of the full significance of one's actions.... after being inscribed in the look of the Other, one suddenly recognizes that one is performing an act that one could 'call' shameful" (78). The "look of the dominant Other" constitutes the minority subject's sense of self by forcing the individual's recognition of his or her actions as "shameful" (or as cause for fear, or pride, etc.), thus reinforcing the individual's sense of his or her "place," and the limitations inherent in that place, in the world of others.

8. In his discussion of Himes's autobiography, *The Quality of Hurt*, Gary Storhoff observes that the "most troubling aspect of Himes's autobiography is his frank description of his mistreatment of women" (41). This brutality, Storhoff argues, "stems from his *over*-conformity to a masculine code of toughness, and his unquestioning acceptance of a social construction of masculinity that enshrines the strong, autonomous, violent male" (41). In his representation of Madge's character, Himes does not go much beyond caricature, and this portrayal seems in line more generally with his "troubling" relationships with women. Phyllis Klotman argues that we should look at Himes's representation of Madge in context of other black writers of the period and in Western culture generally: "The archetypal figure of the female as seducer, betrayer, destroyer," Klotman writes, "has its roots in the myths of legends of Western Civilization" (96). This archetype is often adapted by black writers as "the symbol of the repressive white society which denies complete manhood to the black male" (99). We might also think of Madge in terms of contemporary incidents in which black men were arrested on false accusations of rape, one of the most famous being the 1931 "Scottsboro Boys" case. Nine young black men between the ages of thirteen and twenty-one were prosecuted in Scottsboro, Alabama, accused of raping two white women with whom they were riding in a freight train car. Despite testimony that no rape had taken place from doctors who examined the women, eight of the men were convicted. Various legal battles in the

years that followed eventually resulted in reversals, paroles, and pardons, and although the eight were originally sentenced to death none were executed.

Chapter 5

1. An expatriate like other African American writers living in France (Richard Wright, James Baldwin, Chester Himes), Smith worked as a journalist for Agence France Presse in addition to writing fiction. After Wright's death in 1960, the French press turned to Smith as an informal spokesperson on African American issues. His small canon of fiction results in part from his concentration on other genres of writing and in part from his own propensity for losing manuscripts. As Michel Fabre notes, "Smith had actually written ten novels," including a sequel to *The Stone Face,* which he had sent to critic Jerry Bryant and which "got lost in the end-of-the-year mail when he returned it" (254).

2. Smith himself traveled to France in 1951 and lived there until his death in 1974. As Fabre notes, although Smith "refrained from airing his views in interviews" for fear of losing his job and "being expelled from the country for interfering in French politics," his sympathies, like those of many of the African American expatriates in Paris, "were with the Algerians, a colored, colonial people who suffered from police harassment and from the racist behavior of many French people" (248–49).

3. James Baldwin's short story "This Morning, This Evening, So Soon" addresses similar concerns about the relationship between his African American protagonist and oppressed North Africans living in Paris. The story was originally published in 1960 and was reprinted in the collection *Going to Meet the Man* (1965). Baldwin's narrator observes that he had "once thought of the North Africans as my brothers," but his success in France as an actor and singer leads to a sense of division between himself and these "brothers" (156). Perhaps, he states, "I identified myself with those who were responsible for this misery" (157). Although the Algerians hate the French, "I could not . . . because they left me alone. And I love Paris, I will always love it, it is a city which saved my life. It saved my life by allowing me to find out who I am" (157). As the story progresses, a North African, a former prizefighter named Boona, joins with the narrator and a mixed group

of Americans and French for a night on the town. Boona is accused of theft, and Baldwin's narrator is forced to face the dilemma of choice he has been avoiding.

4. "The exercise of colonial power through discourse," according to Bhabha, depends on the "articulation of forms of difference—racial and sexual" (67), with the essential difference revolving around the dichotomy between the colonizing subject and the colonized object, the master and the slave, the civilized and the savage. The articulation of the dichotomy between master and slave, however, can be disrupted by the "unhomely moment" that negates the "fixity" of such categorization (67). It is by "occupying two places at once," Bhabha argues, that "the depersonalized, dislocated colonial subject can become an incalculable object, quite literally difficult to place" (62).

5. This representation of a counter patriarchy is quite common to black nationalist writing in the 1960s. E. Frances White, in "Africa on My Mind," is critical of such black nationalist discourse that has constructed a patriarchal African past, a golden age of Africa that existed before colonization, as a way to counter the dominant culture's images of Africa. Such a myth of an Edenic patriarchy existing before the "fall" of colonization not only alters the history of African tribal social structure (as White provides evidence to suggest) but justifies a conservative agenda on gender behavior. *The Stone Face*'s privileging of "African tribal feeling" likewise participates in the conservative aspects of the black nationalist agenda by positing an Edenic patriarchy existing in the social structure of the Algerian brotherhood.

Chapter 6

1. Appearing two years after the publication of *The Man Who Cried I Am*, Ishmael Reed's *Yellow Back Radio Broke-Down* (1969) picks up on Williams's revision of frontier mythology and spins out its own surrealistic pastiche of both the Western genre and the genre of black social protest. *The Man Who Cried I Am*'s Alliance Blanc conspiracy reappears in Reed's novel in the form of Christian efforts to stamp out "Hoo-Doo, an American version of the Ju-Ju religion that originated in Africa" (Reed 152). Like Max Reddick, Reed sees writing in terms of jazz, although he goes much further than either Reddick or Williams in rejecting the conventions of social realism in favor of an improvisational style. As the Pope (who arrives in town riding "on

a loud red bull in front of a great stagecoach full of attendants")
observes concerning the Loop Garoo Kid (the book's hero), "Loop
seems to be scatting arbitrarily, using forms of this and adding his
own. He's blowing like that celebrated musician Charles Yardbird
Parker—improvising as he goes along" (147, 154). Captured early in
the novel by "Bo Shmo and the neo-social realist gang," the Kid asks,
"What's your beef with me Bo Shmo, what if I write circuses? No one
says a novel has to be one thing" (34–36). While Reed's improvisational pastiche signifies on some of the same frontier motifs discussed
throughout this study, he goes a step further in his revision by also
parodying the conventions of realist writing that the other writers
have maintained.

2. John M. Reilly notes that the "deliberately imperfect parallels
between fictional character descriptions and actual people" in *The
Man Who Cried I Am* highlight the act of narration, of "historical
interpretation" (32). Although the president in the novel participates
in key events associated with the Kennedy administration (the Bay of
Pigs invasion, for example), Williams departs from history by not representing or referring to the Kennedy assassination, which con-
tributed to the heroic Kennedy myth. Williams's president remains in
the narrative a duplicitous figure, expressing public support for the
African American cause but secretly knowing and supporting the
King Alfred Plan. It is the president who has the authority to put this
plan into action.

3. Williams himself experienced the retraction of an Arts and Letters fellowship from the American Academy in Rome in 1962. As
Gilbert Muller describes the incident, Williams accepted the fellowship and went for an interview—supposedly a mere formality—with
"Richard Kimball, a Yale-trained architect who was the Director for
the American Academy in Rome" (14). Although the interview was
"cordial enough according to Williams," and although Williams had
been selected unanimously by a panel "composed of John Hersey,
Dudley Fitts, Louise Bogan, Phyllis McGinley, S. J. Perelman, Robert
Coates, and John Cheever," he soon after the interview received a
letter indicating that "the American Academy in Rome had rejected
the recommendation" of the panel (15). "Quite clearly, it was Kimball
who obstructed Williams's nomination" (16). Kimball has never
explained or clarified the situation, but Muller speculates that
Williams's novel *Night Song* (1961), the work that garnered him the

recommendation of the panel, bothered Kimball, who seemed to have "believed Williams to be an extension of the world he had written about in the novel, notably in relation to the use of drugs," an assumption that was completely "erroneous" (16). As Muller notes regarding the fictionalized version of this incident that appears in *The Man Who Cried I Am,* "That Williams chose to place a key autobiographical event into the novel through Ames rather than through Reddick suggests the author's degrees of identification with his two main male characters" and suggests as well the shaping and revision involved in Williams's use of historical material (80).

4. Bryant notes that Williams refers explicitly to *Native Son* in the Boatwright episode by establishing connections through naming (Wright and Boatwright) and through chronology (emphasizing that Boatwright's crime and execution take place in 1939–1940, coinciding with *Native Son*'s publication date). Reilly points out that one of Boatwright's speeches echoes "the final words of Bigger Thomas" (31). Bigger delivers his speech to Mr. Max, the communist who defends him, and Boatwright speaks to "his own Mr. Max," Max Reddick (31).

5. The chronology of the novel appears in the narrative in a non-linear form, and Max's travels to the European and African frontiers do not follow each other in a clear progressive line. Rather, trips to Africa and Europe are mixed throughout the book. For the sake of clarifying the individual aspects of my own argument, I am separating these two frontiers more than they are separated in the narrative. Although I discuss Max's relationship with Margrit before I examine the African frontier, Max's time spent in Africa is actually the catalyst for proposing to Margrit. As Anneliese Smith notes, Africa "brings Max into the potential wholeness of being his marriage might mean" (26).

6. Anneliese Smith notes the "basic soundness" of their relationship: "there is never any doubt that Margrit loves Max and not some abstraction of the black man or some sterile notion of an integrated society" (27). As he does so often in the novel, Harry Ames provides a point of comparison as well as contrast to Max, particularly in Williams's juxtaposition of the two sets of interracial couples, Max and Margrit, Harry and Charlotte. As Ronald Walcott notes, for Charlotte, Harry's white wife, "marriage is an act made in defiance of others, rather than in affirmation of the self. Unsurprisingly, unable to live their lives merely in opposition to others, they come to oppose

one another" (31). According to C. Lynn Munro, "By counterposing
the two couples, Williams is ... attempting to dispel the myths which
shroud the mixed couple and to demonstrate that the underlying
dynamics are as varied as those of white-white and black-black relationships" (87).

Bibliography

Allmendinger, Blake. "Deadwood Dick: The Black Cowboy as Cultural Timber." *Journal of American Culture* 16.4 (winter 1993): 79–89.

———. *Ten Most Wanted: The New Western Literature*. New York: Routledge, 1998.

Althusser, Louis. *Lenin and Philosophy*. Trans. Ben Brewster. London: Monthly Review Press, 1971.

Ammons, Elizabeth. "Afterword: *Winona*, Bakhtin, and Hopkins in the Twenty-first Century." Gruesser 211–19.

Anderson, Robert Ball. *From Slavery to Affluence: Memoirs of Robert Anderson, Ex-Slave*. Steamboat Springs, Colo.: Steamboat Pilot, 1967.

Andrews, William L. "African-American Autobiography Criticism: Retrospect and Prospect." *American Autobiography: Retrospect and Prospect*. Ed. Paul John Eakin. Madison: University of Wisconsin Press, 1991. 195–215.

Atkinson, Michael. "Richard Wright's 'Big Boy Leaves Home' and a Tale from Ovid: A Metamorphosis Transformed." Rampersad 129–39.

Baker, Houston A., Jr. *Blues, Ideology, and Afro-American Literature: A Vernacular Theory*. Chicago: University of Chicago Press, 1984.

———. *Long Black Song: Essays in Black American Literature and Culture*. Charlottesville: University Press of Virginia, 1972.

Baldwin, James. *Going to Meet the Man*. 1965. New York: Vintage, 1995.

Bederman, Gail. *Manliness and Civilization: A Cultural History of Gender and Race in the United States, 1880–1917*. Chicago: University of Chicago Press, 1995.

Belsey, Catherine. "Constructing the Subject: Deconstructing the Text." *Feminisms: An Anthology of Literary Theory and Criticism*. Ed. Robyn R. Warhold and Diane Price Herndl. New Brunswick, N.J.: Rutgers University Press, 1991. 593–609.

Bernert, Annette. "The Four Fathers of Isaac McCaslin." *Critical Essays on William Faulkner: The McCaslin Family.* Ed. Arthur F. Kinney. Boston: G. K. Hall, 1990. 180–89.

Bhabha, Homi K. *The Location of Culture.* London: Routledge, 1994.

Bonner, Thomas D., ed. *The Life and Adventures of James P. Beckwourth.* 1856. Lincoln: University of Nebraska Press, 1972.

Bontemps, Arna. *God Sends Sunday.* 1931. New York: Harcourt, Brace, 1972.

Bowser, Pearl, and Louise Spence. *Writing Himself into History: Oscar Micheaux, His Silent Films, and His Audiences.* New Brunswick, N.J.: Rutgers University Press, 2000.

Bradley, David. Foreword. Wright, *Eight Men* ix–xxv.

Brown, William Wells. *Clotel, or, The President's Daughter: A Narrative of Slave Life in the United States.* 1853. Ed. Robert S. Levine. Boston: Bedford/St. Martin's, 2000.

Bruce, Henry Clay. *The New Man: Twenty-nine Years a Slave, Twenty-nine Years a Free Man.* 1895. Lincoln: University of Nebraska Press, 1996.

Bryant, Jerry H. "Individuality and Fraternity: The Novels of William Gardner Smith." *Studies in Black Literature* 3.2 (1972): 1–12.

———. "John A. Williams: The Political Use of the Novel." *Critique: Studies in Modern Fiction* 16.3 (1975): 80–100.

———. "The Violence of *Native Son*." Rampersad 12–25.

Burke, William M. "The Resistance of John A. Williams: *The Man Who Cried I Am.*" *Critique: Studies in Modern Fiction* 15.3 (1974): 5–14.

Byrd, James W. "Afro-American Writers in the West." *A Literary History of the American West.* Ed. Thomas J. Lyon. Fort Worth: Texas Christian University Press, 1987. 1139–47.

Campbell, James. *Exiled in Paris.* New York: Scribner, 1995.

Carby, Hazel. Introduction. Hopkins, *Magazine Novels* xxix–l.

———. *Race Men.* Cambridge, Mass.: Harvard University Press, 1998.

———. *Reconstructing Womanhood: The Emergence of the Afro-American Woman Novelist.* New York: Oxford University Press, 1987.

Chow, Rey. *Writing Diaspora: Tactics of Intervention in Contemporary Cultural Studies.* Bloomington: Indiana University Press, 1993.

Cleage, Pearl. *Flyin' West and Other Plays.* New York: Theatre Communications Group, 1999.

Cooper, James Fenimore. *The Deerslayer.* 1841. Oxford: Oxford University Press, 1987.

Cripps, Thomas *Slow Fade to Black: The Negro in American Film, 1900–1942.* 1977. New York: Oxford University Press, 1993.

Cunningham, George P. "'Called into Existence': Desire, Gender, and Voice in Frederick Douglass's *Narrative* of 1845." *differences* 1.3 (1989): 108–36.

Cutler, James E. *Lynch Law: An Investigation into the History of Lynching in the United States.* 1904. New York: Negro Universities Press, 1969.

Davis, Thadious M. Introduction. Gordon ix–xviii.

Denning, Michael. *Mechanic Accents: Dime Novels and Working-Class Culture in America.* London: Verso, 1987.

Diawara, Manthia, ed. *Black American Cinema: Aesthetics and Spectatorship.* New York: Routledge, 1993.

Dorsey, Learthen. Introduction. Micheaux xi–xxi.

Douglass, Frederick. *My Bondage and My Freedom.* 1855. Ed. William L. Andrews. Urbana: University of Illinois Press, 1987.

———. *Narrative of the Life of Frederick Douglass, An African Slave. Written by Himself.* 1845. *The Classic Slave Narratives.* Ed. Henry Louis Gates Jr. New York: Penguin, 1987. 243–331.

Du Bois, William Edward Burghardt. *The Souls of Black Folk.* 1903. New York: Penguin, 1989.

duCille, Ann. *The Coupling Convention: Sex, Text, and Tradition in Black Women's Fiction.* Oxford: Oxford University Press, 1993.

Eagleton, Terry. *Ideology.* London: Verso, 1991.

Ellison, Ralph. *Invisible Man.* 1952. New York: Vintage, 1980.

Equiano, Olaudah. *The Life of Olaudah Equiano, or Gustavus Vassa, the African.* 1789. *The Classic Slave Narratives.* Ed. Henry Louis Gates Jr. New York: Penguin, 1987. 1–182.

Fabre, Michel. *From Harlem to Paris: Black American Writers in France, 1840–1980.* Urbana: University of Illinois Press, 1991.

Fanon, Frantz. *The Wretched of the Earth.* Trans. Constance Farrington. New York: Grove Press, 1963.

Faragher, John Mack. Introduction and afterword. Turner 1–10, 225–41.

Faulkner, William. *Go Down, Moses.* 1942. New York: Vintage, 1990.

Fiedler, Leslie. *Love and Death in the American Novel.* 1960. New York: Anchor Books, 1992.

Flamming, Douglas. "A Westerner in Search of 'Negro-ness': Region and Race in the Writing of Arna Bontemps." *Over the Edge: Remapping the American West.* Ed. Valerie J. Matsumoto and Blake Allmendinger. Berkeley and Los Angeles: University of California Press, 1999. 85–104.

Fleming, Robert E. "The Nightmare Level of *The Man Who Cried I Am.*" *Contemporary Literature* 14.2 (1973): 186–96.

Flipper, Henry O. *Black Frontiersman: The Memoirs of Henry O. Flipper, First Black Graduate of West Point.* 1916. Ed. Theodore D. Harris. Fort Worth: Texas Christian University Press, 1997.

Flowers, Sandra Hollin. *African American Nationalist Literature of the 1960s: Pens of Fire.* New York: Garland Publishing, 1996.

Fontenot, Chester J., Jr. "Oscar Micheaux, Black Novelist and Film Maker." *Vision and Refuge: Essays on the Literature of the Great Plains.* Ed. Virginia Faulkner. Lincoln: University of Nebraska Press, 1982. 109–25.

Friedman, Joseph. "The Unvarying Visage of Hatred." *New York Times* 17 November 1963: 53.

Gaines, Jane. "Fire and Desire: Race, Melodrama, and Oscar Micheaux." Diawara 49–70.

Gallop, Jane. *Reading Lacan.* Ithaca, N.Y.: Cornell University Press, 1985.

Gates, Henry Louis, Jr. "Criticism in the Jungle." *Black Literature and Literary Theory.* Ed. Henry Louis Gates Jr. New York: Methuen, 1984. 1–24

——. *The Signifying Monkey.* New York: Oxford University Press, 1988.

Gayle, Addison, Jr. *The Way of the New World: The Black Novel in America.* New York: Anchor Press/Doubleday, 1975.

Gibbs, Mifflin Wistar. *Shadow and Light.* 1902. Lincoln: University of Nebraska Press, 1995.

Gilroy, Paul. *The Black Atlantic: Modernity and Double Consciousness.* Cambridge, Mass.: Harvard University Press, 1993.

Gordon, Taylor. *Born to Be.* 1929. Lincoln: University of Nebraska Press, 1995.

Green, J. Ronald. *Straight Lick: The Cinema of Oscar Micheaux.* Bloomington: Indiana University Press, 2000.

———. "'Twoness' in the Style of Oscar Micheaux." Diawara 26–48.

Griggs, Sutton E. *Imperium In Imperio.* 1899. New York: Arno Press, 1969.

Gronniosaw, James Albert Ukawsaw. *A Narrative of the Most Remarkable Particulars in the Life of James Albert Ukawsaw Gronniosaw, An African Prince, Written by Himself.* 1770. Potkay and Burr 23–66.

Gruesser, John Cullen, ed. *The Unruly Voice: Rediscovering Pauline Elizabeth Hopkins.* Urbana: University of Illinois Press, 1996.

Harper, Frances E. W. *Iola Leroy, or Shadows Uplifted.* 1892. New York: McGrath, 1969.

Hebert, Janis. "Oscar Micheaux: A Black Pioneer." *South Dakota Review* 11.4 (1973–1974): 62–69.

Hedin, Raymond. "Paternal at Last: Booker T. Washington and the Slave Narrative Tradition." *Callaloo* 2.3 (October 1979): 95–102.

Hemenway, Robert. Introduction. *Born to Be.* By Taylor Gordon. 1929. Seattle: University of Washington Press, 1975.

Himes, Chester. *If He Hollers Let Him Go.* 1945. New York: Thunder's Mouth Press, 1986.

Hoch, Paul. *White Hero Black Beast: Racism, Sexism and the Mask of Masculinity.* London: Pluto Press, 1979.

hooks, bell. *Black Looks: Race and Representation.* Boston: South End Press, 1992.

Hopkins, Pauline. *Contending Forces: A Romance Illustrative of Negro Life North and South.* 1900. Schomburg Library of Nineteenth-Century Black Women Writers edition. New York: Oxford University Press, 1988.

———. *The Magazine Novels of Pauline Hopkins.* Schomburg Library of Nineteenth-Century Black Women Writers edition. New York: Oxford University Press, 1988.

———. *Winona: A Tale of Negro Life in the South and the Southwest.* 1902. Hopkins, *Magazine Novels* 285–437.

Hughes, Langston. *The Big Sea.* 1940. New York: Hill and Wang, 1993.

———. *Not without Laughter.* 1930. New York: Macmillan, 1969.

Jameson, Fredric. *The Political Unconscious.* New York: Cornell University Press, 1981.

JanMohamed, Abdul R. "Negating the Negation as a Form of Affirmation in Minority Discourse: The Construction of Richard Wright as Subject." Rampersad 107–23.

Jarrett, Michael. "The Tenor's Vehicle: Reading *Way Out West*." *Lit* 5.3–4 (1994): 227–46.

Johnson, Michael K. "Migration, Masculinity, and Race in Taylor Gordon's *Born to Be*." *Moving Stories: Migration and the American West, 1850–2000*. Ed. Scott E. Casper. Reno: University of Nevada Press, 2001. 153–76.

Jones, Daryl. *The Dime Novel Western*. Bowling Green, Ohio: Bowling Green University Popular Press, 1978.

Kaplan, Amy. "Romancing the Empire: The Embodiment of American Masculinity in the Popular Historical Novel of the 1890s." *American Literary History* 2.4 (1990): 659–90.

Katz, William Loren. *The Black West*. 1987. New York: Touchstone, 1996.

Kimmel, Michael. *Manhood in America: A Cultural History*. New York: Free Press, 1996.

Klotman, Phyllis R. "The White Bitch Archetype in Contemporary Black Fiction." *Bulletin of the Midwest Modern Language Association* 6.1 (spring 1973): 96–110.

Kolodny, Annette. *The Lay of the Land: Metaphor as Experience and History in American Life and Letters*. Chapel Hill: University of North Carolina Press, 1975.

———. "Letting Go Our Grand Obsessions: Notes toward a New Literary History of the American Frontiers." *American Literature* 64.1 (March 1992): 1–18.

Kowalewski, Michael, ed. *Reading the West: New Essays on the Literature of the American West*. Cambridge, Eng.: Cambridge University Press, 1996.

Krupat, Arnold. *Ethnocriticism*. Berkeley and Los Angeles: University of California Press, 1992.

Lacan, Jacques. *Écrits: A Selection*. Trans. Alan Sheridan. New York: Norton, 1977.

Lawrence, D. H. *Studies in Classic American Literature*. 1923. New York: Viking Press, 1968.

Leverenz, David. "The Last Real Man in America: From Natty Bumppo to Batman." *Fictions of Masculinity*. Ed. Peter F. Murphy. New York: New York University Press, 1994. 21–53.

Limerick, Patricia Nelson. *The Legacy of Conquest: The Unbroken Past of the American West.* New York: Norton, 1987.

Locke, Alain. "The New Negro." Introduction. *The New Negro.* Ed. Alain Locke. 1925. New York: Macmillan, 1992. 3–16.

Loftis, John E. "Domestic Prey: Richard Wright's Parody of the Hunt Tradition in 'The Man Who Was Almost a Man.'" *Studies in Short Fiction* 23.4 (fall 1986): 437–42.

Love, Nat. *The Life and Adventures of Nat Love, Better Known in the Cattle Country as "Deadwood Dick."* 1907. Lincoln: University of Nebraska Press, 1995.

Marrant, John. *A Narrative of the Lord's Wonderful Dealings with John Marrant, A Black.* 1785. Potkay and Burr 67–105.

McCarthy, B. Eugene. "Models of History in Richard Wright's *Uncle Tom's Children.*" *Black American Literature Forum* 25.4 (winter 1991): 729–43.

McDowell, Deborah E. "In the First Place: Making Frederick Douglass and the Afro-American Narrative Tradition." *African American Autobiography: A Collection of Essays.* Ed. William L. Andrews. Englewood Cliffs, N.J.: Prentice-Hall, 1993. 36–58.

McKay, Nellie Y. Introduction. Gruesser 1–20.

Micheaux, Oscar. *The Conquest: The Story of a Negro Pioneer.* 1913. Lincoln: University of Nebraska Press, 1994.

Milliken, Stephen F. *Chester Himes: A Critical Appraisal.* Columbia: University of Missouri Press, 1976.

Mitchell, Lee Clark. *Westerns: Making the Man in Fiction and Film.* Chicago: University of Chicago Press, 1996.

Mogen, David, Mark Busby, and Paul Bryant, eds. *The Frontier Experience and the American Dream: Essays on American Literature.* College Station: Texas A&M University Press, 1989.

Morrison, Toni. *Paradise.* New York: Knopf, 1998.

Muller, Gilbert H. *John A. Williams.* Boston: Twayne, 1984.

Munro, C. Lynn. "Culture and Quest in the Fiction of John A. Williams." *College Language Association Journal* 22.2 (December 1978): 71-100.

Nadel, Alan. "My Country Too: Time, Place and Afro-American Identity in the Work of John Williams." *Obsidian II: Black Literature in Review* 2.3 (winter 1987): 25–45.

O'Brien, John. "Interview: The Art of John A. Williams." *American Scholar* 42.3 (summer 1973): 489-96.

Painter, Nell Irvin. *Exodusters: Black Migration to Kansas after Reconstruction.* 1976. New York: Norton, 1986.

Palumbo-Liu, David. "The Minority Self as Other: Problematics of Representation in Asian-American Literature." *Cultural Critique* (fall 1994): 75–102.

Patterson, Martha H. "'kin o' rough jestice fer a parson': Pauline Hopkins's *Winona* and the Politics of Reconstructing History." *African American Review* 32.3 (fall 1998): 445–60.

Potkay, Adam, and Sandra Burr, eds. *Black Atlantic Writers of the Eighteenth Century: Living the New Exodus in England and the Americas.* New York: St. Martin's Press, 1995.

Rampersad, Arnold, ed. *Richard Wright: A Collection of Critical Essays.* Englewood Cliffs, N.J.: Prentice-Hall, 1995.

Reed, Ishmael. *Yellow Back Radio Broke-Down.* 1969. McLean, Ill.: Dalkey Archive Press, 2000.

Reid, Mark A. *PostNegritude Visual and Literary Culture.* Albany: State University of New York Press, 1997.

———. *Redefining Black Film.* Berkeley and Los Angeles: University of California Press, 1993.

Reilly, John M. "Thinking History in *The Man Who Cried I Am.*" *Black American Literature Forum* 21.1–2 (summer–spring 1987): 25–42.

Roosevelt, Theodore. *The Winning of the West.* 1889–1896. Lincoln: University of Nebraska Press, 1995.

Rotundo, E. Anthony. *American Manhood: Transformations in Masculinity from the Revolution to the Modern Era.* New York: Basic Books, 1993.

Rowlandson, Mary White. *The Soveraignty and Goodness of GOD, Together With the Faithfulness of His Promises Displayed; Being a Narrative of the Captivity and Restauration of Mrs. Mary Rowlandson.* 1682. VanDerBeets 41–90.

Sartre, Jean-Paul. *Being and Nothingness.* Trans. Hazel E. Barnes. New York: Washington Square Press, 1956.

Scott, Joyce Hope. "From Foreground to Margin: Female Configurations and Masculine Self-Representation in Black Nationalist Fiction." *Nationalisms and Sexualities.* Ed. Andrew Parker, Mary Russo, Doris Sommer, and Patricia Yaeger. New York: Routledge, 1992. 296–312.

Sedgwick, Eve Kosofsky. *Between Men: English Literature and Male Homosocial Desire.* New York: Columbia University Press, 1985.

Segal, Lynne. *Slow Motion: Changing Masculinities, Changing Men.* London: Virago, 1990.

Silverman, Kaja. *The Subject of Semiotics.* Oxford: Oxford University Press, 1983.

Skinner, Robert E. "Streets of Fear: The Los Angeles Novels of Chester Himes." *Los Angeles in Fiction.* Ed. David Fine. Albuquerque: University of New Mexico Press, 1995. 227–38.

Slotkin, Richard. *The Fatal Environment: The Myth of the Frontier in the Age of Industrialization.* 1985. New York: HarperPerennial, 1994.

_____. *Gunfighter Nation: The Myth of the Frontier in Twentieth-Century America.* New York: Atheneum, 1992.

_____. *Regeneration through Violence.* Middletown, Conn.: Wesleyan University Press, 1973.

Smith, Anneliese H. "A Pain in the Ass: Metaphor in John A. Williams' *The Man Who Cried I Am.*" *Studies in Black Literature* 3.3 (autumn 1972): 25–27.

Smith, Henry Nash. 1950. *Virgin Land: The American West as Symbol and Myth.* Cambridge, Mass.: Harvard University Press, 1973.

Smith, Sidonie. *Where I'm Bound: Patterns of Slavery and Freedom in Black American Autobiography.* Westport, Conn.: Greenwood Press, 1974.

Smith, Valerie. *Self-Discovery and Authority in Afro-American Narrative.* Cambridge, Mass.: Harvard University Press, 1987.

Smith, William Gardner. *The Stone Face.* 1963. Chatham, N.J.: Chatham Bookseller, 1975.

Stepto, Robert B. *From Behind the Veil: A Study of Afro-American Narrative.* Urbana: University of Illinois Press, 1979.

Storhoff, Gary. "Slaying the Fathers: The Autobiography of Chester Himes." *a/b: Auto/Biography Studies* 11.1 (spring 1996): 38–55.

Sundquist, Eric J. *Faulkner: The House Divided.* Baltimore: Johns Hopkins University Press, 1983.

Tate, Claudia. *Domestic Allegories of Political Desire: The Black Heroine's Text at the Turn of the Century.* New York: Oxford University Press, 1992.

Taylor, George Rogers. *The Turner Thesis: Concerning the Role of the Frontier in American History.* Lexington, K.Y.: Heath, 1972.

Taylor, Quintard. *In Search of the Racial Frontier: African Americans in the American West, 1528–1990.* New York: Norton, 1998.

Thompson, Era Bell. *American Daughter*. 1946. St. Paul: Minnesota Historical Society Press, 1986.

Thurman, Wallace. *The Blacker the Berry*. 1929. New York: Simon and Schuster, 1996.

Tompkins, Jane. *West of Everything: The Inner Life of Westerns*. New York: Oxford University Press, 1992.

Tonkovich, Nicole. "Guardian Angels and Missing Mothers: Race and Domesticity in *Winona* and *Deadwood Dick on Deck*." *Western American Literature* 32.3 (November 1997): 240–64.

Turner, Frederick Jackson. *Rereading Frederick Jackson Turner: "The Significance of the Frontier in American History" and Other Essays*. Ed. John Mack Faragher. New York: Holt, 1994.

VanDerBeets, Richard, ed. *Held Captive by Indians: Selected Narratives, 1642–1836*. 1973. Knoxville: University of Tennessee Press, 1994.

Walcott, Ronald. "*The Man Who Cried I Am*: Crying in the Dark." *Studies in Black Literature* 3.1 (spring 1972): 24–32.

Wallace, Maurice. "Constructing the Black Masculine: Frederick Douglass, Booker T. Washington, and the Sublimits of African American Autobiography." *Subjects and Citizens: Nation, Race, and Gender from Oroonoko to Anita Hill*. Ed. Michael Moon and Cathy N. Davidson. Durham, N.C.: Duke University Press, 1995. 245–70.

Washington, Booker T. *My Larger Education*. New York: Doubleday, 1911.

———. *Up from Slavery*. 1901. Ed. William L. Andrews. New York: Norton, 1996.

Wax, Darold D. "The Odyssey of an Ex-Slave: Robert Ball Anderson's Pursuit of the American Dream." *Phylon* 45.1 (1984): 67–79.

Wheeler, Edward J. *Deadwood Dick, The Prince of the Road; or, The Black Rider of the Black Hills*. 1877. *Reading the West: An Anthology of Dime Westerns*. Ed. Bill Brown. Boston: Bedford Books, 1997. 269–358.

White, E. Frances. "Africa on My Mind: Gender, Counter Discourse and African-American Nationalism." *Journal of Women's History* 2.1 (spring 1990): 73–97.

White, Hayden. *Tropics of Discourse*. Baltimore: Johns Hopkins University Press, 1978.

White, Richard. *"It's Your Misfortune and None of My Own": A History of the American West*. Norman: University of Oklahoma Press, 1991.

Will, Barbara. "The Nervous Origins of the American Western." *American Literature* 70.2 (June 1998): 293–316.

Williams, Brackette F. Introduction. Love. vii–xviii.

Williams, John A. *The Man Who Cried I Am.* 1967. New York: Thunder's Mouth Press, 1992.

Williamson, Peter. *French and Indian Cruelty Exemplified in the Life and Various Vicissitudes of Fortune of Peter Williamson.* 1775. Van-DerBeets, 202–42.

Wintz, Cary D. *Black Culture and the Harlem Renaissance.* College Station: Texas A&M University Press, 1996.

Wister, Owen. *The Virginian: A Horseman of the Plains.* 1902. New York: Penguin, 1988.

Wright, Richard. *Eight Men.* 1961. New York: Thunder's Mouth Press, 1987.

————. *Uncle Tom's Children.* 1940. New York: HarperCollins, 1993.

Wyatt, David. *Five Fires: Race, Catastrophe, and the Shaping of California.* New York: Oxford University Press, 1999.

Yarborough, Richard. Introduction. Hopkins, *Contending Forces* xxvii–xlviii.

Young, Joseph A. *Black Novelist as White Racist: The Myth of Black Inferiority in the Novels of Oscar Micheaux.* Westport, Conn.: Greenwood Press, 1989.

Zafar, Rafia. *We Wear the Mask: African Americans Write American Literature, 1760–1870.* New York: Columbia University Press, 1997.

INDEX

Abolitionist, 120, 132, 138–39, 142, 144

Actaeon (mythic figure), 159, 174, 176

Adams, Henry, 12, 252n.4

Africa, 12, 16–17, 177, 180–81, 207, 209–10, 222–23, 262–63n.3, 265n.5; as frontier, 12, 17, 228–33, 240, 242. *See also* Algeria; Liberia; Nigeria

African American literature: and parody of, in *Yellow Back Radio Broke-Down* (Reed), 263–64n.1; and social protest, 14, 17, 98, 102, 118, 124, 146, 148, 175, 180, 185–86, 202, 204, 215–16, 218–19. *See also* Domestic fiction; Slave narrative

African Americans: and freedom. *See* Frontier, and freedom from racial oppression

African Americans: and the frontier myth. *See* Frontier myth, adaptation of, by African Americans. *See also* Liberia: as African American frontier

African Americans: and violence. *See* Violence, and the work of African American writers

Aldridge, William, 31–32, 253n.3

Algeria: representation of Algerians in *The Stone Face*, 16, 187, 191, 193–95, 201, 210, 232; substitution of Algerians for Amer-

ican Indians in *The Stone Face*, 181, 192–93, 195–96, 202–204, 241

Algerian war for independence, 16, 180, 191, 262n.2

Allmendinger, Blake, 77–78, 101–102, 105–106, 108–109; *Ten Most Wanted*, 77

Althusser, Louis, 29, 107, 251n.3, 256n.6; *Lenin and Philosophy*, 257n.6. *See also* Interpellation (or hailing)

American Daughter (Thompson), 15, 242–44, 249

American Indian, 7, 8, 15, 32, 62, 106, 109, 115, 124, 160, 181, 192, 240–41, 257–58n.10; and Cooper, 47–48, 171; and Love, 109–10, 125, 240, 257–58n.10; and Marrant, 36–45; and masculinity, 28, 30, 49, 51–53; and Micheaux, 75, 240; and representation as object of exchange, 55–59, 110; and the ritual hunt, 52–53, 150; and Roosevelt, 49–53; and transformation of the white hero, 26–28, 30, 41, 47–53, 195, 203; and Turner, 24–28, 30. *See also* Cherokee Indians; Delaware Indians; Huron Indians; Iroquois Indians; Sac and Fox Indians; Seneca Indians; Sioux Indians

279